IN LEICHHARDT'S
FOOTSTEPS

IN LEICHHARDT'S FOOTSTEPS

AN INVESTIGATION INTO ONE OF AUSTRALIA'S MOST ENDURING MYSTERIES

BRUCE SIMPSON

ABC
Books

To my son Ranald

Published by ABC Books for the
AUSTRALIAN BROADCASTING CORPORATION
GPO Box 9994 Sydney NSW 2001

First published November 2007

National Library of Australia
Cataloguing-in-Publication entry
Simpson, Bruce (Bruce F)

In Leichhardt's Footsteps.
Bibliography.
Includes index.

ISBN 978 0 7333 2242 6

1 Leichhardt, Ludwig, 1813–1848.
2. Simpson Bruce (Bruce F.)
Drovers – NorthernTerritory – Biography.
I.Australian Broadcasting Corporation.
II. Australian Broadcasting Corporation.
III Title
919.40420924

Cover design by Christabella Designs
Set in 11/16pt Sabon by Kirby Jones
Colour reproduction by Graphic Print Group, Adelaide
Printed in Hong Kong, China by Quality Printing

5 4 3 2 1

Contents

ACKNOWLEDGMENTS

THE AUTHOR WOULD like to thank the following people for their help in the preparation of this book:

The staff of the Caboolture Shire Council Library; the staff of the John Oxley Library; Mr Tom Baird; Mr Greg Czechura and other senior staff at the Queensland Museum; Mrs Gillian Nielsen of Caboolture, for her help with the maps; Mr Steve Millard, Group Pastoral Manager of North Australian Pastoral Company; Mr and Mrs Mal Debney of Glenormiston Station; Mr Bob Iles of Redcliffe; Mr John Reynolds of the Department of Primary Industry, Longreach; Ms Marlene Elson-Harris of the Department of Primary Industry, Indooroopilly; Mr Glen Hasted of Winton; Mr Chris Gladwell of the Stockman's Hall of Fame Office, Brisbane; Mr Ian Mossop of Sydney; Mr Peter Evert of Winton; Mr Bob Kirk of Herbert Downs; Mr Barry Sorenson of Winton; Mrs Peter Clauson of Middleton Hotel; Mr Alex Long of Caboolture; Mr Ray Gilham of Mackay; Mr Dennis Schulz of the ABC in Darwin; Andrew Hume of the South Australian Museum; Mr Bob McNamara of Cloncurry; Mr Bill Kitson of the Queensland Landcentre, Brisbane; Mrs Jan L'Estrange of Tambo; Joe Freckleton of Camooweal; Kerry Kendall of Mackay; John and Ailsa Hay of Taroom; Harold Rennick of Chinchilla; Ted Long of Pittsworth; Nicki Radeski of Pittsworth;

Roy Flynn of Millmerran; Adam Clark of Taroom; Colleen McLaughlin of Springsure; Jack Arden of Brisbane; Ray Gillham of Mackay; Matthew Higgins, Senior Curator, National Museum of Australia, Canberra; Greg Blackmore of Emerald; Wayne McCullouch of Mareeba; George Harriman of Reedy, Brook Station, North Queensland; Jim Pola, North Queensland Register, Townsville; Keith Luscombe of Pittsworth; Don McKinlay of Pittsworth; and Josephine Sheahan of Ingham.

Special thanks to Bill Gammage, Canberra, and to my daughter, Fiona.

Last but of course not least, I would like to thank each and every member of the Glenormiston Expedition.

PICTURE CREDITS

Special thanks to the following for their generous permission to reproduce photographs:

Dr Glen McLaren of Ascot, W.A. (pp. 28, 31, 46, 49, 51, 52); Miss Dolores Dwyer of Mt Isa for the photograph taken by her late brother Jim (p. 214); Greg Blackmore (p. 252); Ailsa Hay (p. 246); Ted Long (p. 248); Harold Rennick (p. 250); Jack Arden (p. 250); Ray Gilham (p. 247); Mr Mark Poole and Mr Peter Smith of Caboolture (pp. 148, 157, 164); Mr Ian Tinney of Brisbane (pp. 4, 184, 190, 201 (both), 208, 213 (both), 251); Mr Peter Treloar (p. 4); Mr Robert McQueen of Winton (p. 129); Mr Bob Nash of Pinnacle (p. 193); the John Oxley Library of the State Library of Queensland (pp. 17 (both), 69, 92, 246 (no. 196943), 248 (no. 145198), 249 (nos 45813 and 196944), 251 (no. 116942), 253 (nos 44969 and 196941)); the Image Library and the Mitchell Library of the State Library of New South Wales (pp. 14, 30, 35, 58, 59, 64, 85); State Library of South Australia (p. 65); and the South Australian Museum (p. 107).

Where Leichhardt Lies

Is this the land where Leichhardt lies,
Unfound though the years have fled?
Stark red desert 'neath blazing skies,
Where the ghostly pools of mirages rise,
From the claypan's barren bed.
Where is the spot that he lies at rest,
By channel or gibber-plain?
Did he grimly hold to the journey west
Or, disillusioned and sorely pressed,
Did he turn to the north again?
Did he turn to the north as the Israelites
Once turned to the promised land?
Through days of torture and nightmare nights
To a fate unknown went the ill-starred whites
To death in the black men's sand.

This is the land where the whirlwind goes
In the path of the men who fell;
Where the stars are pale and the min min glows,
And the sandhills shift when the storm wind blows
From the south like a blast from Hell.
Sweeping north go the dull red waves,
Storm-crests of a long-stilled sea—
Deep down under in smothered caves
Do they shield forever the long-lost graves,
And the key to the mystery?
Did he die a hero or die accursed
By the comrades he had led?
Did he fall to fever or blinding thirst?
Was he trapped by flood when the channels burst,
And the north-spawned waters spread?

This is the land where the desert blacks
Still wander, a scattered band.
Do they mutter low of the 'debil tracks'
In the long-ago, and of fierce attacks
In the heart of their sacred land?—
Where the fine red dust of the Centre cloaks
In a close embrace and strong,
The spinifex hills by the rock-bound soaks
Where the twisted limbs of the desert oaks,
Are crooning a deathless song.
Is this the land where Leichhardt lies?—
Land of the 'great unknown'.
Grim red desert and blazing skies,
Guard well your secret from questing eyes
For this is his land alone.

Bruce Simpson

THE GLENORMISTON RELICS

The disappearance of Ludwig Leichhardt's expedition is a mystery that has confounded historians, explorers and bushmen for almost a century and a half. That a fully equipped expedition could vanish as it did seems inexplicable. However, the Australian outback is a vast and sparsely populated region, and it is possible that the key to the enigma may even now be found.

As a boy I read of Ludwig Leichhardt, and the story of his disappearance fired my youthful imagination. Later, while working as a stockman on Glenormiston Station my interest in the lost explorer was rekindled when, with three other stockmen, I disdiscovered relics that may yet solve the mystery of Ludwig Leichhardt's disappearance.

Glenormiston is a well-known cattle station, 6,920 square kilometres in area, lying directly west of Boulia, a one-pub outback town on the banks of the Burke River in far western Queensland. Glenormiston's western boundary is the Northern Territory border. Its southwestern boundary is the Toko Range. On the north it joins Linda Downs and Roxborough Downs, in the east Herbert Downs, and in the south Marion Downs. Situated in a low-rainfall belt, Glenormiston is well watered on its eastern side by the Georgina River and Lower Pituri Creek, but the western part is arid with little surface water. The Mulligan River rises in the Toko Range and runs through the southwest of the property, however it is poor cattle country and the Mulligan water is often brackish. Between the Mulligan and the Georgina there are mud springs, formed, I believe, by artesian water escaping to the surface through faults. Sand and dust build up in the moisture and form mounds. Some of these mounds are quite large and contain pools of reasonable drinking water on the top. The Glenormiston Station homestead is on Lake Idamere, one of two large lakes in Pituri Creek. The other, Lake Wanditta, is further north up the creek.

Both lakes teem with waterfowl and hold a plentiful supply of mussels. There is no doubt the Wonkajera tribe, which once hunted in the area, had bountiful tribal lands. Pituri Creek is named after the pituri plant which once grew in the area and from which pituri, a much sought-after drug with narcotic properties, was made. Pituri was not only used by the local tribe, it was also a valuable commercial commodity, traded by the Wonkajera along well-established trading routes. When working on Glenormiston, I often picked up axe heads of green diorite. I don't know where the nearest deposit of this stone is, but it must be hundreds of kilometres away. There is no doubt that trade was responsible for the presence of those artifacts. Pituri grows no more on Glenormiston; it too has vanished like the Wonkajera from the sand hills west of the Georgina.

My working on Glenormiston was due more to a buckjumping mare than to anything else. Buckjumpers are horses that buck to try to throw off their riders. Those days, most station horses would buck when fresh in from a spell in the horse paddocks between musters, but died-in-the-wool buckjumpers never gave up the habit of trying to unseat their riders.

'Cockroach', the mare referred to above, was always ready to catch me in an unguarded moment. I could ride her without any trouble if I knew she was going to buck by the change in her behaviour, but when she caught me unprepared she took some riding. One morning the mare got stuck into me and bucked over the bank of a creek. I did not get clear of her and badly injured my back. After lying semiconscious in the camp for a couple of days, I went back to work without seeking medical help. But my back continued to grow progressively worse, and finally, succumbing to the inevitable, I went to Brisbane early in April 1947. The doctors at the Brisbane General, not impressed by my tardiness, treated my back without much success. After they had done what they could, they told me the back might improve, but there was some permanent damage. They advised me to avoid hard work and on no account go back to horse work.

It was not the type of prognosis calculated to gladden the heart of a horseman. I tried working in Brisbane and stuck it out for three months. Then, as my back had improved, I decided to go back to the bush and to hell with the advice of doctors. I went to see D. M. Fraser at the office of the North Australian Pastoral Company. I had worked for the company before on Alexandria Station in the Northern Territory. Fraser told me there was a job for me on Glenormiston and wished me well.

To get to Glenormiston in 1947 meant a tortuous rail journey to Selwyn via Townsville, Cloncurry and Malbon. From Selwyn the trip was by mail truck to Boulia and then on to Glenormiston by the same means. After almost four days of travel, I arrived at the station and was met by Martin Hayward, the manager. Martin informed me that the stock camp was up at Lake Wanditta branding calves and that he would run me out there the following morning. I went over to the men's quarters and threw my swag on a stretcher. The station buildings were right beside Lake Idamere. I looked the place over and had time for a shower before the bell went for the evening meal.

I slept well, to be awakened by the breakfast bell. One eats beef three times a day in cattle country, and the traditional breakfast of steak and onion gravy welcomed me back to the fold. After thanking the cook, I rolled my swag and waited by the office for the manager. Martin appeared soon after with mail and some bread for the stock

3

A bronco panel on Glenormiston showing the slope of the rail.

camp. I threw my swag in the utility parked nearby and we were off. We arrived at the bronco yard at Lake Wanditta to find branding in progress. Seeing us pull up the men knocked off for smoko.

Bronco branding was done in a large yard built of wooden posts linked by plain wire strands. A large yard could hold 1,000 head of mixed cattle, and usually a wing or fence ran out from one side of the wide wire gate to facilitate yarding the mob. A bronco panel was built in the yard, near one side and sometimes towards a corner. Stockmen riding bronco horses (heavier types than stockhorses), caught the calves with green-hide ropes called bronco ropes or head ropes. These ropes were fastened to the bronco harness, heavy straps that passed over the saddle and around the horse. Attached to a collar or breastplate, this harness enabled a bronco horse to pull up a fully grown beast.

When the catcher on the bronco horse had roped a calf, he dragged the animal past the side of the bronco panel that was built with a sloping rail. He then rode away at an angle, causing the rope to slide up the rail and drop into the gap between the posts, pulling the beast towards the panel. Once the calf neared the panel, leg ropes were put on and held at the panel, the calf was put to the ground and the head rope released. If there were two working on bronco horses, then by the time one calf was branded, earmarked and castrated, another calf was on the way up to the panel. A good team of two catchers and six to eight men on the ground could put through up to 80 calves an hour.

Open broncoing was sometimes done in those days using a bronco panel built out on the flat. A large team of men was required, however, since the cattle had to be held in the open by mounted stockmen while branding was in progress.

Broncoing was introduced into Australia by Ambrose Madrill, a Mexican who came to this country in the latter part of the nineteenth century. Thomas Elder, part-owner of Blanchewater Station in South Australia, imported two Spanish jack donkeys from Mexico to breed large mules; Madrill came over with them, stayed and showed Australians the Mexican method of branding cattle. Bronco branding is one of those skills that has been almost lost.

Open broncoing with the bronco panel built out on the flat.

Martin introduced me to Ted Bannah the head stockman, then to the rest of the stockmen, or ringers as they were called those days. They were all Aborigines, the four full-bloods were Paddy, Tiger, Tommy and Charley Trottman. The others were Jack 'Snapshot' Hansen, so-called because of his prowess with a rifle, Val Crawley, Alex Wilson and Alex De Satge, the grandson of an early pioneer of the Georgina. Snapshot's wife Topsy was the camp cook. After smoko, Martin departed dropping my swag off at the camp on the way. As the branding resumed, I grabbed a leg rope. I had always prided myself on my skill with a leg rope and was soon in my element. I found out pretty quickly, however, that although I was fit enough for the work, I was not acclimatised. It was bloody hot, and underfoot it was heavy going with loose sand and dust. By the time the branding was done I was completely stuffed. We went back to the camp for a bite to eat, before setting out on horses to let the

'Snapshot' Hansen on a bronco horse at Glenormiston Station.

cattle out and make sure they didn't rush towards water. This gave the cows a chance to find and mother the calves that had become lost in the hurly-burly of the bronco yard.

I needed no rocking to sleep when I crawled into my swag after that first day back in a stock camp. It took the best part of a week before I was back on top form. I was lucky that the horse string I had been given were not fresh, but had already been worked in the camp. I had to keep alert when I was riding one of them—a brown mare called Woolly, who had suffered very severe cuts on barbed wire when young and would panic if she heard wire twang or rattle. One day she trod on a piece of wire near a bronco yard and started to pigjump—a less violent form of bucking. She was not hard to ride and I was delighted to find that my back stood up to the jarring quite well. During my time on Glenormiston I continued to be wary of rough horses. Where once I had been keen to ride buckjumpers I was now happy to let someone else tackle them. Despite this I rode whatever horses were given to me. It was a matter of pride with ringers that no one else took the sting out of their horses.

The ringers were a fairly happy bunch, and like in all camps those days the men had to make their own fun. Outback humour is rather basic, and one of the camp's favourite yarns, told with great amusement, was of a past dogger on Glenormiston who decided to end it all. The man shot his horse and piled a great heap of wood on top of the animal. He planned to put all his worldly goods on top of the heap, light it and then crawl on top and shoot himself. Everything went to plan: he lit the fire, then had second thoughts. He stood with nothing but what he had on and a rifle as everything else he owned went up in smoke.

I saw a funny incident myself in the camp one evening. Topsy was a very good cook and had just spread the evening meal out on a camp trestle table. There was curry and rice, rice custard and a dish of stewed apricots. She was standing at the end of the table about to call us when a king brown snake crawled up almost to her feet. She screamed and did a back flip landing flat on her back on the tucker.

We killed the snake then turned our attention to the cook. She was in some kind of a fit and as stiff as a gidgee post. Snapshot and Ted lifted her off the table and carried her to her swag with most of the evening meal clinging to her back. We knew she had not been bitten, and in due course she recovered while we attempted to salvage what was left of our meal.

Work in the stock camp finished up in early November. The two Alexs and Val departed and Ted Bannah went to Boulia. Ted was a great character, a tough old bushman who played up like Old Harry when in town. He often went into Boulia for a week or two and stayed at the pub. There was no running water in the rooms back then, each room had a marble-topped washstand. Placed on this piece of furniture was a large enamel or china wash dish together with a matching 2-gallon (10-litre) jug. One of Ted's favourite tricks was to walk stark naked down the pub veranda early of a morning with a full jug of water suspended from his erect member.

I spent most of the slack months doing leather work, and made a complete set of pouches for the camp gear. Then the cowboy pulled out and I was asked to take his job on for a while. On Australian stations, the cowboy is an odd-job man who milks the house cows, cuts the wood and so on. I never liked the job and in a few days found my back playing up. Martin generously relieved me of the task. Later I did up the station packs ready for the coming season.

Before the muster started in 1948, Ross Ratcliffe, Bruce Hanson and Lloyd Linson-Smith arrived, having been employed from head office. Both Ross and Bruce had worked on Glenormiston before, and I became great mates with the three of them. Later, after the muster had started, Keith Arnold joined the team. It was one of the happiest camps I have ever worked in.

Early in May 1948 the mustering of two mobs of cattle started. One sunny morning a couple of weeks later, Charley Trottman, Ross Ratcliffe, Bruce Hanson and I were riding out from the stock camp through a patch of gidgee when something caught my eye. It was a piece of iron lying in ground that had been scorched by fire and turned up by a horse's hoof. Charley Trottman and I dismounted to have a better look and discovered part of a saddle tree half buried in the dirt. Bruce and Ross joined us and we soon uncovered other bits of steel from packs and riding saddles. The relics were mostly just under the soil and scattered over a fairly large area. When we uncovered steel buttons and buckles from clothing, it became obvious to us that this was the site where an entire camp must have perished many years before. Because of the items of clothing found, there was a strong possibility that lives had been lost.

Being very busy mustering at the time we could not remain long at the site. But as I rode away I spotted an odd-looking stirrup iron half buried in the ground. Jumping off my horse I pulled it free to find its mate lying underneath. The irons were of a design I had never seen before. Over the years I have described them to many bushmen; all of them agree they have never seen stirrup irons of the same pattern. I kept the stirrup irons for many years in my droving plant (a droving plant is the collective term for a drover's horses,

On Glenormiston in 1948. From left to right: Ross Ratcliffe, Bruce Hanson, Bruce Simpson and Charley Trottman.

packsaddles, riding saddles, equipment for the horses, and all the camp gear), which I later gave to my brother to use. I was not present when the droving gear was eventually sold and I think the stirrup irons must unfortunately have gone with it.

Back on the muster, I asked Charley Trottman if he knew anything about the site. Charley had lived in the area for 50 odd years, having come in from the Jervois Range district with his kinfolk when he was a child. Charley was very proud of the fact that he and his wife had been married by a Salvation Army chaplain in Boulia. Charley, or Trottie as he was called, would certainly have known if a disaster of these proportions had occurred since he'd been there. But Charley could throw no light on the mystery. No one else I spoke to later knew anything about the relics either. Glenormiston had been settled for just over 70 years, and it seemed strange indeed that no one had any knowledge of what had obviously been a disaster of some magnitude. The only likely explanation was that the incident had occurred before settlement. Ross Ratcliffe was convinced that we had stumbled on the remains of the Leichhardt expedition, last heard of in 1848 when Leichhardt was attempting to cross the continent from east to west. Iron and steel will survive for a very long time in the low humidity and arid soil of the semi-desert, so he might be right.

There is a story of a massacre of Chinese on Glenormiston by the Wonkajera tribe sometime in the 1880s, shortly after settlement. It apparently took place at Lake Wanditta many miles from the relic site we found. The unfortunate victims were engaged in building a dam across Pituri Creek. In the early pioneering days, gangs of Chinese were engaged in this work on many outback stations. Using wheelbarrows and the traditional pole and baskets to collect flagstones, they built dry stone overshot dams across the channels. Evidence of their industry is still to be seen on the Georgina and · Diamantina rivers.

The story of the attack was told to Snapshot Hansen by Billy Brady, who was probably the last of the full-blood Wonkajeras. As a boy he was taken from the tribe in the 1890s. The man responsible for his abduction was James Clarke, who was head stockman on Marion Downs, a property adjoining Glenormiston. Brady was to spend the remainder of his life on Marion Downs, becoming a reliable and highly respected employee. He died in 1962 at an approximate age of 75. Snapshot Hansen, who was in the Glenormiston camp at the time the relics were found, passed Brady's story on. Snapshot Hansen was a part-Aborigine, whose mother came I believe, from further up the Georgina River. At the time of his birth, around 1906, the tribal system was already breaking down, and Snapshot spent all his working life in the Glenormiston area.

The fact that this story was remembered and re-told adds weight to the theory that the relics we found pre-date settlement. The lack of information from the period prior to this may be attributed to the disintegration of the Wonkajera tribe resulting in the loss of their oral history and tribal lore.

Ross, Bruce and I planned to return and fully investigate the site when we got the chance. Fate, however, decreed otherwise. At the end of the muster I had a falling out with Martin Hayward, the manager. I pulled out and despite my efforts to dissuade them, Ross and Bruce also left the station. Martin was a good manager, however he and I could not see eye to eye about the deployment of the stockmen. With our departure the relic site was left untouched—and the Leichhardt mystery remained unsolved.

LEICHHARDT'S FORMATIVE YEARS

Friedrich Wilhelm Ludwig Leichhardt was born on 23 October 1813, at Trebasch, a small town in the Mark of Brandenburg in Prussia. It was a time of celebration, for Prussia and its allies had just defeated Napoleon at the battle of Leipzig. Ludwig was the sixth child of Christian and Sophie Leichhardt. Christian, who owned a farm was able to augment his meagre income when he was appointed Royal Peat Inspector, but it is doubtful whether the salary was as grand as the title.

Leichhardt was a studious child, and his parents gave him every encouragement. At an early age he was sent to school at Cottbus Gymnasium, and emerged from that institution at age 18, proficient in a range of subjects, including languages, natural history and geography. Leichhardt had also gained social skills, learnt to play the piano rather indifferently, and had become quite a good swimmer. Although Leichhardt senior had meanwhile divorced and remarried, putting further strain on his resources, he sent his talented son to Gottingen University in Hanover. There Leichhardt studied to be a teacher and, while there, became friendly with Englishman John Nicholson, a fellow student. Later Leichhardt met John's brother William, a medical student who persuaded Leichhardt to accompany him to the university in Berlin. There the pair studied both medicine and natural science. The move was to have a profound influence on Leichhardt's future.

Both young men talked of travel overseas, and during breaks from their studies they went on walking tours throughout Europe, collecting specimens and doing scientific field work. Leichhardt continued his studies in both medicine and science in France and England, spending time with the Nicholson family in Bristol. Though he never formally qualified, the thought of foreign travel was always with him, and by 1840 he knew that his future lay overseas where his scientific training in botany, zoology, and geology would help him to make his mark. He considered going to the Americas, but given his affinity for the English via the Nicholsons and the natural lure of an unexplored land, by 1841 he was committed to seeking his fortune in England's colony of New Holland.

Leichhardt's friend, William Nicholson, who had always planned to go with Leichhardt, pulled out of the proposed trip. Disappointed, Leichhardt went ahead with his preparations. He read as much as he could about the colony, its flora and fauna, the extent of exploration, and its vast unknown regions. As a scientist he saw what opportunities lay in exploring that wilderness. At 28 years of age Ludwig Leichhardt was ready for the challenge that lay ahead; all he lacked was the means. The death of his father in 1840 had in no way benefited him, but when William Nicholson's father died he left his son relatively well off, and perhaps as compensation for having let his friend down, William Nicholson agreed to underwrite Leichhardt's journey to the colony.

Leichhardt was clearly disappointed with the lack of interest shown in his trip by the English scientific establishment. However, when he sailed on 26 October 1841, he had with him a letter of introduction from Professor Richard Owen, the well-known anatomist, to Sir Thomas Mitchell, the Surveyor-General of New South Wales. As the good ship *Sir Edward Paget* made her way out of the English Channel, Leichhardt must have been well pleased. The

Ludwig Leichhardt.

great adventure had begun and his letter to the Surveyor-General was sure to open the right doors.

Although reserved in character, Leichhardt joined in the social life aboard ship. His education made it easy for him to mix with the professional people on board, however Leichhardt was no intellectual snob. He befriended the Murphys, an emigrant family hoping to start a new life in New South Wales, taking a special interest in the Murphy's young son John, who was a hunchback. After arriving in the colony, he continued to keep in touch with the boy, and when Leichhardt led his expedition to Port Essington in Arnhem Land, the teenager John accompanied him. Two others aboard ship, travelling to try their luck in the new colony were John Calvert and his brother. Leichhardt and John hit it off at once and later John was also a member of the Port Essington expedition.

After landing in Sydney in 1842, Leichhardt took lodgings with a man called Marsh, a music teacher, who had also travelled out on the same ship. In the colony of New South Wales, then consisting of the territory covered by the present states of New South Wales and Queensland, there was a lot of talk of exploration, but little action. Leichhardt nevertheless waited for an opportunity to present his letter of introduction. He hoped to be able to join the Surveyor-General's next trip as a naturalist. For some time in the colony there had been speculation about the opening up of an overland route to the far northern settlement of Victoria at Port Essington, established late in 1838. On 17 June 1840, almost two years before Leichhardt's arrival, Edward John Eyre had left Adelaide with an expedition attempting to reach the isolated outpost at Port Essington. His proposed route was to take him through the centre of the continent, but Eyre had got no further than Lake Eyre South, finding the salt-lake country impassable. Turning back to his depot at Mount Arden, Eyre instead successfully completed his famous marathon trip to the Swan River in Western Australia.

The New South Wales colony was short of money, Sir George Gipps and Sir Thomas Mitchell were at loggerheads, and prospects of a new attempt to reach Port Essington seemed remote. When Leichhardt finally met with the Surveyor-General, he came away with little hope of joining an expedition. Nor did there seem to be any call for his services in the tiny scientific establishment in Sydney, and his application for the position of Superintendent of the Sydney Botanic Gardens was turned down. Had he been successful, the history of exploration in this country may have been a lot different. At this point fate stepped in. Leichhardt met Lieutenant Robert Lynd, the Barrack Master of the 63rd Regiment; Lynd befriended the disillusioned young scientist and invited him to share his bachelor establishment. This meeting with Lynd, like his job rejection, was to play an important part in Leichhardt's future.

To keep busy, Leichhardt gave lectures in botany and went on collecting excursions in the areas around the city. In August 1842, he accepted an invitation from Alex Scott to go to Newcastle. Scott, a wealthy grazier, made Leichhardt welcome and left him to his own devices. It was the opportunity Leichhardt had been looking for. He tramped farther and farther afield, collecting hitherto unknown botanical specimens and gaining valuable bush experience. The Spartan-like self-discipline he had subjected himself to on his collecting tours in Europe now stood Leichhardt in good stead. In December he purchased a horse and set out to travel throughout the newly settled districts of New South Wales.

After checking Scott's grape-growing enterprise in the Hunter Valley, Leichhardt set out on a lengthy bush apprenticeship. It would be May 1844 before he returned to Newcastle, bush-wise and loaded with specimens. On his journey, sleeping on the ground in the bush between the scattered stations of the settlers, Leichhardt rode north and crossed the Great Dividing Range into the Moreton Bay area. Then as a guest of the Archer brothers, he made Durundur his headquarters for trips into the Wide Bay area. In their struggle to repel the settlers, the Aborigines of Wide Bay had gained a formidable reputation. They had been responsible for spearing many shepherds and station hands, and had generally made life difficult for the whites

ABOVE: Durundur Station.

RIGHT: John Archer of Durundur, which Leichhardt made his base during his trips into the area around Wide Bay in Queensland.

in the newly opened pastoral lands. To the consternation of the settlers, Leichhardt went among the local tribes unarmed and unmolested; he sat at their fires and learned all he could from them. While the settlers thought him crazy, Leichhardt collected not only specimens but knowledge that later he would put to good use.

From Durundur Leichhardt rode west over the ranges, with letters of introduction to the settlers of the Darling Downs. On the Downs he listened to much discussion about the proposed route to Port Essington. The settlers were impatient with the colonial administration and talked of a settlers' expedition to open up the north to the tiny outpost of Victoria, named in honour of the Empire's Queen. The great dream of trade with Asia had led to the establishment of Victoria, and Port Essington had been chosen as its site because it was where trepang fishermen from the Strait of Malacca and the Celebes anchored to replenish water supplies and to recruit Aborigines to help gather the grey sea slugs that were a delicacy in Asia. During the season there were hundreds of proas (boats) working the north coast of Australia. The genetic influence of the Malay and Macassar seafarers is still evident today in the coastal tribes of the far north. The settlers on the Darling Downs were aware that Fort Dundas on Melville Island and Fort Wellington at Raffles Bay had been abandoned in 1829, and were convinced that without a road from the south to open up grazing land and alleviate the isolation of the settlement, Victoria too, would wither on the vine.

Leichhardt listened and did his own planning. While others had talked, he would act; he would go to Port Essington himself. Before he left to return to Sydney, he was sure he had the full support of the settlers on the Downs. By the middle of 1844 Leichhardt was back in Sydney. He returned a very different man to the new chum who had landed in the colony some two and a half years before. In Sydney there was disenchantment with the long delay in organising an expedition to Port Essington. The colony was united in its opinion about the importance of the venture, but nothing was being done about it. The Surveyor-General was still waiting for a grant from London to finance his trip, and the colony was in economic depression; the Governor, Sir George Gipps, could offer no solution.

Leichhardt took stock of the situation, saw his chance, and put his plans into operation. He still had some money left but not enough. He sold specimens and fossils collected on his journey through the north, and raised loans for the balance required to put a small private expedition in the field. He purchased 13 horses—he had hoped to buy mules as well, but his meagre resources had to be conserved. He spent some money on necessary instruments, restricting himself to the basics—a chronometer, a thermometer, a hand-held compass, and a sextant and artificial horizon. Leichhardt also took with him the map by Arrowsmith that showed little more than the northern coast.

Leichhardt was disappointed in the response from the Downs settlers. Their talk of a settlers' expedition appeared to be just that, and he was forced to look elsewhere for men who were prepared to join him. Leichhardt really had little to offer and found his scope for recruiting limited. He finally settled on a party of six others that included John Calvert; the teenaged John Murphy; John Roper, who had once worked for Alex Scott at Newcastle; William Phillips, a convict; and two Aborigines, Harry Brown and Charley Fisher.

Many Sydneysiders believed the expedition was doomed to failure and were careful to dissociate themselves from it. However, there were others, influenced by Lynd and by the Reverend William Branwhite Clarke, the influential ex-headmaster of Sydney's The King's School, who thought that the rather eccentric German scientist might just win through. In any case it was the only expedition they had. Early in August 1844 Leichhardt was ready to leave Sydney; the journey, he believed, should take seven months from a starting point on the Darling Downs.

NORTH TO PORT ESSINGTON

Leichhardt was not the only explorer preparing to head north. Charles Sturt was also about to leave Adelaide to explore the centre of the continent. The South Australian colony, more financial than New South Wales, had allocated a sum of £4,000 to Sturt and agreed that the members of the expedition would be on the colony's payroll. Charles Sturt believed, like many others, that the centre of the continent held a vast inland sea. He would skirt around the salt-lake country that had foiled Eyre in his attempt to reach the centre and go up the Murray to its junction with the Darling, then up the Darling to where Mitchell had camped in 1836. From the Darling he planned to head northwest into the centre. With Sturt went a nuggetty Scot named John McDouall Stuart. It was a name the colonists would later have cause to remember.

The contrast between Leichhardt's and Sturt's expeditions was striking to say the least. Sturt took with him 16 men, six drays, one cart, one boat, a number of saddle horses and numerous draught animals. When Leichhardt eventually left the Darling Downs, he took nine men, 17 horses, 16 head of cattle, plus instruments and supplies. The explorer also took with him three kangaroo dogs. Unfortunately none of them survived the journey. These dogs, usually a type of greyhound cross, were very fast and greatly prized by the early settlers for their ability to run down kangaroos—hence their name.

Leichhardt and his party left Sydney on 13 August 1844 aboard the *Sovereign* with Captain Cape at the helm. With Leichhardt went the party's personal effects and 13 horses. It was the first leg of an amazing journey that must rank high in the annals of exploration. Leichhardt was to lead his party overland for 4,800 kilometres through the unknown wilderness of northern Australia; the trip would take a little over 14 months, and for a great part of that time the exploration party would live off the land. Leichhardt had a philosophy, simple yet radical for the times: where indigenous people could live and thrive on what nature provided, so too could he and his party.

Nine months into the marathon journey, Leichhardt wrote in his journal that although ragged and at times weary, the party was in good health despite having no flour or salt left. Flour and salt were not the only provisions the party was to do without: bush honey would take the place of sugar, and long before the tea was exhausted Leichhardt had discovered not one, but two coffee substitutes. Nothing that grew, swam, crawled, hopped, ran or flew escaped his scrutiny. His knowledge of botany was invaluable, and he had a scientist's curiosity coupled with a willingness to try anything.

After seven rather rough days at sea, the *Sovereign* docked at Brisbane where Leichhardt received an enthusiastic welcome. He purchased equipment and supplies including 1,200 pounds (550 kilograms) of flour; 200 pounds (90 kilograms) of sugar; 80 pounds (40 kilograms) of tea; and 20 pounds (10 kilograms) of gelatin. To help transport all this to the Darling Downs, from where he intended to set out north, friends gave Leichhardt the loan of a dray, and the explorer bought a light spring cart. There had been heavy rain in Brisbane and over the Downs for some time and, as a result, the roads were in a bad state. The cart was involved in an accident and a shaft was broken. Undaunted Leichhardt swapped it for three

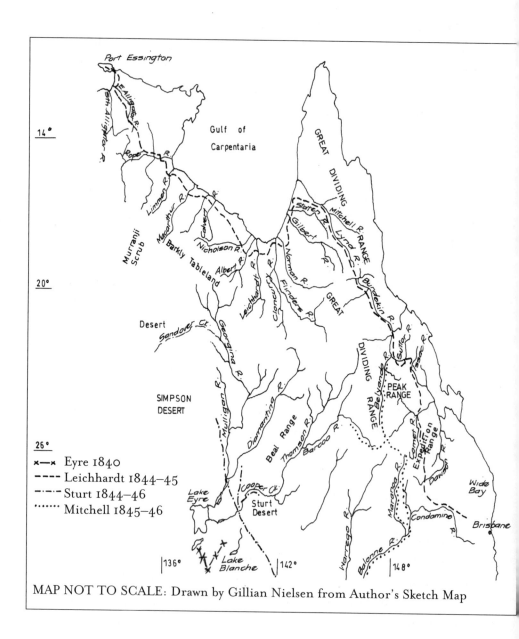

Port Essington

14°

Gulf   of

Carpentaria

GREAT DIVIDING RANGE

Mitchell R.

Staten R.

Gilbert R.

Lynd R.

Norman R.

Flinders R.

Burdekin R.

Muranji Scrub

Barkly Tableland

Macarthur R.

Calvert R.

Nicholson R.

Albert R.

Leichhardt R.

Flinders R.

Cloncurry R.

Limmen R.

Rope R.

E. Alligator R.

Sth. Alligator R.

20°

GREAT

DIVIDING RANGE

Suttor R.

Belyando R.

Isaac R.

PEAK RANGE

Desert

Sandover Ck.

Georgina R.

SIMPSON DESERT

26°

×—× Eyre 1840
---- Leichhardt 1844–45
—·—·— Sturt 1844–46
······ Mitchell 1845–46

Mulligan R.

Diamantina R.

Beal Range

Thomson R.

Barcoo

Comet R.

Expedition Range

Dawson R.

Maranoa R.

Wide Bay

Condamine R.

Brisbane

Warrego R.

Balonne R.

Lake Eyre

Cooper Ck.

Sturt Desert

Lake Blanche

|136°

|142°

|148°

MAP NOT TO SCALE: Drawn by Gillian Nielsen from Author's Sketch Map working bullocks and thereafter put his faith in packs. Leichhardt's decision was a good one considering the unknown terrain that lay ahead of the expedition. The advantage of drays and carts is that they have a greater carrying capacity than packs. This is more than offset, however, by the problems they create. Wheeled vehicles are slower than pack animals; crossings are difficult over creeks and gullies; tracks must be cut through scrub; while swamps, flooded streams and ranges are virtually impassable.

When droving, I always preferred to use packs, a habit vindicated when in 1954 I bought a light wagonette from George Booth senior. George had just retired from droving and he threw in a couple of wagonette horses with the vehicle. Later, travelling down the Northern Territory–Queensland border fence with a mob of bullocks a wheel fell off the wagonette. Luckily I had two packs on board in case of trouble: taking these my horse tailer packed two horses with the essentials and caught up with the cattle. I managed to borrow additional packs until I could get my own sent, and completed the trip with them. I decided that the faith I had always had in packs had not been misplaced. Utilising both horses and bullocks for the job, Leichhardt was to find that packs gave him complete mobility. When the supplies carried by a pack animal were consumed, the explorers could eat the animal.

John Roper's horse was to meet this fate when it broke a leg as the party crossed rough country on the upper Burdekin River. Nothing was wasted when a beast was slaughtered. The meat was jerked (cut into thin slices and sun dried), the fat was rendered down for cooking and for greasing the saddles and packs, even the skin was saved. Leichhardt wrote in his journal that a nourishing thin soup could be prepared from the cured hide. Around the Gulf the expedition passed through flying fox habitats, so into the pot went the flying foxes. This addition to the explorers' diet was later to raise some eyebrows among the refined Sydney folk for whom the eating of fruit bats was obviously not the done thing; Leichhardt of course could not afford to be quite so fastidious.

Setting up camp.

While he was preparing for his departure from the Darling Downs, Leichhardt was persuaded to have three more men join the expedition: Pemberton Hodgson, who was a resident of the district; Caleb, an American Negro; and John Gilbert, a naturalist and a collector for the well-known John Gould. Leichhardt had some misgivings about including Gilbert in his party, and right from the outset there was a misunderstanding on Gilbert's part about the collection and destination of specimens other than birds. The three new members added four horses and two bullocks to the stock numbers, and Leichhardt bought five working bullocks. These, together with the gift of four ration steers from John (Tinker) Campbell and his partner Steppes, and a bullock from Mr Isaac, brought the expedition's total stock numbers to 17 horses and 16 head of cattle of which 12 could carry packs.

Leichhardt spent some time at Campbell's Westwood Station on the Darling Downs where he made preparations, such as breaking in the bullocks to pack work and altering packs. The packs used by Leichhardt would have been a far cry from the pack saddles designed later; and in all probability were military saddles adapted for the job. When faced with a long trip, it is essential that pack saddles are fitted well to the animals that will be carrying them. Badly fitting pack saddles will cause them galling and sore backs. It is also important that there is no confusion about which pack is carried by which of the various pack animals. Once a pack saddle is fitted to a horse, or in Leichhardt's case a bullock, that animal always carries that particular pack saddle. Mountings for pack saddles include cruppers, girths and flank girths, breast plates, breechings, and a long surcingle that goes over the whole load and is fastened near the girth. Balancing the load a pack animal is to carry is very important if the pack is to remain stable. Badly balanced pack bags can cause the pack saddle to chafe the pack animal, and in extreme cases can result in the pack rolling. Balancing the weight in pack bags is an acquired skill, done by lifting a bag in each hand and comparing the weight of each. On the stock routes, horse tailers were past masters of the art. Because gear was taken from at least some of the pack bags overnight, each morning bags had to be weighed again. I have seen a horse tailer take the bags of a dry ration pack, frown, transfer a packet of tobacco from one bag to the other, then satisfied, pack the horse! He may well have been playing to the gallery, but it was one of those tasks horse tailers took pride in.

It is possible, of course, even when everything is done correctly to have disasters when using packs. Prior to taking delivery of a mob of Territory bullocks, I was travelling through timber country on Willaroo Station, south of Katherine in the Northern Territory, when Red Ned, a packhorse, went berserk. He had bumped into a branch containing a wasp's nest. These short-tempered little insects will descend on any intruder like small avenging angels with fire in their tails. Anyone riding a horse stung by these little scourges is guaranteed to have his hands full keeping control of the mount. Packhorses unrestrained by human hand are free to give full rein to their feelings of pain and outrage. Red Ned certainly did just that. He put on a show that would not disgrace a station outlaw. The pack rolled, the surcingle burst and Red Ned bolted, kicking the pack saddle and bags to pieces as he went. We managed to pull him up about half a kilometre away, he had been carrying the corned beef pack and his route was strewn with beef, broken strapping and bits of pack saddle. Luckily I had a day to spare before taking delivery of the bullocks. We camped at a nearby creek and I set about the task of repairing the pack saddle and its mountings. The scattered pieces of corned beef were gathered and dusted off, proving to be none the worst for their wild ride.

Leichhardt was finally ready to make a start at the end of September. Already he found the stock numbers inadequate for the party that now numbered ten, and on alternative days some of the expedition's members had to walk. The expedition began when Leichhardt led his party out from Jimbour (also known as 'Jimba'), the farthest flung station on the Downs, on the first of October. Travelling northwest he had made the Condamine River by 7 October. Faced with thick scrub Leichhardt left the river and was caught in heavy rain for almost a month at a lagoon he called Kent's Lagoon. It was here that Leichhardt realised that handling a group of unpaid volunteers would be no easy job. It did not help matters that Gilbert regarded his role as that of a freelance naturalist and collector because of his association with John Gould. After an extended argument on the morning of 17 October, Charley Fisher threatened to shoot John Gilbert. Leichhardt intervened, took all issued equipment from the Aborigine and banished him from the camp. Charley returned before dark, and after apologies to both Gilbert and Leichhardt was reinstated. On another occasion young John Murphy and Caleb became lost and were away for two nights before being found and brought back. This was to happen to all the members of the expedition at various times, and was hardly surprising considering the nature of the country.

By the end of October Leichhardt came to the decision that stock numbers and ration usage made reducing the men by at least two an absolute necessity. In fairness to the original members it was agreed that Caleb and Gilbert, the last two to join, should be the ones to return. Gilbert, however, persuaded Pemberton Hodgson to go in his stead. It was a fateful decision on the part of the naturalist. Before Hodgson and Caleb left the party, Leichhardt slaughtered one of the small steers and the meat was jerked. The experiment was entirely successful and yielded 65 pounds (30 kilograms) of dried meat.

Now with his reduced party all mounted, Leichhardt left Kent's Lagoon, and on 6 November discovered and named the Dawson River. By 27 November the expedition was at a range Leichhardt called the Expedition Range. The explorer established a firm routine for shifting the camp forward. Reconnoitring parties would be sent ahead to find water and to establish the best route to take. These scouting parties consisting of two, sometimes three, usually included Leichhardt himself, and were often away overnight. The explorer obviously realised that the fitness of the stock was of the utmost importance if he was to be successful. Soft going for the pack animals and good grazing close to camp were made top priority. Only when Leichhardt was satisfied did he shift the main camp. At night the horses were hobbled—their legs loosley linked together— and the cattle put to graze on the best feed available. These practices demonstrated excellent stock husbandry; keeping animals well fed and well watered ensured they remained in good condition and pre- vented straying—elements vital to the success of the venture. Caring for the hooves of travelling stock is another important factor in the completion of a long journey, and picking the best route showed good stock management. In handling the number of stock he could afford to take with him, Leichhardt demonstrated all the attributes that were later to identify a good drover. The men took turns at night watch, with always someone awake by the fire. During Leichhardt's absence, Gilbert as the next most senior member, was left in charge. It may have been an unfortunate choice, as we will see later, but Leichhardt had little option.

The expedition suffered the loss of some of its precious flour when a bag was ripped in scrub. Leichhardt set all hands to work scooping it up. The residue had a little too much of the environment in it to be added to the general supply, so it was cooked up as a gruel. Leichhardt wrote that it was quite good; I dare say it was rich in natural fibre.

Early in December the expedition was on the Comet River, one of the tributaries of a river Leichhardt was later to call the Mackenzie. On the morning of the 7th, the party received a nasty shock. Charley, whose job was to bring in the horses, galloped into the camp saying that the Aborigines were attacking the stock. On investigation the only tangible evidence of the alleged attack was what appeared to be a slight spear wound in the shoulder of one of the horses. As Leichhardt patched up the wound, he must have been keenly aware of his position: he was responsible for the safety and welfare of the men; the fitness of the stock, which was essential to the success of the expedition; and above all he carried the onerous burden of guiding the expedition through the wilderness to Port Essington, still some 2,500 miles (4,000 kilometres) away. To add to Leichhardt's woes, he did not have a happy camp. He had been

Close to the place on the Mackenzie River where Leichhardt began to head northwest.

unable to weld the exploration party into a unified team and this incompatibility was to prove costly to the explorer's reputation.

Before reaching the Mackenzie River, the explorers found the framework of a hut that was obviously of European design, the poles having been cut by a steel axe. Leichhardt deduced that it must have been the work of an escaped convict. If he was correct, the absconding prisoner had certainly put some considerable distance between himself and the authorities. In the early days of settlement, the Aborigines were known to be hospitable towards lone white men who strayed into their tribal areas. A typical example of this is the case of James Murrell, a man who lived with the Aborigines on the central coast of Queensland for some 17 years. There may have been other men—convicts who went bush and who took axes or other tools with them. I tend to think that this is the only feasible explanation for the hut seen by Leichhardt.

It was on the Mackenzie that the explorer found the first coffee substitute, a sprawling vine growing in the river sand yielded a bean that when roasted and ground produced a very acceptable brew.

Despite his problems, Leichhardt made reasonable progress, naming rivers and geographical features after members of his party, and in honour of prominent citizens of the colony. Those people who had been afraid that the north would be festooned with foreign place names need not have worried. All sources suggest that Leichhardt was influenced far less by his roots than by colonists from the British Isles.

As the expedition continued north, it encountered numerous Aborigines. Leichhardt's policy was to be friendly but not intimate with the indigenous population. He exchanged presents with them whenever possible and did everything he could to avoid trouble. In fact until 28 June 1845, the only trouble he had with Aborigines was with the two members of his own party. On 25 January that year, both Harry Brown and Charley Fisher deserted. Leichhardt was not unduly worried; he knew they would not go far, being out of their own area, and true to form the two returned next day, and after a

Charley and Brown, members of Leichhardt's original party.

good talking to were reinstated as members of the expedition. On 19 February more trouble flared when Charley Fisher struck Leichhardt in the face after being taken to task for gathering honey when he was supposed to be bringing in the horses. He was again banished, and Brown went with him in sympathy, but soon returned to the fold. Charley asked for forgiveness the following day, and after having his prized honey-gathering tomahawk confiscated, the Aborigine was once again reinstated.

Leichhardt's critics were to interpret this leniency with the two Aborigines as weakness. It must be remembered that this was at a time when flogging was a common practice in enforcing obedience, and by no means restricted to the punishment of convicts. There were others, however, who regarded the explorer as a martinet. It seems that as far as Leichhardt's critics were concerned, he was on a hiding to nothing, regardless of the course of action he took.

When the Mackenzie River turned northeast, Leichhardt left it and turned northwest, discovering and naming the Peak Range. From there he led the expedition on to the Isaac River, naming it after one of his supporters. After travelling up the Isaac for some 110 kilometres, Leichhardt reconnoitred ahead and finally found a route through a gorge to the headwaters of a stream he would later call the Suttor. As the Suttor was flowing in the direction the explorer wished to go, he followed it right down to its junction with the Burdekin River. Leichhardt had somehow missed seeing the Belyando join the Suttor; this may have been because of the way the two rivers meet.

On 3 April, Leichhardt started up the Burdekin River, the party feasting on figs as they went. The expedition was to travel up the Burdekin for over a month. On the night of 10 April, Leichhardt camped on the river at a spot just short of latitude 20 degrees south. It must have been very close to the present site of Sellheim. On the 6 May Roper's horse broke a leg and was promptly dispatched. The meat from the unfortunate animal was cut into strips and dried in the sun. This method was used whenever one of the expedition's bullocks was slaughtered as well as with the kangaroos and emus shot by the party.

Looking north from Leichhardt's campsite 121 on the Burdekin River.

Unlike many other explorers, Leichhardt learnt from the Aborigines. Every freshly deserted camp he came across was of vital interest to the explorer. He studied the food the Aborigines ate and the method of preparation. As a botanist Leichhardt was fascinated by the native plants and fruits eaten by the Aborigines, and his interest was to have practical long-term benefits—no member of his party suffered from scurvy on the long journey to Port Essington. This is in marked contrast to the disasters visited on other explorers by this disease, which is caused by the lack of vitamin C. The title of 'Doctor' given to Leichhardt was a honorary one only, nevertheless his scientific training was both extensive and widely acclaimed. If Leichhardt took a sample of food from an Aboriginal camp, he always left a gift in return. How to deal with the seeds of the pandanus palm had him puzzled for a long time, but the secret of how to roast, grind and soak the seeds (thus rendering them harmless) was revealed at last in an Aboriginal camp by the Gulf of Carpentaria. Leichhardt had put his plan to utilise bush tucker into effect as soon as the trip started, and wildlife had been used to augment supplies right from the outset.

When catching their horses, members of the expedition had been in the habit of grabbing their mounts by the tail to prevent them walking away, and on 10 May Roper tried out this novel method on his new mount. The startled horse responded by felling Roper with a double-barrelled kick to the chest. Roper was lucky to escape with nothing more than injured pride and severe bruising.

The numerous groups of Aborigines the party had encountered during the trip had not caused any trouble. Leichhardt's policy of arm's length friendliness had, to his knowledge, been adhered to, and been remarkably successful. Perhaps an element of complacency had replaced earlier caution, however, Leichhardt may not have been so confident of avoiding trouble had he been aware of what had gone on at times when he was absent from the camp.

THE DEATH OF GILBERT

The attack on Leichhardt's party, which resulted in the death of John Gilbert and the wounding of John Roper and John Calvert, was so uncharacteristic of the Aborigines' behaviour to that point that it warrants special attention. Leichhardt had led the expedition up the Burdekin as far as he could, then after finding a way over the rough watershed, he had crossed over on the head of a river he called the Lynd. He had followed the Lynd down in a northwesterly direction until it met the Mitchell, before he turned west around the Gulf of Carpentaria coast. This had taken the expedition a lot further north than it needed to go, but Leichhardt may have chosen this route because of the soft going for his sore-footed stock: the country away from the river flats was rough and stony. On the way, the Aborigines the party encountered had, as usual, appeared quite friendly.

On 27 June 1845, the expedition camped at a lagoon close to a dry creek. Brown and Charley went out hunting in the afternoon to bag something for the pot. Shots were heard and they returned with the news that they had disturbed Aborigines attempting to drive off the cattle and spear them. The two said they had sent the natives packing and brought back a dilly bag of yams taken from the Aborigines' camp, which was located just 250 metres from the explorers' own camp.

This rather startling news by all accounts brought little or no reaction from Leichhardt or his companions. There is no record of extra precautions being taken to guard either the camp or the stock. This seems extraordinary as at any time during the evening or night the Aborigines could have speared the stock at their leisure. That they did not, then or later, is significant. The night watch so conscientiously adhered to earlier in the journey was at this stage virtually nonexistent. There had been no trouble from the Aborigines to worry about, and Leichhardt found it impossible to police the system.

The next day, 28 June, the expedition travelled on and camped by one of a chain of lagoons in which the water had dried back a fair distance, and was surrounded by a belt of tea trees. Smoke had been seen rising from a number of points during the day indicating that Aborigines were active in the area. Apparently no concern was felt by any of the party and the camp was set up with William Phillips rigging his tent on the other side of the water hole from everyone else. Gilbert and young Murphy set up their two-man tent in the trees with the entrance away from the fire and the packs. Calvert and Roper did the same but with the tent opening towards the camp. It was Leichhardt's habit to stretch out close to the fire, and the two Aboriginal members of the expedition usually did likewise. From Leichhardt's account of the night's events in his journal, there is nothing to indicate that trouble was expected and this is borne out by the fact that he did not issue the necessary percussion caps to Charley and Brown that would allow them to fire their guns. The stock had been turned out to graze as usual, and after a gourmet meal of whistling ducks and teal, the explorers settled down for the night.

At approximately seven o'clock, before any of the party were asleep, Leichhardt, by the fire, was startled by a shout, and a shower of spears lanced out of the darkness. A few were thrown at the fire and at Phillips' tent, but the two tents in the trees bore the brunt of the attack. John Murphy slipped out of his tent and, jumping behind a tree, opened fire at the Aborigines, wounding at least one. Gilbert,

The camp at Dried Beef Creek.

who followed him, was apparently struck by a spear as he left the tent. Meanwhile the attackers had overrun the other tent spearing and striking both Calvert and Roper with waddies. Brown and Charley, after obtaining caps from Leichhardt, joined Murphy in firing at the Aborigines, who melted into the night dragging at least one wounded tribesman with them.

The assault was over in a matter of minutes leaving the party stunned by its ferocity. Gilbert had been killed almost instantly, and Roper and Calvert were both in a serious condition with multiple wounds inflicted by spears as well as waddies. Roper had spear wounds to the head; another spear had penetrated his cheek damaging an optic nerve. He had another spear wound in the loins, and yet another spear was still stuck through his left arm. Calvert had been struck a number of times with waddies. The most serious was a blow to the face that had crushed his nasal bones. He also had serious wounds in the groin and knee where he had been hit with barbed spears.

The spear was the main weapon used by Aborigines for both hunting and fighting, and launched from a woomera or spear thrower, these weapons could reach with deadly accuracy up to a distance of 100 metres away. Approximately 3 metres in length, the spears were barbed, making it more difficult for a wounded kangaroo or emu to escape by dislodging it. Spears were usually tipped with fire-hardened wood or with secured points of quartz, flint or jasper. In most tribal areas, 'quarries' can be found where spear points, scrapers and knives were chipped by the tribe's toolmakers. For fishing, the Aborigines used spears with the head split into two or three points without barbs. Fishing spears were thrown down into the water by hand. After white settlement, Aborigines in the north made what were called shovel-nosed spears; in place of points these had large flat blades of sharpened iron or steel that could disembowel a bullock as easily as a man.

Aborigines used the waddy, or nulla-nulla, for delivering the coup de grâce to game. These strong heavy clubs, about 1 metre in length, were formidable weapons at close quarters and were also used by the Aborigines for hand-to-hand fighting among themselves.

Both Calvert and Roper were in great pain, and Leichhardt did what he could for them in the darkness. He cut the barbed spear from Calvert's groin, and was forced to break off the head of the barbed spear in Roper's arm before it could be removed. It must have been a night of terror for them all, suspecting that at any moment another attack might erupt out of the gloom.

Before daylight, wailing was heard in the distance indicating that the natives did not escape without loss. As soon as he could see, Leichhardt again tended to the wounded. In the light of day he was better able to assess the extent of their wounds and to clean and dress them more professionally. Later in the morning Leichhardt reconnoitred around the camp to find the Aborigines gone and the stock unmolested. Gilbert was buried that afternoon with Leichhardt reading the Church of England funeral service over the body of the unfortunate naturalist.

Leichhardt now found himself in the position of having to balance the needs of the wounded against the safety of the whole party; every hour he stayed in the camp increased the risk of another attack on either the party or the stock, yet he had to wait until he thought Calvert and Roper fit enough to travel. With the nearest help well over 1,500 kilometres away it is difficult to imagine a more parlous situation. It is a tribute to Leichhardt's strength of purpose that he never lost sight of his goal in this time of crisis.

The added workload on the other members of the party helped, as it gave them little time to reflect on their predicament. Under Leichhardt's care, the wounds of Calvert and Roper responded well, although they were both still in pain. On 1 July, Leichhardt made the decision to move on. He had stayed three days in the camp and must have felt that to stay longer would have been tempting fate. He took the expedition on 20 kilometres to a campsite by a creek. It must have been hell for the wounded men, who rode and suffered without the benefit of painkillers of any kind.

Leichhardt's critics were to have a field day over the events of the 28 June: 'He had camped in the wrong place'; 'The camp could not be defended!'; 'He should have been better prepared for an attack!'.

The criticism is not entirely without foundation. It was a stupid place to camp, for an attacking party was given every advantage by the nearby tree cover allowing a close approach. Being scattered all over the place like a dog's breakfast, the camp could not be defended, but as things turned out, however, that fact probably saved the expedition from annihilation. Had they been camped together in one small area there is every chance the entire party would have been wiped out. The fact that Leichhardt and his companions were certainly unprepared is puzzling. With the benefit of hindsight it is easy to criticise this lack of vigilance, yet there appears to have been some cause for concern. Why these concerns were not acted on warrants closer scrutiny.

A lot of the information regarding the attack was recounted or written by the survivors long after the event, and is confused and conflicting. Let us then look at the accepted facts.

i. The attack was just after dark and was fiercely driven home.
ii. The attack was aimed at the humans not the stock.
iii. Smoke signals had been observed during the day of the attack while travelling to the fatal campsite.
iv. There had been a clash of some sort with the Aborigines on the afternoon of 27 June.
v. The explorers were totally unprepared for any attack.

The ferocity and determination of the attack indicates that it was a retaliatory one directed against the men only, but initiated by what? Had the explorers camped on a sacred water hole? If the hole had been a large permanent one, a native well, or an isolated rock hole, it may add weight to this possibility, but as it was, the hole was one of a number, all of which were fast drying up.

The only other possibility is that the attack was a direct result of what had occurred the day before. The smoke signals seen as the explorers were shifting camp indicate that their progress was being monitored by the tribe Charley and Brown had clashed with the day before. Were the two telling the truth about the contact? Or had they invented a story to explain the shots? Gilbert doubted their story, so did Phillips. In his book *Strange Journey*, naturalist Alec Chisholm quotes these extracts from the journals of the two men. Firstly from the diary of the dead ornithologist:

I am inclined to think that the real cause was that our blackfellows surprised them at their camp, and as I know Charley would not be very particular in his treatment of a native woman if he caught one, it seems to me that the men perhaps resisted, when the boldness of our fellows in the superiority of their weapons effectually drove them off; and as Charley and Brown well know the Dr [Leichhardt] would not at all consent to such conduct, they saw the necessity of making up an excuse.

Chisholm continues:

That Gilbert was not alone in his doubts is indicated by Phillips, who in his notes on the events of the 28th had this to say: 'On the first view of the case this certainly appears to have been an atrocious act on the part of the natives, but on careful reflection there is little doubt that it was only natural retaliation for some insult or injury, fancied or real, offered to them at the last camp by our blackfellows; for it is certain that it was the same tribe who followed on our tracks, and shrewd suspicions were entertained by one or two of the party, that like all other mischief there must have been a woman at the bottom of it.'

The above allegations, though supportive of one another, are of course suspicions only. More notice can be taken of Gilbert's opinion as it was expressed before the attack and only hours before he was killed. Phillips on the other hand wrote his account some time after the event. If their doubts regarding Charley and Brown's story were real, why did they not warn Leichhardt of their concern? If their concern was genuine, there must have been a reason for their reluctance to inform their leader. Could it have been that to do so may have implicated themselves? E. M. Webster, in her book *Whirlwinds in the Plain,* has this to say regarding Gilbert's control of the camp in Leichhardt's absence:

Another situation perhaps less familiar to modern readers, occurred when Gilbert was in charge of the camp during Leichhardt's absence. On January 18th 1845 Gilbert noted with humorous appreciation the 'slyness' with which a native offered the explorers the use of women, and two days later, as John Murphy reveals, the travellers 'had some gin'. Whatever the nature of the gin the party enjoyed under Gilbert's auspices, the incident was not one he wished to submit to future readers.

The author was reluctant to include the above in her book, and only did so to show that Gilbert's diary was not a perfect check on

Leichhardt's account of the journey. Alec Chisholm's book was very anti-Leichhardt, and in part was based on Gilbert's journal.

If then, the whites had themselves abused Aboriginal women and were reluctant to advise Leichhardt of the possible danger, why did they not take precautions themselves? The only possible answer can be that it had happened before without Leichhardt's knowledge and there had been no reprisals on those occasions.

Some of the most vexing questions about the attack concern the circumstances of Gilbert's death. Accounts of the attack agree that both Charley and Brown were close to Leichhardt at the fire at the outset and had to wait for the explorer to find percussion caps before they could fire on the attackers. Various accounts also agree that Gilbert was killed almost instantly early in the assault, as he followed Murphy out of the tent. This tent was placed in the trees some distance from the fire, with its entrance facing in the opposite direction. Drawing on Charley's retelling of Gilbert's death, based on the stories of the other expedition members, here is Alec Chisholm's account of Gilbert's death:

> There was no time for reflection. Gilbert grabbed his gun and scrambled out of the tent. In that moment a spear flew through the half-light, by the greatest mischance it struck Gilbert in the chest.
>
> He staggered and groaned; but with a supreme effort, he kept his feet.
>
> 'Here Charley' he gasped. 'Take my gun! They have killed me!'
>
> Grasping the hilt of the spear in both hands, Gilbert pulled it from his breast and sank to the ground.

Here is Leichhardt's version:

> Nor seeing Mr Gilbert, I asked for him, when Charley told me that our unfortunate companion was no more! He had come out of his tent with his gun, shot, and powder, and handed them to him,

when he instantly dropped down dead. Upon receiving this afflicting intelligence, I hastened to the spot, and found Charley's account too true. He was lying on the ground at a little distance from our fire. And, upon examining him, to my sorrow, saw that every sign of life had disappeared, the body was however, still warm, and I opened the veins of both arms, as well as the temporal artery, but in vain; the stream of life had stopped, and he was numbered with the dead.

This is Leichhardt's description of the wound:

> The spear that terminated poor Gilbert's existence, had entered the chest between the clavicle [collar bone] and the neck; but made so small a wound, that for some time, I was unable to detect it. From the direction of the wound, he probably received the spear when stooping to leave his tent.

Both above accounts of the fatality are based on details given by Charley. Chisholm has obviously embellished his version a little: it has a 'Boys' Own Annual' ring to it. Leichhardt's account does not mention Gilbert's removal of the spear at all. Charley could not have been in two places at the one time, so did this happen before or after he received caps from Leichhardt? Charley Fisher's description (via Chisholm) of the victim's actions after being mortally wounded lacks credibility—for Gilbert to retain his grip on his gun when struck by a spear thrown with enough force to kill him is astounding. The mind boggles, however, when the dying man is supposed to have handed the firearm to a companion, then removed the spear himself; this was no flesh wound, the spear would have been jammed between the collar bone and the neck muscles and lodged deep in the chest of the victim.

If, then, Gilbert did not remove the spear who did? Was it Charley? Did the fact that Gilbert died immediately after the removal cause him to lie, possibly believing he had, by his action, caused Gilbert's death. If Gilbert was speared at the front of his tent how did his body end up a little distance from the fire (accepting Leichhardt's version)? Or was the supposed site of his wounding wrong? Could he have been hit by a missile as he ran bent over towards the fire?

Leichhardt's description of the wound raises further questions. The spear that struck Gilbert may not have been a barbed one, nevertheless it would have had a stone head attached to its shaft; the small wound that Leichhardt had difficulty in locating is not consistent with it being the combined entry and exit wound of a spear. Leichhardt's description of the wound sounds in fact more like the typical entry made by a rifle ball. The expedition carried both no. 4 and no. 6 shot as well as ball. There were four men firing guns during the attack (Leichhardt never used guns due to poor eyesight). In the darkness and confusion could Gilbert have been killed by a stray round as he ran to the group by the fire? The only certainty is that we will never know.

If Leichhardt had been careless and complacent prior to Gilbert's death, the events of the 28th were a bitter lesson. That he learned from the lesson is evident from what he later wrote:

Since Mr Gilbert's death, the arrangements of our camp have been changed. I now select an entirely open space, sufficiently distant from any scrub or thicket, even if we have to go a considerable distance from water. Our pack saddles are piled in two parallel lines close together, facing that from which a covert attack of the natives might be expected. We sleep behind this kind of bulwark, which of itself would have been a sufficient barrier against the spears of the natives. Tired as we generally are, we retire early to our couch; Charley usually takes the first watch, from half past six to nine o'clock; Brown, Calvert, and Phillips follow in rotation; while I take that portion of the night most favourable for taking the latitude. John Murphy has his watch from five to six. We generally tether three horses, and kept one bridled; and with these arrangements we slept as securely and soundly as ever.

Leichhardt's use of the packs to construct a palisade was typical of the resourcefulness he had shown when organising the expedition and on other occasions during the journey. Time and again he was forced to improvise, achieving the desired result with what was on hand or with what he could find. Bush ingenuity, as shown by Leichhardt, really knows no bounds. The humble pack saddle can be used in many ways. It has often served as a mosquito-net peg on which to rig a bush net, and I have seen pack saddles utilised to make a quite serviceable boat: the pack saddles are placed end to end and upside down in the middle of a tarpaulin; whatever gear and rations are needed are placed within the flaps of the saddles; then the ends and sides of the tarpaulin are thrown over and lashed tight. The resulting makeshift boat can then be steered across a flooded creek by one or two swimmers. The benefit of using this method is that rations like flour and sugar are not damaged by water. If loaded packhorses are put across a flooded stream, these rations have to be covered and tied on top of the pack saddles; even with these precautions water damage can result if a packhorse gets into trouble.

The measures Leichhardt put in place were a little like shutting the stable door after the horse had bolted. Nevertheless, it indicates that the explorer had regained full control of the expedition.

Gilbert's death was a tragedy, and a loss to the infant scientific establishment in the colony. He was Gould's most able and most active collector, and he had sent specimens of both birds and mammals to Gould in England from Tasmania, Swan River, and Port Essington, where he had spent a number of months prior to joining Leichhardt's expedition. In his book *Furred Animals of Australia*, Ellis Troughton pays tribute to Gilbert as a collector. Gilbert's arrangement with Gould seems to have been a purely financial one. Gilbert did the collecting while Gould did the classification, naming and cataloguing of the specimens sent to him. In short Gilbert got the cash and Gould got the credit. Of the 700 species of native birds in Australia, 215 are credited to Gould, none to Gilbert. Gould did honour Gilbert by naming the Gilbert Whistler after his collector, as well as a very rare marsupial listed in *Furred Animals of Australia* thus: Gilbert's rat-kangaroo, *Potorous gilbertii*, Gould 1841. In all likelihood it was a specimen sent to Gould by Gilbert during the latter's sojourn at Swan River. After 1879, there were no official sightings of the potoroo for 115 years, and the little marsupial was thought to be long extinct. However, in November 1994 two researchers from the University of Western Australia discovered a small but thriving colony of the long lost potoroos at Mount Gardiner. Like the Leichhardt mystery, Gilbert's rat-kangaroo has survived the passage of time.

Port Essington and Fame

By 5 July 1845 the expedition had travelled some 80 kilometres from the camp where Gilbert had been killed. It was a red letter day, for at last the party had reached the Gulf coast. Everyone rejoiced at the sight of the shimmering waters of the Gulf of Carpentaria. Leichhardt gave the latitude of this position as 16 degrees 27 minutes 26 seconds. In his book of the expedition, Leichhardt wrote how the pessimists of the party, who had despaired of ever reaching the Gulf, now changed their attitude. The passage smacks of personal triumph, forgivable I dare say under the circumstances.

On 7 July, an Aboriginal man walked into the camp just on dusk mistaking it for his own. He walked up to the fire, then realising his mistake bolted and shinned up a nearby tree. Nothing would induce the Aborigine to descend. Charley Fisher thought it might be a good idea to dispatch the yowling intruder with a well-placed shot. Leichhardt quickly vetoed that idea, and after the party had withdrawn some distance from the tree in which the Aborigine was perched, he slid down and disappeared.

Some days later, on 12 July, Leichhardt crossed a river he named the Gilbert in honour of the dead naturalist. Calvert's wounds were responding well, but Roper was growing increasingly weak. On the 15th, Leichhardt decided to stop for two days to give him a chance to recover. By the 19th, the explorer wrote that Roper was greatly improved, although he still found riding a severe trial. While out scouting with Brown on the 20th, Leichhardt met and made friends with a group of Aborigines. He gave them some small gifts, and persuaded them to accompany him back to the camp. Leichhardt records that the Aborigines showed great interest in the clothes and hats of the party. These locals guided the party along the banks of a river Leichhardt called the Yappar (this was later to be called the Norman due to confusion over its location). As the party journeyed on around the Gulf coast, they were living to a large extent off the land; bush tucker and game were adequate in keeping the men in reasonable physical condition. Their diet included native fruit and yams, while pigeons, ducks, geese, fish, flying foxes, 'roos and emus all went into the pot.

After skirting south around tidal creeks, the expedition was forced to camp without water on 25 July. Charley, who was in charge of the cattle, allowed them to stray as the horses were being hobbled by the

The point where Leichhardt crossed the river he called the Yappar, later renamed the Norman.

others, and the next morning, after he and Murphy went out to muster them and did not return for some hours, Leichhardt sent the rest of the party back to water at the previous camp while he waited for Charley and the bullocks. The explorer spent a thirsty day and night with just his equally thirsty horse for company. He dozed by the fire with the reins in his hands, and to add to his discomfort, during the night the restless nag stepped on his head. John Murphy and Charley finally arrived back at 7 am with some water and promptly boiled the billy for their perishing leader. The bullocks had been found, and the party regrouped at the old camp.

Leichhardt's behaviour throughout this crisis demonstrates again bushmanship and clear thinking. Many cases of death by perishing are the result of panic and lack of logical thinking. I once knew a character with the nickname of 'Spinifex', who left Urandangi in central Queensland with a horse plant (a number of horses) to travel up the Georgina River. Somehow he became disorientated and perished within sight of the river channels. In another incident, two young new chums who had grown disillusioned with stock-camp life decided to leave the Morstone Station camp in secret and walk to Camooweal (northwest of Mount Isa) some 50 kilometres away. In those days Camooweal aerodrome had a rotary beacon just visible on the horizon from the camp. The lads set off at night taking a tin of preserved peaches with them, but no water. Everything went well until daylight came and of course the light vanished. The lads became disorientated and began walking in a circle, as lost people often do. By this time the pair were very thirsty and the sweetened fruit did nothing to assuage their craving for water. They were all but done for, when by sheer luck the pair stumbled on the tank at the *whim* (a well) on Morstone. When they were found, the lads were lying in the water in a serious condition.

Again at Camooweal one summer during the 1950s two young chaps went through on a motor bike en route to Darwin. They were advised to take water with them but chose to ignore the advice. The bike broke down between Camooweal and the Three Ways. Before

47

another vehicle came along, one of them was dead and the other close to death. It doesn't take long to become dehydrated in mid-summer.

Motor vehicles can give a false impression of distance, which is fine while ever the motor is running. If a vehicle breaks down, however, the scenario is very different. I once found a family standing beside a broken-down sedan between Winton and Boulia in central Queensland. There were three young children in the group including a babe in arms, and they did not have a drop of water with them. I managed to help them overcome their danger, but could not begin to understand the recklessness of the parents. The one thing they had done correctly was to stay with the vehicle. My advice to people in the bush who become lost, separated from their companions or are the victims of a motor breakdown is simply: stay cool, stay where you are and above all, always carry water.

While looking for the straying bullocks, Murphy and Charley had found a creek containing large deposits of salt. In less than ten minutes the pair had collected enough of the salt to last them the remainder of the trip. Salt is an important element in the human diet; among primitive tribes it was, and in some remote areas still is, a much sought-after trade commodity. In developed countries salt is present in most of the processed foods sold, but a diet completely free of salt is not very pleasant—I can vouch for that from personal experience. In 1954 I took a short cut down the Victoria River with cattle from a property on the Western Australian border. We ran into a late wet season and were without salt for over a week. We were without a lot of other rations too, but it was the salt we missed the most. Animals as well as humans need salt, herbivores gaining it from the minerals and salts occurring naturally in grass and foliage; carnivores from the flesh and blood of their prey. Some salt licks occur naturally, others are prepared licks put out by graziers. One has only to observe how popular these are with stock to appreciate that their need for salt is as great as ours.

The expedition was now making good progress inland from the coast, and on 6 August, Leichhardt began following the course of a river he believed to be the Albert, named by Lieutenant John Stokes when he surveyed the area in 1838. In this he was wrong; the river in question was later named the Leichhardt by A. C. Gregory. The mistake is understandable when one realises Leichhardt did not have Stokes's maps; they were not printed until 1846. The only map he did have was Arrowsmith's, a map that lacked detail and was later found to be not entirely accurate.

By 18 August, the party was on the true Albert, which Leichhardt named the Beames, and two days later reached the Nicholson, which Leichhardt named after his one-time host in England, Dr W. A. Nicholson. The expedition made good progress despite having to cross numerous creeks, many of them tidal. On 31 August rain fell most of the day, forcing the explorers to rig the tents for the first time since Gilbert's death. On 2 September the party camped on a creek Leichhardt named Turner's Creek. Early the next morning

Leichhardt mistook this river for the Albert, which had been named by Stokes. A. C. Gregory later renamed it the Leichhardt.

Brown had a very lucky escape when he was returning from a call of nature and mistaken for a wild Aborigine; his frantic shout just saved him from being shot.

Leichhardt named the Calvert River on 8 September, and on 14 September, after seeing a flock of seven emus near a river, called the stream Seven Emus. The birds had been feeding on a fresh shoot of grass, which the expedition's stock hoed into as well; unfortunately it went through them like a dose of Epsom salts, doing little for their already weakened condition. This type of grass, called goose picking by drovers, doesn't have the bulk to satisfy hungry animals. Its nutrient value, already low because of the high water content, is almost completely lost due to the scouring it causes. In 1958, I struck goose picking when travelling down the Georgina stock route with a mob of Eva Downs bullocks from the Northern Territory. The Eva mobs usually did not give a lot of trouble, but on this particular trip they received a bad fright, and rushed (the equivalent of America's stampede) every night for over a week. When we hit the goose picking, the mob, already nervy and stirred up, began to lose condition quickly.

A drover's overriding responsibility is to the cattle under his control, and his reputation depends on his ability to keep his charges in the best possible condition. The time-honoured law of the stock routes is simple: if there is no grass on the route, go where the grass is. Never one to ignore tradition, I surreptitiously took the mob out on to station grass every few days and filled them up before returning to the light pickings on the stock route. By these means I managed to keep the bullocks in reasonable condition until the grass on the route improved.

Leichhardt continued his naming of rivers. On the 16th the expedition was on a river Leichhardt called the Robinson, and on the 21st he named the McArthur River in honour of the Macarthur family of Camden, New South Wales. The party had now been travelling for almost 12 months, and their clothes bore testimony to the rigours of the trip. Shirt tails and sleeves had been sacrificed to

Frank Shadford, owner of Seven Emus Station, at the place on the Robinson River where cliffs prevented Leichhardt and his party from crossing.

patch the more important parts of their apparel, and to ease the situation Leichhardt split Gilbert's clothing up among the men. The next day, 22 September, saw the last of the tea finished. Leichhardt experimented with sterculia seeds as a substitute and after roasting the seeds, a quite reasonable brew was produced.

Groups of Aborigines were often encountered, most of whom were friendly and seemed to have a knowledge of both knives and guns. In his book Leichhardt put this down to contact with the Malay fishermen, who for centuries had anchored on the northern coast to replenish water supplies.

On the McArthur, the coffee first found on the Mackenzie was again rediscovered. Leichhardt sent the men to collect as much as they could while he and Charley went ahead to scout for water. On their return the whole party enjoyed a drink of 'bush coffee'. The collected beans lasted for three weeks, and this brew together with the sterculia 'coffee' greatly compensated for the lack of tea.

On 1 October the expedition camped at longitude 136 degrees on a river Leichhardt called the Red Kangaroo River. This may be the river now called the Batten. Six days later one of the weak pack bullocks was slaughtered and its load transferred to one of the horses. To enable the meat to be carried, some of the party's collected specimens had to be abandoned. At the time the party was camped on a river Leichhardt called the Limmen Bight River, as he surmised from Arrowsmith's map that the river would empty into Limmen Bight. The group travelled on to the northwest, meeting Aborigines who showed more and more the influence of contact with the seafaring men from the Strait of Malacca. On 16 October the expedition lost their remaining kangaroo dog through sickness. It was sadly missed, for the dog was a link with the past, and there was no guarantee they would not meet the same fate. Then on 18 October, Roper reported seeing a large tidal river. In recognition of his companion's scouting efforts, Leichhardt called it the Roper. Game abounded and the hunters of the party shot 51 ducks and two geese. That night the explorers sat down to a veritable feast.

The Limmen Bight River where Leichhardt made a crossing.

In Leichhardt's estimation the Roper was some 700 yards (640 metres) across. On 20 October, the party travelled 16 kilometres up the Roper and camped a few kilometres past a fresh-water tributary. Next morning, 21 October, there were grim tidings for Leichhardt. Charley Fisher came back from getting the horses with the news that three of the strongest horses had drowned during the night. They had gone into the river and the steep muddy banks, combined with the restriction caused by the hobbles, had given the horses little chance. Horses unfortunately cannot reason: there was water in the river and they were thirsty. Had they been given a late drink at the creek the explorers had passed, the tragedy may have been avoided. Leichhardt was devastated. As it was impossible to increase the loads on the remaining pack animals, the explorer was forced to give up his complete botanical collection. He had faithfully collected and preserved leaves, flowers and fruit from hundreds of plants but was forced to burn the lot. It must have been with a heavy heart that he watched the flames consume the work of over 12 months.

The next day Aborigines from the Roper River were met, who from their behaviour had seen Europeans before. Leichhardt continued on up the Roper and on 23 October he named the Hodgson and the Wilton rivers. That night the expedition camped on the banks of the Roper close to its junction with the Wilton. Leichhardt thought the site would be a safe watering place, however two of the horses got into trouble trying to climb up the bank. Panic led to the animals becoming bogged. Leichhardt decided his only chance was to wait for high tide. He watched the horses all night, and next morning stripped off, went into the river and swam one of the horses to safety. The other, however, got itself tangled up in the lead rope and drowned. The Roper proved to be something of a nemesis for the beleaguered explorer. The number of horses was now reduced to nine, and slowly but surely the strain of travel was beginning to tell on them. After a late start the next morning, the expedition crossed the river at the now well-known Roper Bar.

The Roper Bar must have seemed like the end of the earth to Leichhardt and his companions as they struggled across it towards the end of 1845. In less than 27 years the same bar would become a hive of industry; ships that had navigated the river unloaded supplies there for the building of the Overland Telegraph Line, which largely followed the route taken by John McDouall Stuart between 1861 and 1862. Another intrepid explorer, who like Leichhardt refused to admit defeat, Stuart was stopped twice by the tangled scrubs of the Murranji and forced to return to Adelaide. But McDouall Stuart was not to be denied, and on his third attempt to cross the continent from south to north in 1862 he broke through the Murranji barrier north of the site of Newcastle Waters. Ten years later the Overland Telegraph Line was completed and the young colonies were in direct contact with the outside world. Leichhardt too had pioneered an important route—the coast stock route around the Gulf coast to the Roper River. D'Arcy Uhr in 1872 made the first epic trip along the coast road with cattle from Charters Towers. In the years that followed, thousands upon thousands of cattle were moved up the coast road to stock the newly established stations in the northwest.

Leichhardt led the expedition up the northern bank of the river but on 26 October, Brown's horse was exhausted, forcing the party to hold up for a day. On 28 October the expedition passed a large spring flowing from the bottom of a rise. The weather was now very hot, heat rash was becoming a problem and Leichhardt had also developed boils on both knees, making riding uncomfortable. The party had a day's spell on 31 October, as Brown's horse was again in trouble. While out hunting, the expedition's two Aborigines saw the first crocodile yet seen by the group. The party continued to successfully live off the land, and it was about this time that Leichhardt collected the first specimen of the mainland spectacled hare-wallaby. John Gould later gave the marsupial the scientific name, *Lagorchestes conspicillatus leichardti*, in honour of the explorer, but omitting the second 'h' from Leichhardt's name.

During the first week in November the expedition travelled through country that was part of the watershed of the Roper River. They came across large numbers of Aborigines and saw their roomy native huts constructed with both stringy bark and tea-tree bark. Still making progress, they were held up on 7 November when a bullock was slaughtered, forcing the party to remain in camp while the meat was dried in the sun. On the 12th another horse was lost through being staked by a large piece of broken timber it had run into, thereby throwing more strain on the party's mobility. Leichhardt had been heading northwest leaving the Roper creeks behind him and endeavouring to cross the divide onto South Alligator River water. He calculated the division lay on longitude 133 degrees 35 minutes east. On 17 November the expedition came to the brink of the basalt tableland and saw before them a sheer drop of over 200 metres. Below them stretched an extensive river valley with a number of tributary creeks feeding into the main stream. It was not until the 20th that the expedition was able to descend by a route found by Charley. The second last bullock was butchered on the 21st, having refused to travel further, and the party stayed in camp until the 23rd in order to dry the meat. The results were not the best, storms were becoming more frequent and the meat became flyblown.

By the night of 24 November the expedition had camped on the South Alligator at latitude 13 degrees 5 minutes 49 seconds south. Leichhardt calculated the expedition's position was only 140 miles (220 kilometres) from Port Essington, news that must have been reassuring to the rest of the party who for many months had failed to share their leader's confidence. The expedition had next to cross swampy country that proved very difficult to negotiate. Charley almost sank out of sight trying to retrieve a goose he had shot, and after the next day's stage, Leichhardt chose a camp close to open forest country where game was abundant. Charley who had been commissioned to shoot waterfowl for dinner returned with a whole tribe of Aborigines. They had in their possession a steel tomahawk and cloth of English make, and to Leichhardt it was obvious that the tribe had been in contact with either Malay boat people or other foreigners. The Aborigines became a little over-friendly after gifts were exchanged, so Brown mounted a horse and encouraged the natives to leave. They were back next morning in time to see the explorers eat breakfast, showing great interest in the food, but declining to sample any. Just then Brown returned to the camp with the one remaining bullock. The beast took one look at the Aborigines and charged scattering them left and right. After chasing them for some distance the bullock returned, the Aborigines did not.

On the morning of 2 December, an unarmed Aborigine came to the camp and greeted the explorers in English, calling Leichhardt 'Commandant'. Presents were exchanged with the friendly Aborigine, who knew of the settlement of Victoria, referring to it as 'Balanda', a corruption of 'Hollander', a word the Malays used to describe whites. Leichhardt had with him a small list of Aboriginal words compiled by Gilbert when he was at Port Essington, and it was to prove a great help in gaining information. Redmond, the last remaining bullock, was still striking terror into the hearts of the indigenous population, and when Leichhardt managed to retain the services of two Aborigines as guides, they stuck close to the leader for protection from the temperamental and racially prejudiced bullock.

Next day, 3 December, the expedition encountered a river Leichhardt thought was the East Alligator. Aborigines were again in attendance, and gifts were once more exchanged. (Leichhardt had commenced the expedition with a variety of trinkets for such purpose; however, by this time he was reduced to offering odds and ends of camp gear that were no longer needed, as well as pieces of iron.) On the 5th Leichhardt decided to spell for a day to let the horses recover. The local Aborigines visited the camp and gave the explorers a gift of fish. After receiving presents in return, the Aborigines became rowdy and showed signs of taking over the camp in a friendly way. Brown mounted his trusty steed and restored order, the visitors retiring to the other side of the lagoon from the one the explorers had camped on. Buffalo tracks were seen for the first time earlier in the day. On the 8th, after covering 14 kilometres, the party camped off the East Alligator River at latitude 12 degrees 6 minutes 2 seconds. Aborigines again visited the camp, and among them again was a character who spoke some English and called Leichhardt 'Commandant'. His name he said was Bilge. Most of the Aborigines the group was now meeting had a smattering of English and most had a knowledge of the settlement at Victoria. The Aborigines were rather contemptuous of the explorer's food, saying that at Balanda there was plenty of flour, rice and so on.

On 11 December Brown and Roper, who was still not completely fit, tracked and shot a young buffalo. The meat was shared with the local Aborigines who called the buffalo 'Anaburro'. The rest of the meat was dried in the usual way, probably saving Redmond from a like fate. The buffaloes may have come from the abandoned settlement at Raffles Bay.

Two days later, on 13 December the expedition reached the coast at Mount Morris Bay and turned northwest along the Cobourg Peninsula. On 17 December Leichhardt led the expedition out of the bush and into the tiny isolated settlement of Victoria on Port Essington. He had achieved the incredible. He had converted a dream into reality. He had covered 4,800 kilometres through an unknown wilderness, and had been on the road for a little over 14 months. For a great deal of that time he and the rest of the party had lived off the land. The survival of the party on 'bush tucker' was the key to the expedition's success, and probably Leichhardt's greatest triumph. Roper once said that he doubted if there was a place in Australia where Leichhardt would not survive. There were few, however, who learnt from his experience, as we will see. Burke and Wills certainly did not, leaving it until it was too late to ask for help from the people they had hitherto treated with contempt.

At Victoria the exploration party was greeted with pleasure and surprise by the commandant, Captain John McArthur. The lonely little outpost of the empire saw few visitors, and Leichhardt and his

Landing Place Port Essington
1848

Port Essington in 1848. Leichhardt's goal was successfully reached in 1845 after travelling 4,800 kilometres through unknown territory in just over 14 months.

ragged companions were made welcome by all while being plied with questions about the epic journey. To McArthur, bored to distraction at his isolated post, it must have been a delight indeed to have a traveller as erudite as Leichhardt at his table. The exploration party relaxed and enjoyed the meagre trappings of civilisation offered by the outpost. They were to spend the festive season at Victoria, but after a diet of jerked meat and flying foxes, every day must have seemed like Christmas Day to them.

Leichhardt spent the time at Victoria working on his journal and his maps. If he noticed any disenchantment the residents of Victoria felt about their lot he did not mention it. The tiny settlement, established just seven years before, was already in decline. Within four years it would be abandoned like the earlier settlements. The great dream of establishing a gateway to Asia would again be put on hold. Leichhardt found a good friend in John McArthur. At the same time the commandant of Victoria quietly assessed the character of the explorer's companions. He was not impressed by some of them, and later was forthright in voicing his opinion of them.

Within a month of the expedition reaching Port Essington the settlement received an unexpected visit from the little schooner *Heroine*. Captain Martin McKenzie chanced to call in on his way from Bali to Sydney. The commandant at Victoria arranged passage for the explorers with his fellow Scot, and when the *Heroine* left her berth at Port Essington the little schooner carried a party of men who had been given up for dead months before.

Meanwhile, back in Sydney, the powers that be, believing that Leichhardt and his party had perished through causes unknown, at last managed to stir the Surveyor-General, Sir Thomas Mitchell, into action. Mitchell received £2,000 to finance his attempt to reach Port Essington from a starting point of Fort Bourke on the Darling River.

Sir Thomas Mitchell,
Surveyor-General of the
Colony of New South Wales,
and Leichhardt's great rival.

Mitchell intended to travel up the western side of the Great Dividing Range. The difference between his and Leichhardt's expedition was remarkable. Mitchell took with him two boats, three carts, eight bullock drays, over 100 bullocks, 13 horses and some 250 sheep. The personnel of the expedition consisted of Mitchell, his personal servant, two free men (ex-convicts) and 23 convicts. Mitchell believed in a level of obedience difficult to achieve with free men, and ran the operation along army lines.

The expedition finally got underway on 17 November 1845. There were now three major expeditions in the field. In the far north Leichhardt and his party were on the head waters of the East Alligator River. While, to the west of Mitchell, members of Charles Sturt's expedition were struggling to get back from the centre of the continent to their base, lower down the Darling River. Sturt's health was broken, unable to walk or ride he was carried along in a dray.

Mitchell had trouble getting his cumbersome convoy of bullock drays, carts, and stock moving. He decided not to go as far west as Fort Bourke before heading north. In fact the Surveyor-General kept close to newly settled areas, and his progress was painfully slow. By the middle of March his expedition was no further north than the Barwon River, and was still close to stations established on that river. Despite his closeness to civilisation Mitchell sent no progress reports to Sydney, possibly with good reason considering his tardiness. Mitchell, who had always claimed that the trip to Port Essington could be accomplished in seven months, had now been on the road for four months, and was hardly out of sight of settlement. By this time the 130-ton (133-tonne) *Heroine* had negotiated the largely uncharted Torres Strait, and was sailing down the east coast to Sydney. Charles Sturt had been back in Adelaide for some time having failed to find a route north through the centre; what with Eyre's impassable salt lakes and the waterless inhospitable deserts that defeated Sturt, Port Essington, it seemed, would not be reached from Adelaide. However Sturt had, nevertheless, discovered Cooper Creek and had followed it up stream to the northeast for some distance. It was valuable information that set another missing piece of the jigsaw in place.

In camp on the Balonne on 18 April 1846, Mitchell received news of Leichhardt's triumphant return to Sydney. It was a devastating blow to the Surveyor-General. Despite his slowness to move, he had always believed that he alone should be the one to open the road to Port Essington. Now a rag-tag and bobtail private expedition led by a German opportunist had stolen his thunder. Antipathy and resentment towards the man he regarded as a foreign usurper consumed Mitchell. Leichhardt without knowing it, had made a bitter and influential enemy. The expedition was still in a position to receive the Sydney papers, and none of what Mitchell read pleased him. There was praise for Leichhardt, and even worse, a none too flattering comparison between him and the German. Mitchell's relentless vendetta against Leichhardt may well have had its beginning in a camp by the Balonne River.

Mitchell led his expedition north, travelling up the Maranoa River then northeast down the Belyando. His route was converging quickly with that taken by Leichhardt. Before abandoning the journey north and returning, he had got closer than 80 kilometres to Leichhardt's track. Mitchell would later claim credit for discoveries already mapped by the earlier explorer.

The *Heroine* docked in Sydney on 24 March 1846. Captain McKenzie had with him a report from the commandant at Victoria to the governor of the colony, together with a request for payment of four pounds, four shillings and five pence expended on clothing for Leichhardt and his ragged companions. Let us hope that the colonial bureaucrats enabled Captain McArthur to balance the books at Victoria before the settlement was abandoned.

The totally unexpected return of Leichhardt and his party caused a furore in the city. Most of the population had given them up for dead long before. Their apparent return from the grave was greeted with a euphoria that continued unabated for weeks. The colony had been disappointed and saddened by Charles Sturt's failure, but while they commiserated with Sturt they wanted a winner. Leichhardt had returned to them triumphant after lifting the veil from 4,800 kilometres of unknown wilderness, and the city paid him the homage they felt was his due. Dr Lynd, who had prepared his friend's obituary, was delighted to celebrate Leichhardt's return, and found himself basking in reflected glory that was not entirely unearned.

Some were to view with jaundiced eyes the adulation received by Leichhardt; over 100 years later Alec Chisholm, in the book *Strange Journey*, wrote this:

> Neither Sturt nor Mitchell, for all their labour, ever received a fraction of the public acclamation that came the way of Leichhardt. This was a curious yet more or less logical state of affairs. The Britishers did their jobs according to schedule and the public accepted their successes as normal developments. The eccentric German, on the other hand, was not expected to succeed, and when he did make a sudden reappearance in Sydney, months behind time, there was a strong and extravagant reaction from the attitude of 'I told you so!'. His very blundering had caused him to become a public idol.

Chisholm's criticism is quite unfair. While it is true that Leichhardt took far longer than expected to reach his destination, that estimated time of arrival was based on the opinion of Sir Thomas Mitchell, and at best that was no more than an educated guess, for neither Mitchell nor anyone else had any knowledge of what lay between the Darling Downs and the tiny northern outpost. Just how unrealistic this estimate was can be judged by Mitchell's own painfully slow progress on his expedition north: after five months' travelling from his starting point east of the Darling he was still able to obtain current Sydney newspapers. All things considered it is doubtful if anyone else, given the meagre resources available to Leichhardt, could have succeeded in reaching Port Essington.

The Failed Trip to the West

When Leichhardt and his six companions disembarked in Sydney on 25 March 1846, it was more than three months since they had achieved their destination of Victoria. The recuperative rest they had had at Victoria and the leisurely sea trip aboard the *Heroine* back to Sydney had done a great deal to restore them to health and fitness. It was fortunate, for the demands made on them by the good citizens of Sydney were considerable. Leichhardt, while flattered by the attention, was busy with plans for the future. His first priority was to publish a book based on his journals of the expedition. Within days of his return his strip maps of the route were placed, by order of the Governor, in the hands of Captain Samuel A. Perry, the Deputy Surveyor-General. Perry was commissioned to produce a to-scale map suitable for inclusion in Leichhardt's forthcoming book. The task would bring him no plaudits from his master, Surveyor-General Sir Thomas Mitchell, who had clashed with the Governor, Sir George Gipps, more than once over the years, and who regarded Perry as a toady. Nevertheless, with vice-regal approval Perry got on with the job of tidying up Leichhardt's maps.

Leichhardt found it difficult to concentrate on his book in the hurly-burly of Sydney. The Macarthurs of Camden had invited him to stay with them and Leichhardt gladly took up the invitation, escaping to the tranquillity of the countryside. In June he was back in Sydney to finalise work on the maps and to consult with Captain Phillip Parker King, who had undertaken to edit Leichhardt's manuscript. The explorer wrote English fluently, but King considered that the sensitivities of readers need not be subjected to details such as Leichhardt's opinion of the flesh of the dingo he sampled; the flying fox diet however, survived the editing. In June, Leichhardt received a letter from the Colonial Secretary advising him the administration would make a gratuity £1,000 available to the explorer and members of the expedition—£600 going to the leader, the balance to be split up among the others. The *Sydney Morning Herald* also started a public fund that would later hand £800 to Leichhardt, £150 each to Calvert and Roper, £80 to Murphy, £50 plus a pardon to Phillips, and £25 each to Brown and Charley. Captain McKenzie, who had not been paid by the government for

Captain Phillip Parker King, who undertook the editing of Leichhardt's manuscript.

the explorers' fares, was reimbursed from public funds and presented with a silver snuff box. Roper thought that more of the money should have gone to the rank and file. Leichhardt, however, had debts to clear and was already planning another exploration, matters that Roper neither knew nor cared about.

As though driven by some urge to further prove himself worthy of the recognition bestowed on him, Leichhardt could not rest on his laurels, he felt he had to do more—this time he would cross the continent from east to west.

As he went ahead with his plans, whispers circulated in Sydney that not all had been well with the expedition. Leichhardt, it was rumoured, had not in fact been the true leader of the party. John Roper tended to fantasise when talking of the trip. He was always the unsung hero and the real man in charge. Not certain of the facts and doubtful of what action to take, Leichhardt wrote to Calvert, one man the explorer knew to be totally loyal. In a quandary as to what he should do, Calvert showed Leichhardt's letter to Lynd, who advised him to front Roper. This he did. The confrontation resulted in Roper writing emotional letters to both Leichhardt and Lynd denying all guilt, and there the matter rested.

Leichhardt's approach to the government for funds for his next expedition met with a blunt refusal. There would be no further financial help for the explorer. There would be no convicts allocated to him, and no pay for members of any expedition he undertook. Leichhardt was one explorer who, it seemed, would be paid retrospectively, and then only on results. Considering the importance of the proposed exploration and Leichhardt's reputation, the government's attitude is difficult to understand. This may have been due to the influence of the Surveyor-General. Although Mitchell was not on good terms with Sir George Gibbs, the Governor, he had many powerful friends who could have lobbied on his behalf. The refusal to finance the trip may, on the other hand, have been due solely to the chronic shortage of money in the colony. It must be remembered that the finance for Mitchell's 1845 expedition came directly from London.

John Calvert, John Roper and John Murphy, long after their epic journey
to Port Essington.

If the trip was to go ahead, Leichhardt would again have to depend on unpaid volunteers, at best an unreliable method of assembling an exploration party, and one that was fraught with danger.

Disappointed, but determined to proceed, Leichhardt worked on his proposed route. He knew from the reports of both Eyre and Sturt that the southern half of the continent should be avoided at all costs, and he made no secret of his intended route. In his attempt to reach Swan River in Western Australia he would skirt Sturt's desert, going as far north as the Peak Range before turning west. There was a lot of conjecture about what would be found in the interior of the continent at that time. Sturt and many others believed in the inland sea theory; Sir Thomas Mitchell clung to the optimistic belief that great forests, lakes, and streams would be found there; others, including Leichhardt considered the deserts found by Sturt had provided the clue to the interior. Leichhardt held to the hope that Mitchell would have returned by the time he was ready to start out, providing valuable information on the country west of the Dividing Range.

At a dinner in Sydney, Leichhardt met John Mann, a surveyor and member of a well-respected English family. Mann had arrived in Sydney the same year as Leichhardt. He was 27 years of age, keen on exploration, and before he and Leichhardt parted that night, Mann had agreed to join the expedition to the Swan River. The next volunteer was Hovenden Hely. The son of a wealthy family, his father had held numerous positions before he died, the most important being the Superintendent of Convicts in the colony. Hely took over the family estates at Brisbane Water in 1841. He was 23 when he met Leichhardt and was used to the good life of Sydney society. The fact that he was related to Mann by marriage may have influenced the explorer in accepting him as a member of the party. John Roper was known to Mann and Hely. Both may well have heard criticism of Leichhardt from the unhappy Roper, who believed that he should have received a greater share of both recognition and cash for his services.

It is not hard to feel some sympathy for John Roper. He was an ineffectual type of fellow who had lost the sight of an eye in the attack that killed John Gilbert. But his lack of loyalty and his small-mindedness tend to negate any such feelings. Roper's feathers were further ruffled when a piece written by Leichhardt's supporter of old, the Reverend William Clarke, appeared at that time in the *Sydney Morning Herald*. Clarke expressed the hope that the explorer might engage companions who would not disgrace him. Roper took umbrage at the unfortunately timed article, and the relationship between him and Leichhardt was put under further strain. Even though Roper wasn't in the new party, he continued to nurse a grudge against Leichhardt and his contact with Mann and Hely may have planted seeds of future trouble.

Other members to join the expedition were: James Perry, a saddler; Daniel Bunce, a gardener-cum-botanist; Henry Boecking, who would do the cooking; a man called Meyer, who like Boecking was a German; and Harry Brown of the Port Essington expedition. The party travelled to the Hunter River by boat, embarking on 1 October 1846. John Mann did not accompany the main party. He was given the task of taking the stores direct to Brisbane by ship. Leichhardt and the rest set up camp at Stroud, New South Wales, where pack mules for the trip were purchased and broken in. Hely was commissioned to travel to Lamb's Valley and there pick up 290 goats for meat from W.C. Wentworth's station. An Aboriginal lad named Wommai helped Hely on the three-day droving trip back to Stroud, and after approaching Leichhardt with a request to join the expedition, Wommai became the ninth member of the party. Henry Turnbull, who worked at a local horse stud also successfully applied to join Leichhardt. On 13 October the expedition finally started overland for the Darling Downs, with the goats being driven along behind.

In November the expedition arrived on the Downs, where Mann met them with a dray load of stores. Henry Turnbull also caught up to the relief of some of the party who were growing heartily sick of shepherding the goats, and who welcomed another man to take a turn at the unpopular task. Although willing enough, Meyer, in Leichhardt's opinion, would not be up to the task ahead, and with some regret the explorer dismissed his countryman. The personnel of the expedition was finally settled; Leichhardt and eight companions would proceed to the Swan River settlement in the west.

Henry Russell, one of the settlers on the Darling Downs, met the party and invited Leichhardt to use his station at Cecil Plains as a jumping off point. An early wet had swept in over the Downs making the travelling difficult, however with Russell guiding them over the wet tracks the party reached Cecil Plains, despite trouble with straying stock, and made final preparations for the journey. Russell was one of the settlers who had earlier talked a lot about going to Port Essington, only to disappoint Leichhardt when his services were needed. In his book *Genesis of Queensland*, published in 1889, Russell wrote rather unkindly of Leichhardt's repeated attempts to master a buckjumping mule, but despite the patronising

Cecil Plains Station in 875. Owned by Henry Russell. This station was used as the starting point for Leichhardt's doomed attempt to cross the continent from east to west.

way the story is told, it is clear the explorer's determination overcame the recalcitrance of the mule. Russell's attitude towards the explorer was somewhat paradoxical: he would later describe Leichhardt as a clownish figure who spoke in almost broken English; yet before the explorer left Cecil Plains, Russell gave Leichhardt five cows and a bull with the rather quaint idea of breeding on the trip. One cow was lost with sickness within days of leaving, and the bull expressed its opinion of exploration by badly goring Hely's horse.

There had been no news of Mitchell's return. Leichhardt therefore reverted to his original plan to travel to Peak Range by his old route; he would then attempt to head west across the headwaters of streams running either north or south from the ranges he believed must run parallel to, and inland from, the north coast of the continent. On 9 December, Leichhardt led his party out from Jimbour on the Darling Downs. The expedition's stock was made up of 15 mules, 14 horses, 40 head of cattle, 270 goats, and 108 sheep. To take a menagerie like that into rough country with mainly inexperienced men was folly, and any good stockman could have advised the explorer against it. The settlers on the Downs only added to the problem by donating additional stock. Different types of stock travel at their own particular pace, they have individual grazing habits, and like birds of a feather they stick to their own kind; it was inevitable that Leichhardt would find his stock scattered in four or five mobs each morning.

Leichhardt was by now an excellent bushman. His handling of the limited stock he had taken to Port Essington spoke volumes for the quality of his stock husbandry. However, the explorer was not experienced in handling larger mobs, nor were many of his companions. When travelling stock in hot weather, it is important to get an early start; with the stock Leichhardt had, this was clearly impossible. To make matters worse, the explorer was short of mounts; it would have served Leichhardt better if his friends on the Downs had given him additional horses. To be fair Leichhardt had travelled the route before, at least as far as Peak Range, but in taking the mixed mobs through the rough country he was without the help of the deeply worn stock pads or tracks made by travelling mobs. These were always a boon to drovers when negotiating difficult terrain.

Leichhardt set double watches at night, with one man mounted and the other by the fire. With two tents, Leichhardt split the party into two groups according to social status: the colony at that time mirrored the English class system. It was a decision that did not help engender unity among men thrown together on a lengthy and perilous mission. Leichhardt shared the gentlemen's tent with Mann, Hely and Turnbull; the other three whites slept in the other tent; and the two Aborigines slept under the stars. With the Condamine River in full flood behind them, the exploration party set out on a journey that became an unmitigated disaster. Within the first few days there were quarrels between members of the expedition and especially between Mann and Leichhardt. On the night of the 11th, the stock rushed and were not fully mustered for weeks. Leichhardt held up in the camp until 3 January 1847. His reasons for doing so were twofold: he could not go on without the pack mules that had decamped, and on the 15th news had reached him that Mitchell had returned. Leichhardt sent Hely back to obtain what details he could of Mitchell's discoveries and made every effort in the meantime to muster the missing stock.

On 3 January, the last of the missing pack mules were found; Leichhardt decided to move on. He could not afford to waste any more time even if it meant continuing without the possibly valuable information from Mitchell. He sent Brown and Turnbull to bring back the still-absent Hely, who had spent Christmas Day and New Year's Day with his feet comfortably planted under the tables of settlers back on the Downs. Flies and mosquitoes become a constant torment to the men; John Mann became blind with blight; and most of the party suffered with diarrhoea and vomiting. After six days' travelling, Leichhardt spelled at Dried Beef Creek to wait for the absent three to catch up. The three finally caught up in mid-January with no useful information from Mitchell, news not calculated to please the impatient Leichhardt.

Intermittent rain continued making life miserable. When the party reached the Dawson River, it too was in full flood. After waiting a day, the crossing was made with some difficulty. Swimming the goats and sheep over proved to be an onerous and lengthy exercise. The great adventure must have begun to pall in the minds of the young gentlemen from Sydney.

In the gentlemen's tent, tension between Hely and Turnbull led to Hely being transferred to the 'men's' tent. Bunce, who gave up his place in the tent to Hely, was forced to sleep in the rain with the two Aborigines. Hely was the main cause of the trouble but both he and Bunce resented the move, and both blamed Leichhardt. Sickness was beginning to take its toll on the party, while the weather conditions added to their woes making tempers short and straining tolerance. Petty squabbles broke out among the men and Leichhardt and Hely clashed over Hely's horse that had developed a sore back. The animosity generated by these rather minor disagreements were to loom large when members of the expedition wrote their stories of the trip.

Sore backs on riding horses can be caused by badly lined saddles or by unwashed saddle cloths. The main reason, however, is the riding style of the man on the horse. I have known big, heavy men, who rode lightly and never gave a horse a sore back; on the other hand I have known light-weight men who would cut the back of every horse they rode. Back in the stock-camp days, it was not unusual for someone to say of a horseman's skill: 'Oh! He can hang up [ride a buckjumper], but he has teeth in his backside'. Meaning that the man gave a sore back to every horse he worked. To prevent giving a horse a sore back it is important for the rider to keep his or her weight in the stirrups, and not sit flat in the saddle.

By 31 January the expedition reached Ruined Castle Creek, and that evening in the camp Leichhardt tried unsuccessfully to extract an aching tooth that was tormenting Hely. The instrument he used in the operation was a bullet mould, giving some indication of the extent of the medical equipment carried by the explorer. Hely seemed to obtain some relief from the treatment; perhaps he feared another assault with the bullet mould. On 10 February, the party crossed the Expedition Range with Bunce growing increasingly ill, and the next day both he and Wommai went down with fever. That night the camp was flooded with water from a nearby creek. The rain was incessant and the boggy ground was now making travel difficult, particularly for the sheep.

The stock continued to hold the party up. On the 22nd, a morning's travel was lost owing to the stock having strayed. Later, three mules became hopelessly bogged, and after being relieved of their packs the three mules headed for the horizon. By the 24th the expedition had camped by the Comet River, which was roaring past in full flood, and a day later, when it being too wet to travel, Leichhardt moved the camp 6 kilometres to higher ground. Next day the stock had again strayed, and Hely and Turnbull, who were sent out to muster the strays, did not arrive until after dark with the missing animals. Despite problems with sickness, rain and straying stock, the expedition reached the junction of the Comet and Mackenzie rivers on 5 March. While the Comet was still running a banker, the other tributary forming the Mackenzie was not flowing at all above the junction. Leichhardt now saw his mistake in not crossing the Comet earlier and further south. Had he done so, he could have travelled north on the western side of the flooded river. This would have avoided the problem of having to face a difficult crossing at the junction.

The expedition settled down to wait for the river to fall, and by 12 March most of the party were down with fever, a condition they did not at that time connect with the clouds of mosquitoes making life a misery for everyone. Leichhardt dosed the men with quinine sulphate and calomel without any noticeable improvement in their condition. Leichhardt too caught the fever. He bathed twice a day in the river in an attempt to lower his temperature, and did what he could for his sick companions. Within a week the river was deemed to have fallen enough to allow a crossing, but a plan for the few fit men to establish a camp on the other side had to be abandoned when Boecking, Wommai, and Hely all suffered a relapse. John Mann who resisted the fever, with Bunce, who had now recovered, aided Leichhardt around the camp. Leichhardt must have learnt something of the character of his companions at the camp by the flooded Comet River. Wommai, Hely, and Turnbull were particularly bad patients. In the meantime most of the goats had scattered, some never to be found; the sheep and cattle had also wandered off; the horses and mules, however, were still under control because of their habit of coming to the camp each morning. There they would stand in the smoke from the fire to avoid the attentions of the tormenting flies.

On 20 March, Leichhardt made plans to cross the now-waist deep river in four days' time. Baffled as to what was causing the sickness he blamed the damp flour that had become sour. He withdrew the flour from the ration using it only for skillaglee (a dish of flour and goat's milk). Bunce, who had planted mustard in a small plot by the river, inspected his garden to find the mustard almost picked clean. There was hell to pay as suspicions ran high; Bunce claimed later that Leichhardt admitted to the theft, a damning indictment if true, however it could have been any one of the party, or indeed merely bandicoots. Arrangements for crossing the river went ahead. While a race was being built to push the remaining sheep and goats into the stream, John Mann collapsed with the fever he had been fighting for days. On the 24th, the day they planned to cross, not one horse or mule came to the camp as usual, and the attempt had to be deferred. Next morning there was both good and bad news for Leichhardt: one horse wandered into camp enabling the stock to be mustered; the bad news was that Boecking again went down with fever. Nothing daunted Leichhardt and the few fit men got the remaining goats and sheep over the river. Then Turnbull took sick. That night the tethered horses and mules broke free and had to be mustered again next day.

Finally, Leichhardt got enough pack animals together to take the stores over to the other side. They camped that night with the five sick men still on the southern bank of the Comet with the cattle. Finally the party was united in the new camp, and two days later Leichhardt went back over the Comet and mustered the cattle; most of the others were still sick with fever. Although he now had the river behind him, Leichhardt found travel was impossible because of the condition of members of his party. He looked after the sick, and he and Wommai, the only other fit man, fetched water and cut wood. While the remainder of the party lay about the camp in varying degrees of incapacity, Leichhardt worked and planned to move the expedition forward to the Peak Range where they might at last shake off the fever that was eroding the will of the party. He got little support for the idea from his companions who it seems conserved their energies for complaining about the food. By the end of March Leichhardt must have wondered if any of them had the stomach to complete the trip.

Over Easter, Leichhardt decided on a desperate plan: he would take the sick members of the expedition forward from a camp that was cursed by fever, leaving just Hely and Mann to guard the bulk of the stores until he returned; the remainder of the stock could then be mustered. Following the plan, Leichhardt left the invalids at a water hole on the Mackenzie, then he and Wommai went back to the old camp and began to muster the scattered stock. There was no offer of help from Mann or Hely. After a false start on 9 April, Wommai and Leichhardt moved forward on the 11th and once again the party was united. Leichhardt, who had packed the mules at the old camp, now had to unpack them himself while his younger companions lay in the camp. He too had suffered bouts of fever during the hold up; he had kept going because of a strong will and old fashioned guts, elements sadly lacking it seems in the make up of many of his companions.

In the new camp there was a slight improvement in the health of some of the men, however the stock strayed constantly making it impossible for Leichhardt to control them with so few fit men. Finally he decided to abandon the sheep and goats. On the 17th, after managing to muster the stock, another start was made and Leichhardt led the expedition some 16 kilometres to a camp by a lily-covered lagoon. After a delayed start the next day due to missing stock, the party arrived at a picturesque spot by a creek. It rained heavily that night, and next morning the mules and horses had cleared out. As that morning's start was out of the question, Leichhardt slaughtered a cow and jerked the meat, a risky business with rain about. At one time Leichhardt had thought fatty mutton may have caused the illness among the men, and he may have thought beef would help them to throw off the fever that had paralysed the expedition. Morale was very low. Secretly there was talk among the men of turning back, and they blamed their illness on Leichhardt's failure to carry adequate medicine. The explorer did however have quinine, and long after the cause of fever was known—malaria—and its host identified, quinine was still the standard treatment.

Leichhardt was sure the party's health would improve if he could only reach the higher ground at Peak Range, but the yet-undisclosed desires of others in the party lay in the opposite direction. Constant rain, straying stock and illness kept the expedition from travelling, and on the 27th Leichhardt went down with fever. Two days later he forced himself to go out with Wommai to muster missing horses; they were successful in picking up two. A planned start for the 29th was abandoned when the explorer again fell ill and the cattle could not be found. After six months' travel, the expedition had made little progress. With the best part of 4,000 miles (6,000 kilometres) still ahead of the expedition, Leichhardt felt he had no alternative but to reduce the rations. While this made sense to him, it did not to men who had become disillusioned with exploration and who were now thinking only of themselves. Returning was now openly discussed;

using the leader's health as a valid excuse for going back, Mann was deputised to approach Leichhardt with the proposal that either the party should return or the rations should be restored to what they were. Bunce alone demurred then reluctantly agreed. Neither claim had anything to do with Leichhardt's health, in short the whole proposal was humbug. Leichhardt was dumbfounded and confronted the gathered members demanding of each their opinion. There are a number of different versions of what took place at that confrontation. In the event Leichhardt agreed to increase the flour ration. It was a hollow victory for the men; what they had wanted was to return to the Darling Downs. And it was far from solving the real problem and by no means a satisfactory basis for the continuation of the expedition.

On 1 May everything was ready for departure the following morning. The start was later than planned, and just as the expedition was leaving John Mann collapsed and said he was not up to riding. Leichhardt was not to be thwarted. He dosed Mann with quinine and, leaving Brown with the invalid, took the expedition on. The pair caught up early next morning at a camp from where the Peak Range stood out clearly in the early light. Wommai was missing with the cattle; he had overshot the camp the night before, and on returning had again missed the camp leaving the cattle half way between the old and new camp sites. Determined now to go on Leichhardt sent Hely and Brown back for the missing cattle and moved the expedition to Newman's Creek to wait for the two to catch up. It was as close to the Peak Range as Leichhardt was destined to get.

On the afternoon of 6 May, Brown and Hely turned up at the camp; the pair had no cattle and but one horse between them. Leichhardt, filled with dismay, could do little other than accept their tale of woe. Brown and Hely explained lamely that they had not been able to locate the cattle and had lost the horse when it strayed from a night camp. Next morning Leichhardt sent Hely and the two Aborigines back to muster the missing cattle while he rode out to reconnoitre to the west. Returning late he became slewed, lost his bearings and spent the night away from the camp. Suffering from constant, weakening diarrhoea, he hid his growing despair at the hold-ups from the rest of the party. The bickering and bitterness during this period is clearly shown in the writings of Mann and Bunce: claims of greed in others and injustices to themselves are common. The writing is typical of men with nothing to do save feel sorry for themselves.

The days passed as they waited for the men to return with the cattle. Arguments over food were frequent, Leichhardt had promised them a pudding when they got to Peak Range. Now despite the absence of three of their number they wanted the pudding, and when Leichhardt refused, the men sulked like children. John Mann, Leichhardt's second in charge, had again been spokesman for his pudding-deprived companions. As Leichhardt rode out to find a suitable spot to kill a beast, the explorer must have wondered at the calibre of the men he had chosen to accompany him.

John Mann's description of the failed expedition clearly shows the enmity he felt towards his leader over many issues. With not enough to do he now took up his journal and polished up his already twice-written suspicion that Leichhardt had stolen and eaten over 20 pounds (10 kilograms) of sugar. This time he was satisfied his claim would be believed. Hely and the two Aborigines finally returned on the 17th bringing back just nine bullocks; eight others had escaped while they were looking for water. All in all it was a pathetic result for 10 days' mustering. Leichhardt was now between the devil and the deep blue sea. It was impossible to continue without the missing bullocks, yet he could not rely on his men to bring them to him. The only solution it seemed to him was to take the whole camp back to where the cattle were, muster them and start again. It meant going back two stages to a camp where they had already spent 11 sorry days. The decision must have been galling for the explorer, but it seems he had little alternative. John Mann, for reasons of his own, opposed the move back to pick up the cattle. He and the others had talked of saving face by taking the expedition to the newly established settlement at Port Curtis. Leichhardt's plans to start back the following day had to be postponed as the mules were missing. The explorer, keen not to waste the day entirely, slaughtered one of the bullocks, and that night the party feasted on fresh beef, the remainder being salted or dried, while Boecking undertook to make black puddings.

Later that night the remaining eight bullocks disappeared on Turnbull's watch. It is hard to believe that the constant failure to muster and hold the stock was entirely accidental. It seemed clear that the men were bent on abandoning the idea of going to Swan River. Their open proposal to do so had failed when the explorer had agreed to the ridiculous alternative of increased rations. To achieve their aim they may well have decided on a subtle campaign of passive resistance.

Leichhardt decided to send Hely and Brown back to start the muster, the main party would go back and join them when the meat had dried. The eight bullocks, now mustered again, went bush after Leichhardt handed the watch over to Perry. The meat dried slowly because of rain, and despite being on higher ground the men still fell ill. Their fever notwithstanding, the 36 black puddings made by Boecking quickly disappeared. On 23 May (Whitsunday) the men finally got their long-awaited sweet pudding, but with Hely and Brown back at the old camp missing out. The celebration was marred by an altercation over sugar, now under the control of Leichhardt.

Wommai had twice lost the eight bullocks after mustering them and getting to within a few miles of the camp: the first time the beasts were frightened by a large 'roo; the second time by thunder. On 28 May, Hely and Brown walked into the camp; they were not only minus cattle but minus their own horses. They had both been taken sick they said and had found no cattle. They had by accident found all the missing mules and horses but had lost them again together with their own mounts. Finding that the main party had not arrived at the old camp, they had been forced to walk back. The stock situation was now in crisis; it must have gone close to breaking Leichhardt's resolve. Hely's despair seems to have been limited to his missing out on all the pudding, clear evidence in Hely's mind of his leader's lack of consideration.

The next day Leichhardt himself went out with Wommai and mustered the horses and mules without trouble, securely tethering them for a start back the following day. At the end of May the expedition was back at the camp where the party had killed the cow. Leaving the remainder of the party again down with fever in the camp, this time Leichhardt and Wommai rode out to search for the cattle. The members of the expedition, consumed with self-pity, had become little more than a demoralised rabble.

When Leichhardt and Wommai returned on 7 June after mustering four of the missing bullocks, they found the mules and horses gone and everyone prostrated with sickness. At last Leichhardt acknowledged the futility of it all; he told the men he would take them back to the Downs. The explorer may well have compared his present companions with the members of his first expedition, and if he had done so the comparison would not have been flattering.

The next morning Leichhardt went out and mustered the four bullocks again, now needed for the return trip. By promising extra food he induced his companions to watch the bullocks night and day. He and Wommai then set out to muster the mules and horses; they were barely out of sight when the bullocks too departed. As their leader searched for the missing stock, the members of the expedition lay in the camp bemoaning their fate and cursing Leichhardt for not killing a bullock before he left; his selfishness, in their minds knew no bounds. Bunce's claim that Leichhardt had eaten the mustard, and Mann's allegations regarding the 'stolen' sugar were mulled over until unfounded suspicion became established fact. Taking refuge in their journals they shrouded their own inadequacies by vilifying Leichhardt. Leichhardt was away for ten days. The extended absence of the leader began to worry the men and finding they had to look after themselves brought about an improvement in their condition. While Leichhardt was away, the four missing bullocks were seen feeding near the camp, and after some debate one was slaughtered and the remaining three allowed to go bush. Three mules and two horses wandered into the camp on the 13th, and three days later Hely, Brown, and Turnbull set out to search for their leader.

Leichhardt took little food with him preferring to travel light and live off the land. He and Wommai finally found one mule and six of the missing horses. The tracks of the rest of the missing mules and horses indicated they were well on their way back to the Downs. Leaving the tracks, Leichhardt and Wommai rode on to find all the missing cattle, for once together in a mob. With a camp full of sick men and the decision made to return the cattle were of little use to him. But it must have been with a heavy heart that the explorer rode away and left them. Returning with the mules and horses on the 17th, Leichhardt found Hely and company camped 10 kilometres out from the main camp. Fearing that something serious had happened to Leichhardt, thus leaving them stranded, the three had made a rather lethargic attempt to look for him. The 18th was declared a holiday, and another pudding was consumed. Leichhardt took the opportunity to write up his diary that had been neglected for some time; the improvement in the health of the party now the return was eminent did not escape his notice.

Leichhardt took stock of the situation: he now had ten horses and nine mules for the trip back to the Downs; some stores and packs were left behind, and on 21 June the sorry cavalcade started on the return journey.

In his book, *Genesis of Queensland*, Henry Russell describes the return in July 1847 of the expedition in 'Funereal procession' to his property at Cecil Plains. Russell showered bush hospitality on the weary men. But there is a hint of smugness in his account of Leichhardt's failure. Russell was one of those men who talked about exploration while Leichhardt acted; the tall poppy syndrome may have been alive and well as far back as 1847.

There were many factors that contributed to the failure of this exploration. Singly each one may have been overcome; in concert the problems they created were insurmountable. The mixed stock certainly caused problems, and would have done so even in isolation, but not to the extent of threatening the future of the expedition. The season was a lot wetter than it had been on Leichhardt's first trip; the effect of the weather could have been largely neutralised, however, if Leichhardt had crossed the Comet River high up (further south) rather than travelling down the eastern bank of the river. This mistake resulted in the impetus of the expedition being destroyed. Sickness too was an important factor that impacted on the ability of members of the expedition to function; again this was largely a result of the hold-ups in the vicinity of the Comet and Mackenzie rivers. There is some doubt however whether at least some of the illness may have been feigned; Leichhardt who was older and generally in poorer health than other members of the expedition managed to withstand the effects of the fever quite well. The last factor contributing to the disaster was, I believe, the crucial one, and it may well have destroyed the chances of success even if everything else had gone well. That factor was the calibre of the men Leichhardt had chosen to accompany him; in the final analysis they did not have the stomach for the task. The young men from Sydney had seen or heard of Leichhardt's return from Port Essington—the party looking fit and rested after a sea journey—and they would have witnessed the adulation showered upon the triumphant explorers. It may well have given the young volunteers a very false impression of what exploration was all about. Despite warnings from Leichhardt of what they might expect, the young men had little idea of the privations and rigours that lay ahead of them. When they were needed most, they were found wanting.

The most important message to come out of the failed trip was the problems caused by relying on unpaid volunteers for exploration. The situation could often result where the leader's authority depended on the goodwill of his companions. The disadvantages inherent in this type of operation are obvious when compared with strickly disciplined, government-funded expeditions. It is little wonder Leichhardt ran into trouble, for he found it impossible to exercise his authority over men who had decided on their own agenda.

INTO THE UNKNOWN

Sir Thomas Mitchell returned from his trip in November 1846. In his report he claimed to have discovered a great river that flowed to the Indian Ocean. This river he had named the Victoria, and would, he maintained, provide a safe and direct route to the north. Mitchell had been in the field for 12 months. After abandoning his attempt to reach Port Essington by an alternative route, he must have felt the need to discover something of major importance. Wishful thinking may have led him to assume more than was wise regarding the course of his Victoria.

In his journey north, Mitchell followed the Belyando River almost to its junction with the Suttor, and to within less than 80 kilometres of Leichhardt's track. On 12 August 1846, he gave up the attempt to reach Port Essington and back-tracked up the Belyando to his Camp xliii. On 10 September, Mitchell set out with three men and a month's rations to explore to the southwest. Determined not to return without a discovery that would do him justice, he noted in his journal that he was hopeful of finding a river that flowed to the north Australian coast. Three days into the trip he believed he had found the river he so desperately wanted to discover. For 16 days he and his small party followed this river that continued to flow to the northwest. Mitchell was convinced he had found the door to north Australia. In his journal

The famous *Beagle* was used in the survey of the north coast of Australia in 1839.

Mitchell waxed eloquent about his discovery, giving the river the name Victoria, believing it to be the headwaters of the great river that flowed into the Joseph Bonaparte Gulf near the Western Australian–Northern Territory border. Mitchell claimed his discovery would open up the whole of the interior to settlement. Had he followed it for another few days he would have seen his Victoria turn southwest after its junction with the Alice—it was, in fact, the Barcoo. When surveying the north coast of Australia in the *Beagle* during 1839, Lieutenant John Stokes* discovered and named the Victoria after his young Queen. Stokes took his ship 80 kilometres up the river, and in his report was as optimistic about the potential of his discovery as Mitchell was about *his* Victoria. Stokes, however, based his opinion on facts rather than on assumption. The river Mitchell discovered retained the name Victoria until 1858 when it was renamed the Barcoo by A. C. Gregory.

* Lieutenant John Lort Stokes assumed command of the *Beagle* when Captain J. C. Wickham became seriously ill and was taken off the ship at the Victoria settlement at Port Essington.

There were many who doubted Mitchell's rather fanciful claim. The press took sides, and a heated debate raged on the course and destination of the river. Charles Sturt thought Mitchell was wrong, as did Leichhardt, who had reached the conclusion, based on experience and observation, that all the Gulf rivers and those running south would have their source in ranges inland from the north coast. The colonial administration too was far from convinced that Mitchell's claim was correct. In its infinite wisdom it commissioned Edmund Kennedy to follow the river and settle the matter once and for all. Mitchell, however, was adamant the Victoria flowed to the northwest coast and that was that. He drew up a map showing the course of the Victoria through the unknown vastness of northern Australia to its mouth in the distant Joseph Bonaparte Gulf. The mysterious power that guided his pen during this exercise has never been revealed. Mitchell demonstrated his confidence in his discovery by sailing to England with his map before Kennedy left to trace the river. Mitchell did discover valuable grazing land during his expedition, and unfortunately this fact was overshadowed by the furore over the 'Victoria'. In due course Kennedy returned with the sobering news that the Victoria was a tributary of Cooper Creek; however the name of the river remained unchanged until 1858. In 1848 Edmund Kennedy lost his life in a disastrous attempt to explore Cape York; hostile Aborigines virtually wiped out his party.

After his return to Cecil Plains, Leichhardt did not waste time in bemoaning his fate. If he did not agree with Mitchell about the Victoria, he saw there may be some benefit in checking on Mitchell's inland route to the north, as a way of avoiding the floods and fever encountered on his failed attempt. Taking Perry, Bunce, and Wommai with him, together with Frederick Isaac, a young settler on the Downs, he set out on a trip to reconnoitre the Maranoa. Six weeks later, after a round trip of 1,000 kilometres, Leichhardt resolved that on his next attempt to go west he would travel via the Maranoa. Bitterly disappointed about the failed expedition, Leichhardt was already planning another journey. One disturbing fact emerged during the trip to the Maranoa when Bunce saw fit to acquaint Leichhardt with the full story of the subversive activities of the other members on the disastrous expedition to Peak Range. Meanwhile John Mann, Hovenden Hely, and Henry Turnbull had returned to Sydney. Realising that searching questions would have to be faced on the failure of the expedition, they agreed that if blame was to be apportioned then none of it must settle on their shoulders. Deciding that attack was the best form of defence they set about blackening the name of their former leader.

Back on the Downs, Leichhardt found himself in an invidious position. He had sent a letter to Sydney, already published, that expressed his disappointment at the failure of the expedition while at the same time absolving his companions from any blame or responsibility. That should have been enough for the three gentlemen in Sydney, but guilt spurred them on. Lynd and Clarke listened in dismay to the growing criticism of their friend by men who were respected members of Sydney society. Sir Thomas Mitchell revelled in, and added to Leichhardt's discomfit, by publicly disparaging the importance of the German explorer's first trip, while claiming many of Leichhardt's discoveries as his own.

Leaving most of the expedition's gear with Henry Russell at Cecil Plains, Leichhardt journeyed to Sydney to be greeted with a vastly different reception to the one accorded him after his first expedition. The explorer who had triumphed over the wilderness was now seen to have feet of clay.

It was the beginning of a very difficult period for Ludwig Leichhardt. He now had a number of powerful enemies. To his few friends he told the truth about the failed expedition then threw himself into preparation for another attempt at reaching Swan River. This trying period for the explorer was brightened by the publication of his book, and by the news that the Royal Geographical Society had awarded him its Patron's Medal for 1846. Leichhardt also received word from Prussia that he had been forgiven for sailing to New Holland without fulfilling his compulsory army service obligations; if he wished he could now return to his homeland to a hero's welcome. However, the only plans Leichhardt had for travel were in his adopted country. His approach to the government for funds met with the same response as before. As an explorer Leichhardt had cost the colonial administration very little. The governor saw no reason to upset the status quo. Again the explorer had to search for volunteers to accompany him on his expedition to the west, but the task had been made doubly difficult by the adverse criticism arising from his failed attempt. Leichhardt's plans received another blow when Robert Lynd's regiment was ordered to New Zealand. The barrack master tried unsuccessfully to persuade his friend to abandon his plans for further exploration and to try his luck in New Zealand. Leichhardt was devastated by the news, for in Lynd's going he lost not only a backer, but a true friend and confidant.

Despite all these setbacks Leichhardt was still determined to head west. It seems nothing else was of any importance to him. Getting to Swan River had almost become an obsession. What drove Ludwig Leichhardt is difficult to establish. It certainly was not financial reward—there had been little enough of that. Nor was it fame and glory. Leichhardt could have basked in glory had he wished after returning from Port Essington, but instead he escaped to the Macarthurs at Camden to avoid the public acclaim and hype that followed. Perhaps the thing Leichhardt wanted more than anything else was to be accepted. He had been in the colony for six years and had shown no inclination to leave. The colonists from England, on the other hand, still called England home, and returned at every opportunity. Despite the geographical differences, the social life of the colony was little more than a microcosm of English society, with all its snobbery and class distinction. If, in fact, it was acceptance Leichhardt craved, in all probability he would not have achieved it had he crossed and recrossed the continent half a dozen times. He was a German among Englishmen in an English colony, and he had powerful enemies—enemies that would not be silenced even when it was accepted that Leichhardt had perished.

It was imperative that Leichhardt find a backer for the expedition. He had little money left and royalties from his next book would not be available for some time. Due to John Calvert's good offices, Leichhardt found a backer in John Mackay, a Sydney businessman and exporter, who agreed to underwrite the costs of the expedition.

Having settled one of his major problems, Leichhardt set to the daunting task of recruiting companions for the trip. Financially he could only offer them the hope of a government gratuity at the end of the trip, for the governor had refused to guarantee even that. It was not a prospect that was likely to attract the type of men needed for such an undertaking. Leichhardt had long before this become reconciled to accepting the best of the well-meaning but often ill-fitted volunteers attracted to such a venture. He had made mistakes in the past and would need divine guidance if those mistakes were not to be repeated. Few of the members of the failed expedition interested the explorer. He would have taken Perry, but Perry was newly married and loath to exchange marital bliss for the rigours of exploration. Bunce was initially a member of the new party, but when the expedition reached the Downs, to his disappointment, Leichhardt told him he would not be needed. In dropping Bunce the explorer may well have added another name to the growing list of his detractors. Wommai was the only member of the failed expedition to accompany Leichhardt in his second journey west. The final party was made up of August Classen, a German and a relation by marriage to Leichhardt; Arthur Hentig, another German; Billy Bombat, an Aboriginal youth; Wommai; Donald Stuart, a ticket-of-leave man; and a stockman called Kelly, from Logan River Station.

If Leichhardt had made mistakes in the past no one could accuse him of not learning from them; the goats and sheep had proved to be a menace on the last attempt, this time goats and sheep were not among the stock taken. There would be horses, mules and bullocks only. Sugar had been a contentious commodity, more trouble than it was worth in the opinion of Leichhardt, so sugar was not on the

If handled properly, mules make excellent pack animals.

inventory. Splitting the members of the last expedition into two tents by social class had caused friction, this was to be avoided in the attempt to reach Swan River. There would be just one tent large enough for all.

When his preparations were complete, Leichhardt took a ship to Newcastle, picked up the pack mules held ready for him, and set out overland for the Darling Downs. Mules, if properly handled, make excellent pack animals. They are strong, keep their condition well and never need shoeing. A lot of outback drovers made use of these hardy pack animals that are ideal for long trips. When droving, a packhorse plant, which could contain both horses and mules, could travel 2,000 kilometres without an appreciable spell. I had two mules on the road with me, the smaller of the two carried water canteens and the other carried the cooked tucker pack. This mule named

Monty was a bit of a character and was admired by everyone who got to know him. Monty knew every camp on the road to the west. At any place I had camped previously he would break out of the horse plant and go to stand there. Monty usually took a bit of persuading that this time we were moving on. When we finally got to wherever we were camping, Monty would stalk away from the horses and stand where he considered the tucker pack should be placed. It was quite plain that Monty believed he should be unpacked before any other pack animal, to ignore him was a risky business. We often teased him by pretending to walk past him to the other horses, but only once did I see someone actually bring a packhorse up before Monty had been attended to. The mule put his long ears back and kicked the packhorse in the guts with both hind feet.

Leichhardt arrived at Rosenthal on the upper Condamine River to find the Darling Downs again being deluged by an extended wet. Stores were delayed on the road up from Brisbane but Leichhardt was not too dismayed; if he was going to follow Mitchell's route, surface water would be vital. The expedition's stock was put together in February, numbering 30 head of horses and mules, and 50 head of cattle. As before, Leichhardt put his faith in packs; there would be no drays to restrict mobility. The explorer seemed satisfied with his companions, although initially one of his countrymen had given him some cause for concern. Classen was an ex-seaman and something of a disciplinarian, a characteristic resented by other members of the party. It appears that the problem had been resolved by the time the expedition reached the Downs.

While the explorer waited for the rain to clear, news came of Kennedy's report on Mitchell's 'Victoria'. He had followed the river as it turned southwest and had continued along its course through sandhill and claypan until it became apparent it was in fact Sturt's Cooper Creek. In Sydney, Leichhardt's old friend the Reverend Clarke was ecstatic and his letter in the *Sydney Morning Herald* reflected his mood; the great man had been wrong! His friend Leichhardt had been vindicated as had others.

Although pleased with the news, Leichhardt was more interested in what he could gain from Kennedy's report to help define his own route. Knowing the true course of the so-called 'Victoria' (Barcoo) would save him both time and effort. He decided on a route that would take the expedition down the Condamine, then up the Cogoon River. From there Leichhardt would follow Mitchell's route to the 'Victoria' River. He would then follow the 'Victoria' as far as it took him in the right direction, before striking out in the hope of finding rivers that would lead him north to the rivers of the Gulf of Carpentaria and eventually to the west coast of the continent.

The expedition moved out from Rosenthal on 3 March 1848. Leichhardt broke the journey for four days at Cecil Plains and arrived at Allan Macpherson's station near Mount Abundance, on 3 April. In his last letter from Macpherson's station, Leichhardt wrote of the trip to that date expressing his pleasure at how all the members had travelled. The stock were no trouble, the weather had been fine, and he could not, he wrote, speak too highly of his companions.

William Hill and Allan Macpherson, the owner of Mt Abundance Station, were the last white people to see Leichhardt and his party alive.

Leichhardt added that the party had killed their first bullock, and estimated that the meat would last until the expedition reached the 'Victoria'. After waiting two days for the meat to dry at the camp at Mount Abundance, Leichhardt started for the 'Victoria'. In their camp that night the party was visited by Allan Macpherson and William Hill, who had ridden over from the station. The party talked late into the night. Before leaving the explorers, the two visitors shook hands all round and wished the party godspeed. Macpherson and Hill were the last white men known to see Leichhardt and his party.

MYSTERIES AND RELICS

When Ludwig Leichhardt led his expedition out from Mount Abundance, no one in the 60-year-old colony had any idea what lay ahead of the party. And in the 159 years since he departed, nothing has been found that provides a definite clue to his fate. The circumstances of his party's end is as great a mystery today as it was at the time.

Many theories have been advanced to explain how the expedition vanished as it did; these include fire, flood, fever and attack by Aborigines. Some of Leichhardt's detractors claim he simply led his party out into the desert, past the point of no return. One of these theories may well be right. In the 15 years following Leichhardt's disappearance a number of explorers were active in the interior. After the Burke and Wills tragedy, a number of attempts were made to establish their fate. During this period Augustus Charles Gregory, McDouall Stuart, William Landsborough, John McKinlay and Frederick Walker were all in the field. In 1862 the reports of these explorers were made public. Their description of good grazing land on the Barkly Tableland and in western Queensland led to a great expansion of settlement. Men like John Costello, Nat Buchanan, the Duracks, the Gordons, John Sutherland, and many others were quick to respond to the challenge. In a little over 20 years outback settlement would leapfrog to the East Kimberley region. These men, many of them Celts, were to throw more light on the unknown than many explorers.

There is no doubt that these overlanders and settlers would have been aware of the Leichhardt mystery. But in the 20 intervening years since the explorer had vanished, dingoes and the weather would have played their part, and a person would have had to virtually ride over the scattered remains of a camp to recognise it for what it was.

Although rumours circulated on the Downs that Leichhardt's party had fallen victim to the Aborigines, efforts to establish the fate of the explorers were neither prompt nor efficient. This may have been due in part to the time Leichhart estimated his journey would take; he thought he might be in the field for up to two years. Despite the earlier concern generated by the rumours, it was not until 1852 that a search party was dispatched under the command of Hovenden Hely. Hely had accompanied Leichhardt on the earlier aborted attempt to cross Australia, and had in no way distinguished himself on that trip. Hely ventured no further afield than the Warrego River; his efforts to establish the fate of the lost explorers can at best be described as half-hearted.

The government advanced £2,000 to finance Hely's ineffectual expedition. As no money had been forthcoming to help equip Leichhardt, it appears the government considered the lost explorer was worth more dead than alive.

The only significant attempts by an explorer to discover the fate of Leichhardt's party were undertaken by A. C. Gregory. In 1856 he led an expedition organised under the auspices of the Royal Geographical Society of London. Gregory, who had been exploring the Victoria River district, led his party southeast, parallel with, but further inland than Leichhardt's route to Port Essington. Originally Gregory had no plans to look for Leichhardt, but under pressure from the colonial administrators his charter was extended to accommodate the interests of Leichhardt's friends. On Elsey Creek,

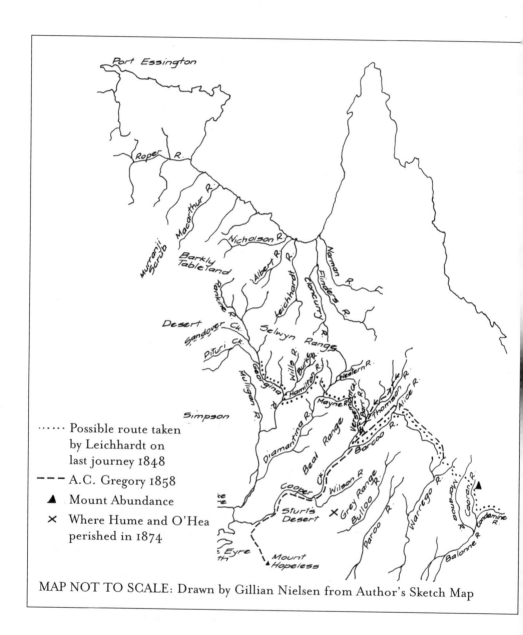

Port Essington

Roper R.

Macarthur R.

Musganji Scrub

Nicholson R.

Barkly Tableland

Albert R.

Leichhardt R.

Calvert R.

Norman R.

Flinders R.

Desert

Sandover Ck.

Tomkins R.

Selwyn Range

Pituri Ck.

Georgina R.

Wille R.

Burton R.

Hamilton R.

Western R.

Mulligan R.

Mayne R.

Vergemont Ck.

Thomson R.

Alice R.

Simpson

Diamantina R.

Beal Range

Barcoo R.

···· Possible route taken
  by Leichhardt on
  last journey 1848

--- A.C. Gregory 1858

▲ Mount Abundance

✕ Where Hume and O'Hea
  perished in 1874

Cooper Ck.

Wilson R.

Grey Range

Bulloo R.

Paroo R.

Warrego R.

Maranoa R.

Condamine R.

Coorani R.

Sturt's Desert

Eyre th

Mount Hopeless

Balonne R.

MAP NOT TO SCALE: Drawn by Gillian Nielsen from Author's Sketch Map

Gregory found evidence that trees had been felled with an axe or with a steel tomahawk. These small axes were greatly prized by Aborigines, and there is a strong possibility that the axe or tomahawk responsible could have come to inland Aborigines from trade with coastal tribes. Coastal tribes had been in contact with seafarers from the Strait of Malacca for centuries, and had been employed by them to harvest and cure by smoking the bêche-de-mer from the northern coastal waters. Articles such as tomahawks may have been given to the Aborigines as gifts or as payment. There was also the possibility that the implements had come from the British settlement at Fort Wellington on Raffles Bay, abandoned in 1829; or from Port Essington, abandoned 20 years later. On his journey to Port Essington in 1845 Leichhardt had seen natives near the East Alligator River in possession of a tomahawk. Steel or iron tools were highly prized by the Aborigines and were a valuable trading commodity.

I found the Aborigines in this area to be excellent stockmen. On Nutwood Downs, south of the Elsey in the Northern Territory, the country was rough and in parts covered with thick lancewood scrub, difficult to ride through and the home of wild scrub bulls. The Aboriginal stockmen seemed to revel in the fast exciting work, constantly striving to outdo one another in the difficult art of throwing and tying down wild cattle. I joined this camp at the start of the bullock muster, as did the new head stockman. This meant that the Aborigines were the only ones who knew the horses. When the stock horses were draughted and allocated, it was no surprise to find the Aborigines had the pick of the horse plant. Good scrub horses are a breed apart, picking their way through the thickest scrub with no help from the rider. In scrub an experienced rider never pulls on the reins. (My string of horses was fair with the exception of one brown mare, who was no good in scrub and so slow you could virtually kick your hat faster.)

Track mustering in scrub country is quite different to other types of mustering. The idea is to ride along the tracks of the cattle until it is evident they are not far ahead. The stockmen then usually dismount, relieve themselves and tighten the girths of their saddles, then continue on. Talking is out, communication is by whistling and signs. When the cattle finally take fright, it means a hell-for-leather ride through the scrub to wheel them. The man on the best horse takes the lead with the rest following in single file behind him. When riding the brown mare, I usually found myself as 'tail-end Charley'. One afternoon I was in that position when I saw the riders ahead skirt around a large wash-out in a gully. I gave the mare her head thinking she would negotiate it as the other horses had. The mare left it a bit too late, the bank gave way under her hooves and in she went. When the dust cleared, I found myself sitting on the edge of the far side of the hole with the mare jammed upside down in the wash-out. I tried to get up but discovered my legs below the knees were trapped against the bank by the mare. She made a few feeble attempts to extricate herself, then threw in the towel. I punched and cursed the brown mare for a few minutes then realised she was not going to budge. I looked around then for a stick to prise my legs loose, but soon found there was none I could reach. I knew it was only a matter of time before the others missed me and ran the tracks back, so I forced myself to relax and make the best of the situation. It could have been a lot worse I knew; I could have been underneath the mare in the bottom of the wash-out.

Dragging my tobacco tin and matches out of my pocket with some difficulty, I rolled a smoke and waited. I was to roll quite a few more smokes before I saw Splinter and another stockman jog out of the scrub just on sundown. They rolled the mare to one side and I managed to drag myself free. I then helped them to get the mare onto her feet. I escaped with no more than bruising to my lower legs. They thought it was a great joke when they saw I was not seriously hurt. I joined in the laughter, probably from relief. I had not relished the thought of spending the night with no company other than the brown mare.

*   *   *

In 1858 Gregory again set out to trace Leichhardt's route to the west. He followed the Barcoo River, first discovered by Thomas Mitchell, down to its junction with the Thomson. Gregory then travelled up the Thomson until he was forced to return back down the river due to a shortage of water and stock feed. He then led his expedition down the Barcoo and Cooper Creek to Mount Hopeless. The only trace of the lost explorer he found was a tree marked with an 'L' on the Barcoo. Ignoring the evidence of the tomahawked trees he had found on his earlier journey, Gregory concluded that the remains of the Leichhardt expedition would be found between the Barcoo and the rivers flowing into the Gulf of Carpentaria. This ended Gregory's attempts to establish Leichhardt's fate.

I've been on the Barcoo and Thomson rivers myself in vastly different conditions. Working with a droving plant of Sam Fuller's, we left Longreach in early April 1951. It was raining when we started out down the Thomson, and light rain fell for the next couple of days. We had a mob of cattle to collect from Braidwood Station to take for sale. We knew the Thomson was running, but when we got to the Braidwood crossing we found the river in full flood. Even to bushmen used to swimming flooded streams it was a daunting sight. Our situation was made even more parlous because none of us knew the horses, we had no idea which horses were good swimmers. Nearly all horses can swim, but really good swimmers are rare. There are horses that will panic and do their utmost to drown the accompanying rider; others will regularly plunge down in an attempt to touch the bottom; on the other hand a good strong swimmer will scarcely wet the rider above the thighs. When crossing a flooded creek without stock, some men prefer to swim behind their mounts hanging on to the tail. To negotiate a stream with stock or a horse plant, however, it is imperative that the rider stay in the saddle. It is impossible to oversee the situation when one's eyes are at water level.

Jimmy Charles, who was in charge of the plant, and I looked at the torrent then at one another. We lit smokes and discussed the situation. As it was mid-afternoon, we decided to put off crossing until the following morning. All the droving gear was being carried in a heavy wagonette and there was no chance of getting it over the river. Fortunately, we had two sets of packs and bags on board, we checked them over and set about selecting a few basic rations and gear to take in the packs. We would be able to carry only two swags, so the four of us would have to sleep head to toe until we could get the wagonette across.

The next morning we packed two horses and picked our mounts. I caught a solid bay gelding and stripped off, tying my clothes and boots to the pommel of the saddle. I looked over as we were about ready to cross, to see Jimmy still fully dressed in coat, leggings and boots. When I asked him what was going on, he told me he could not swim a stroke, if his horse failed him he said it would not matter what he had on. I decided to stick close to him on the way across. We then pushed the plant horses into the flooded Thomson, Jimmy's horse proved to be the best swimmer of all. Everything went well until we reached the other side. One of the packhorses baulked at the bank and turning began to swim down the river, I urged my horse out of the water and rode along the bank as fast as the muddy ground would allow and finally got ahead of the swimming packhorse. Putting my mount back into the flood I gave the frightened and quickly tiring deserter a lead back up the bank. Fortunately he followed me. While the rest of us got dressed, Jimmy lit a fire to boil the quart pots. After a quick drink of tea, we headed for Braidwood.

In 1860, some time after Gregory's search, Nat Buchanan and William Landsborough explored the Barcoo River and went on to look at the area around the present site of Longreach. It must have been a good season, for two years later they returned with three partners and took up Bowen Downs and Mount Cornish. The latter property included a stretch of the Thomson River.

In 1862 McDouall Stuart reported seeing a light-skinned Aboriginal girl, suggesting European paternity, in the Newcastle

Waters area on the Barkly Tablelands. There are also reports that he saw what appeared to be bare footprints of a European.

In the same year Frederick Walker, while searching for Burke and Wills, found the dried tracks of horses and mules, these tracks on the upper Thomson were deep and suggested they had been made during or just after rain.

William Landsborough was also out looking for Burke and Wills that year. Having travelled by sea to the Gulf of Carpentaria, Landsborough searched and named the Barkly Tableland and discovered the Georgina River, calling it the Herbert. He travelled down that river only a short distance past the present site of Camooweal, then returned to his base on the Albert River. After replenishing his supplies, Landsborough searched up the Flinders River, from where he travelled southeast to the Barcoo. He crossed that river below the present site of Tambo and reached the Warrego via Langlo Creek. From the Warrego, Landsborough returned to the Darling Downs.

In 1864 Duncan MacIntyre, a settler looking for good grazing land, found trees marked with an 'L' on the Flinders River. When his discovery became known, an expedition was organised to investigate and search the region. This expedition, called the 'Ladies expedition' because of its support base—the women of Melbourne who had raised the money for the search—was led by a Dr Murray. It proved to be a complete disaster, the party disintegrating when it had travelled no further than Cooper Creek. Duncan MacIntyre, disillusioned by the bickering and fault finding that followed, went on ahead to continue his own search, without success. It was reported that he died from fever shortly afterwards.

In 1867, nearly 20 years after Leichhardt left on his trip, Captain Cadell reported seeing a white man in company with Aborigines while he was exploring the Roper River in the paddle steamer *Eagle*.

Then in 1871 Sub-inspector James Gilmour led a party of native Aboriginal mounted police to investigate reports of a white man living with the Aborigines west of Cooper Creek. The mounted force of Aborigines was used to control the frontiers of settlement. The reputation of these units left a lot to be desired, for they were responsible for some of the worst massacres of their own people. Poor leadership can be blamed for a lot of their damage.

Not a lot is known about Gilmour, but he was reputed to be a good bushman, an ex-Maranoa grazier who had been given an instant commission in the force. Gilmour found no white man in the area he searched; he did, however, find human remains that were later identified as European. Aborigines told Gilmour that *Vinie Vinies* (white men) had been killed there; they later added that the saddle packs and other belongings of the party had been burnt. Gilmour made two trips to the area close to Wantata waterhole. Some relics were found, including scraps of leather and cloth, but there was nothing that could be definitely linked to the Leichhardt exploration.

In her book *The Belle of the Barcoo,* Jan L'Estrange tells of two very old mules found running on Minnie Downs, southwest of Tambo in 1873. It is well known that mules live to a very great age.

A man by the name of Andrew Hume became involved in the Leichhardt mystery during the early 1870s. Hume may well have been a man who confused fact with fantasy; he could, on the other hand, have been merely a con man. In April 1866, Hume was returning south after working on Queensland pastoral properties and stopped for a spree at Baradine, a small town in New South Wales. After a week, he found himself penniless, so he and a misguided mate called Smith decided to hold up Border's inn. The fact that Border's inn was the very pub where they had been making merry did not seem to bother the pair. They were, of course, recognised, and made off with little to show for their effort. During the hold-up, Hume had boasted of being a dangerous bushranger. He soon found himself hoisted on his own petard for the pair were easily captured and Hume received a lengthy gaol term for bushranging.

In what may have been an attempt to obtain his freedom, Hume told prison officials in 1871 that he had information that would solve the mystery of Leichhardt's disappearance. Hume claimed to have lived with the Aborigines for many years, saying he had hunted and camped with them on the lower Cooper Creek and in much of the outback. Hume also told his gaolers that he had crossed Australia from east to west in the far north and returned during 1862. In an area calculated to be near the Victoria River in the Northern Territory, he claimed he met a man who was a survivor of the Leichhardt expedition. Hume further claimed this man spoke a foreign language and was in possession of papers that would prove his identity. Hume could not get this man away from the Aboriginal tribe he was with so he continued his journey.

In fact Hume literally talked his way out of Parramatta Gaol. That the authorities were not only prepared to release him, but to back him in an attempt to bring the white man back to civilisation, speaks volumes for Hume's powers of persuasion. It also demonstrates how desperately people were looking for answers to the mystery of Leichhardt's disappearance. With support and assistance from the government, Hume set out to bring in the man he claimed to have found on the Victoria River. Hume based himself in camps of men working on the Overland Telegraph Line and finally returned to Sydney in 1874. He again claimed to have met the white man and as before had failed to get him away from the tribe. Hume now claimed the man was Classen, and that Classen had told Hume that there had been a mutiny in Leichhardt's party. Leichhardt had been killed and the rest of the men had turned south to get back to civilisation. Classen had survived because he was away looking for water. Hume had brought back with him relics, including a sextant, watch and telescope. He also carried a large bundle of papers that had been buried in a satchel by the white man. When asked by the authorities to present this evidence, Hume claimed someone had stolen the papers and relics during his journey to Sydney. He still had a small telescope in his possession, which he claimed, had belonged to Classen.

Despite growing doubts regarding Hume's reliability, there were still people willing to back him in another attempt to verify his claims. By the middle of 1874 Hume had mustered enough support to lead an expedition into the outback. The route he planned to take was through western Queensland and up Cooper Creek; certainly a rather circuitous way to reach the Victoria River. Hume's drinking had by this time become a problem, and all three of his companions left the expedition before it reached the New South Wales–Queensland border. Timothy O'Hea then joined the expedition at the behest of Eccleston Du Faur, one of Hume's backers. O'Hea was a very brave Irishman (who had been awarded the Victoria Cross for quietening a fire on an ammunition train in Canada), but he was a new chum; his faith in Hume as a leader and as a bushman was later to cost him his life. After leaving Mungindi, Lewis Thompson, a local stockman, joined the party and the three proceeded on horseback to Nockatunga Station on the Wilson River, a tributary of Cooper Creek. Hume led his party out from Noccundra waterhole on Nockatunga in November. Cooper Creek turns almost due west opposite Nockatunga, and Hume was warned to be careful not to miss the track to a newly established station on the Cooper.

Despite this warning Hume took a wrong turn and ended up travelling almost parallel with the river. It was almost too late when they decided to turn back. Thompson managed to get to water by letting his mare find her own way to a creek. After recovering, he filled the water bag and returned to where he had left his two companions but they had vanished. Though still weak and exhausted, Thompson managed to make his way back to the station on his knocked up horse. Although badly dehydrated he led a party back to try to rescue Hume and O'Hea. The tracks told the story; the two men had pulled the packs off the horses and once freed, these horses walked straight to water in the creek where Thompson had filled the water bag. The pair left the horse tracks and perished in the dry and rugged foothills of the Grey Range.

Another man who was involved with relics allegedly from Leichhardt's expedition was John Richard Skuthorpe. Nicknames have always been popular in the outback and Skuthorpe was known as

'Jack Dick'. He was something of a legend in his own life time—in 1904 he was one of the first drovers to bring cattle back through the notorious Murranji Track. The Murranji, as it was known, was part of the main stock route from the west—160 kilometres of tangled lancewood and bullwaddi scrub stretching between Top Springs and Newcastle Waters. In 1904 the only waters on the track were Yellow hole and Murranji hole; both were unreliable as they did not last long after the wet. Later when other drovers and I brought bullocks in from west of the scrub, the track was watered by government bores. Despite this improvement the Murranji was still a difficult and dangerous route that taxed the skills of drovers to the full. Back in 1904 it must have been hell. Skuthorpe's family were later famous as rough riders. Two of them, Lance and Violet, became household names in Australia.

Skuthorpe and his brother took up country on the Diamantina River in 1875. Later his brother managed leases for Walter Douglas, and these leases, west of Boulia later became known as Glenormiston. While on the later-named Glenormiston, Aborigines told Jack Dick of a very old white man who was living with a tribe on the Mulligan River. This man was said by the Aborigines to speak a different language to English. In 1877 Skuthorpe went to the Mulligan in the southwest portion of the station. The Aborigines told Skuthorpe that the old white man had died, but he met two of the man's children, a boy and a girl, who were living with the tribe. The natives also told Skuthorpe that they had buried with the white man a saddle bag containing papers.

In 1880 Skuthorpe met Du Faur in Sydney. Du Faur, who was as keen as ever to solve the Leichhardt mystery, thought the matter should be investigated. He believed the man who had died on the Mulligan may have been Classen. Hume, he thought, may have become confused about where the two had met. He suggested that Skuthorpe should go to the Mulligan taking with him a German-speaking stockman and bring the half-caste children to civilisation. The advice about the German speaker must have seemed a bit odd to Skuthorpe.

Skuthorpe reportedly advised Du Faur that far from being children, the boy and girl were young adults, happy in the tribe and as wild as hawks. Du Faur failed to deliver the money Skuthorpe wanted for abducting the pair and Skuthorpe returned to Queensland.

In the Christmas issue of the Sydney *Bulletin* in 1880 an offer of £1,000 reward was made to anyone who could solve the Leichhardt mystery. Within a month Skuthorpe sent a wire to Du Faur saying he had recovered the papers and relics buried by the Aborigines as well as relics found elsewhere. Skuthorpe added that he would require more than the £1,000 before he handed these over and disclosed where the white man was buried. In September Skuthorpe wrote to the New South Wales Government stating that if £6,000 was paid to him he was prepared to reveal all. When negotiations broke down, Skuthorpe bailed up and refused to cooperate. The relics were not mentioned again. What happened to them is anybody's guess.

In 1886 two prospectors reported seeing a white man with an Aboriginal tribe on the McArthur River near the Gulf of Carpentaria.

Sometime shortly after the turn of the century, a man called Charlie Harding is reported to have found a brass plate on the butt of an old gun. The gun butt was stuck in a tree near the Musgrave Range. (See Appendices, 'The Leichhardt Nameplate'.)

Bob McNamara, an experienced bushman, recently told my brother Jeff of the following incident: in 1923 a man from New South Wales travelled up the Georgina with a mob of horses. This man later told Bob's father of finding the remains of a very old, burnt out camp on Glenormiston country.

In the late 1930s relics, which included coins, and skeletal remains were found on Mount Dare Station on the western edge of the Simpson Desert. Mount Dare is in northern South Australia, and on the opposite side of the Simpson Desert to the Cooper country.

In 1948 unexplained relics were found on Glenormiston Station by me and three other stockmen. In all probability this was the same camp referred to by Bob McNamara.

An 1841 Maundy threepenny piece (left) and a very worn 1817 half sovereign found by the Grenfill–Price expedition at Mount Dare in 1938.

In 1994 Jim Evans, the manager of Durrie Station, found an old clay pipe, buttons and a shot measure near Wantata waterhole. This is in the area searched in 1871 by Sub-inspector Gilmour.

In the years following Leichhardt's disappearance, stories circulated of white men living with inland tribes. These stories are quite apart from the reported sightings of wild white men referred to above and emanated from the Aborigines themselves. Many of these stories may have originally related to John King the survivor of the Burke and Wills expedition. King had lived with the natives on the Cooper for months before he was finally rescued by A. W. Howitt in September 1861.

Rumours that Leichhardt and his party had been massacred by the Aborigines were also common, and again this information came from the natives. Many of these reports originated in the Eyre Creek and Georgina River areas and were quite explicit. It was these stories that led to Hely's ineffectual search.

It is obvious that all the reports of the sighting of white men cannot be linked to the disappearance of Ludwig Leichhardt's expedition. The same must be said for the various relic sites and for the numerous 'L'-marked trees. Let us then examine the information noted above.

The light-skinned girl seen by McDouall Stuart is important, but there was no follow up on this sighting, or on the footprints seen by McDouall Stuart. The fact that there was so much shipping activity over the centuries around our northern coast makes drawing conclusions very difficult. Aboriginal cohabitation with seamen and men from Fort Wellington and from the Port Essington settlement all confuse the issue. Survivors from shipwrecks may have played a part as well. The sightings of white men in the company of Aborigines on the McArthur River and on the Roper River similarly cannot be attributed with any certainty to the fate of the Leichhardt expedition. Before their hunting grounds became threatened, Aborigines tended to look after straying whites. Two well-known cases are those of John King, cared for on Cooper Creek, and James Murrell, who spent 17 years with the Aborigines on the Queensland coast.

As for marked trees reported to be in the desert areas, I am baffled. I am of the opinion that these trees may not be genuine Leichhardt relics. (See Appendices, '"L" Marked Trees in Queensland'.) I base this on the explorer's plans to follow coastal rivers to the West, and on there being no plausible reason for those stated plans to be abandoned. Why would an explorer whose *modus operandi* was to follow rivers—whose plans for his last trip were similar—inexplicably lead the expedition into the desert? One theory is that Leichhardt was trying to get back to the Georgina River, but from where? Why wouldn't he have returned via the route he had safely negotiated on the outward part of the trip? Why would he have ventured into the arid desert when his plan was to use the headwaters of northern-flowing rivers to reach the west? It is one thing to look at a map and say, yes, Leichhardt could have gone here, or he could have gone there. It is a different proposition if one knows the area and its inherent dangers; then one can better understand the hazards of travelling into such country. For

Leichhardt to attempt to cross the inhospitable centre would have been out of character and extremely foolhardy. Leichhardt was not a reckless man. In his book, *The Mystery of Ludwig Leichhardt,* Gordon Connell has explained Leichhardt's presence in the centre of Australia thus: rather than go west from the Elsey into waterless country he turned south. This is nonsense. The Elsey is a tributary of the Roper, a river Leichhardt had followed in 1845 to lead him to northern flowing rivers. From the headwaters of the Roper he would have known that the way west was open. After travelling thousands of miles to the Elsey to skirt the desert, why would Leichhardt have turned back into it, when within a few days' ride he knew he would find a well-watered route to west Australia, a route he had always planned to follow?

The area around Wantata waterhole has figured prominently in scenarios that attempt to explain the Leichhardt mystery. Sub-inspector Gilmour's report of his search of the area in 1871 was inconclusive; that does not, of course, dismiss the possibility that Wantata holds the key. However, searches of the area with metal detectors have failed to discover any of the iron and steel from saddlery and camp gear that would have survived the fire. With regard to the burning of the above items, it is possible that the Aborigines were referring to an incident that happened elsewhere. I have spoken to Jim Evans, who in 1994 found relics in the same area, and he is convinced as I am that white men camped and probably died near Wantata. The question is, were those men members of Leichhardt's expedition? Prior to 1871 there were small parties of whites in the Cooper and lower Diamantina districts looking for grazing land. The movements of these men were little known and deaths and disappearances were not always reported. But more importantly, would Leichhardt have gone so far south when we know he planned to go northwest? Wantata is within 80 kilometres of the South Australian border and close to the inhospitable country that defeated Sturt. Leichhardt knew the substance of Sturt's report on the area, and had he run into trouble on his way west, it is reasonable to assume he would have turned north not south. Leichhardt knew from experience that the north held both water and game in abundance. Many of the theories linking Wantata with the mystery are based in the belief that the party mutinied. I will examine that scenario later.

The chances are that the two old mules running on Minnie Downs in 1873 did belong to Ludwig Leichhardt. The question is, of course, were they mules he had lost, or were they the survivors of a fatal attack on the exploration party? It is well known that mules will make their way home, and when Leichhardt abandoned his first trip to the west his lost mules beat him back to the Darling Downs by a comfortable margin. There is no way of knowing how the mules came to be on Minnie Downs, or how far they had travelled to get there. They may even have been responsible for the tracks seen by Frederick Walker on the upper Thomson in 1862. Walker reported that there were both horse and mule tracks present and one would think Walker would have known the difference. However, in those wet and boggy conditions it is very hard to differentiate between the tracks of a large mule and those of an unshod horse; mud built up around and under the hooves can almost completely disguise the normal characteristics of an animal's tracks.

Two men whose activities are worthy of close examination are Hume and Skuthorpe. Hume was an extraordinary character—one who should at least go down in history as a man who talked his way out of gaol. I have known some garrulous individuals who have talked their way into gaol, but the return trip without ropes, ladders and wire cutters is a different matter! Was Hume a charlatan, or was he a victim of circumstances, who lost his life in trying to vindicate himself? If we are to believe in Hume we must also believe the story he told to gain his release. He claimed he had crossed Australia from east to west in 1862 and returned, all without backup. I have ridden over much of the country he would have had to cross, and I believe his claim to be preposterous. If we are to dismiss that claim we must also dismiss the claim that he met Classen in the far northwest. As a result, the whole fabric of Hume's story is in tatters. The tale of the mutiny, his search from the Overland Telegraph Line, his alleged meeting again with Classen, and his story of the lost relics all depend on his claim that he crossed the continent.

Hume also claimed that he had for many years lived with the Aborigines as far out as Cooper Creek. This may well be true, for he apparently had the reputation among his peers of being a 'white blackfellow', a term in use then to describe a white man who preferred the company of Aborigines to that of his own kind. While living with the tribes in western Queensland, did Hume meet a white man living with a tribe, or merely hear stories of massacres in the west and of white men living among the Aborigines there? While in gaol, did he hear of Gilmour's search of the Wantata area west of the Cooper? Did he invent the story of crossing the continent and meeting a white man in the far northwest so that the authorities would have to rely on him to lead a search? The route Hume took on his last journey appears to indicate an affirmative answer to the above questions. Having carried out the obligatory search in the Victoria River district, he then had a free hand to travel to the source of the rumours, the Cooper Creek and Diamantina River districts. But to state, as he did, that he was going to the Victoria River in the Northern Territory via the Cooper was a nonsense. There was no short cut to the west from Queensland in those days. The overlanders who stocked Wave Hill and Victoria River Downs did not travel the 'coast road' to the Roper River because of the scenery. More than anything else it is the manner of Hume's death that casts doubts on his ability as a bushman. Here was a man who claimed he had crossed Australia twice—who had further claimed to have lived with the Aborigines on the Cooper Creek, yet who perished while well mounted, a few days after leaving Nockatunga Station. In the early 1960s Bob Howard worked as a stockman on Nockatunga and other stations in the area; he scoffed at the suggestion that an experienced bushman might get into trouble there. Thompson, who was with Hume, survived because he was a bushman; Hume and

Bob Howard, once a stockman on Nockatunga Station, argues that it would be unlikely that an experienced bushman would get into trouble in the area.

O'Hea would have survived as well had Hume followed the tracks of the freed packhorses. His own horse would have done the same for him if he'd had the sense to give it its head. I can understand and forgive a new chum for leaving the horse tracks, but not a man who is supposed to be an experienced bushman. O'Hea put his life in Hume's hands and paid a terrible price.

The claims made by Hume and later by Skuthorpe are similar in many ways. Both feature a survivor of Leichhardt's party who speaks a foreign language; neither of these survivors are ever seen by another white person—besides Hume himself; both survivors have papers and relics that are buried; in both stories the claimants recovered these papers and relics, but never presented them for verification. It must also be noted that Skuthorpe met and talked with Hume at Mungindi, when Hume was on his way to the Cooper. Skuthorpe's refusal to accept the £1,000 offered for the relics is puzzling; surely a bite of the cherry was better than no cherry at all, and in 1882 it must be said £1,000 was a rather substantial bite of the cherry. If Skuthorpe was genuine, the only possible explanation must lie in the nature of the man himself. He was by all accounts a rough uncompromising bushman to whom bureaucracy was anathema. Hume's motive is plain enough; Skuthorpe's behaviour more enigmatic. Rather than throw light on Leichhardt's disappearance, Hume and Skuthorpe have, if anything, added to the mystery.

Were there half-caste children living with a tribe to the west of Glenormiston, and, if so, could they have been fathered by early overlanders? Was there a Leichhardt survivor in the channel country? Was Skuthorpe's survivor on the Mulligan River the same man Hume had met or had heard of? Or was there no survivor other than in the minds of men who both had axes to grind?

The relics found at Mount Dare are obviously of European origin. Coins found there pre-date 1848, however this is not as conclusive as it may first appear—the coins may have been in circulation for many years after minting. Skeletal remains were also found in the same area. Mount Dare is in northern South Australia on the western side of the Simpson desert. The South Australian Government responded to the interest aroused by publicity about the find, and in 1936 sent an expedition to investigate. Led by Dr A. Grenfell Price, the party included the Deputy Surveyor-General, A. D. Smith; an ethnologist whose name was not recorded; and a wireless operator and photographer, A. C. Kennear.

The finds had been widely reported in the press, for the Leichhardt mystery has always been good copy. Unfortunately the human remains had become scattered due to cattle in the area. Some bone fragments and teeth were found that were possibly the remains of Europeans. Relics found included scraps of leather and iron together with the coins. The official report of the expedition stated that a connection between the finds and the lost Leichhardt expedition was a possibility only. Because of the remoteness of

Mount Dare from Leichhardt's proposed and stated route, and the extensive desert country lying between, it is highly unlikely the relics are connected with the explorer's disappearance. As stated earlier, Leichhardt's method of exploration was to follow and make maximum use of rivers. He stated before starting out that he would skirt north around Sturt's desert, and made no provision for carrying water over desert country. The geographical position of the site suggests it is more likely that the unfortunate party who met their fate at Mount Dare came from the south.

The lack of local knowledge regarding the relics we found on Glenormiston in 1948 is puzzling. It seemed that whatever drama was acted out there occurred prior to white settlement. The lack of pre-settlement knowledge can possibly be explained by the fact that the station Aborigines in 1948 were not the original inhabitants of the area. The Wonkajeras had virtually vanished many years before, together with their tribal law and oral history traditions.

When assessing evidence relating to Leichhardt's disappearance, it is important that two major influences are not ignored: first, the influence of foreign visitors, who for centuries had contact with the Aborigines of northern Australia; second, the activity of small parties of settlers, who were at times in the field ahead of the explorers. There is no shortage of clues that may or may not relate to the fate of the Leichhardt expedition. The mystery, however, remains.

WHICH WAY WEST?

It may appear futile to speculate on the route taken by Leichhardt on his last expedition, yet I believe if a number of factors are considered it is possible by the application of logic and relevant knowledge to reach conclusions regarding possible routes that would have attracted the explorer. The particular factors are Leichhardt's known plans; his methods as used in earlier expeditions; Kennedy's report on the Victoria River; the condition of inland streams in 1848; and my personal knowledge of the outback.

Leichhardt said many times that to reach the west he would skirt north of Sturt's desert country; even if sorely pressed he would not have turned south to the area that had defeated Sturt. Although he started his journey below the 24th parallel, his planned route would have taken him, with some deviations, to the northwest. We know that he intended to follow Mitchell's so-called Victoria River (Barcoo) as far as it suited his plans. This was in character, for during his trip to Port Essington Leichhardt made full use of rivers and creeks, following them until it became obvious they were no longer of use. It is safe to assume then that the explorer would have stuck to the Barcoo for as long as possible. At the Barcoo's junction with the Alice, the expedition would have been 80 kilometres southwest of the present town of Barcaldine. Leichhardt would then have had three possible options: first to follow the Alice, but the Alice was coming in from the northeast not the direction he wished to go; second to strike due west and try to pick up another river, a risky idea and completely out of character; third to follow the Barcoo although it was now headed southwest, the explorer would have known from Kennedy's report that it was joined by another river, the Thomson. I believe that Leichhardt, cautious as ever, would have taken the third option, following the Barcoo to the junction or to a point from where he could safely cut across to the Thomson.

This is not inhospitable country. I have worked and contract-mustered on both Retreat Station and Thunda Lakes in the district. The Retreat Station homestead is less than 50 kilometres from the junction of the Barcoo and the Thomson. There was an outbreak of contagious bovine pleuropneumonia in the district that year, the first for over 30 years. I found myself in the unique position of being the only man in the area who could inoculate cattle against the disease. In those days the old needle and seaton yarn method was used. The operation was a simple one: a short length of serum-soaked yarn was inserted in the soft tissue at the end of a beast's tail. The instrument used was a bladed needle with an open eye near the point, when the needle was removed the seaton stayed in the tail. Anyone could learn to inoculate, and after half an hour become quite proficient. My reign as the expert did not last long.

To get to Retreat originally we had to cross the Barcoo channels with a wagonette pulled by a five-in-hand team. I usually drove the wagonette, as the cook, who traditionally did the job, could not handle the horses. This type of horse-drawn vehicle had a pole rather than shafts like on a wagon. On wagons, horses called shafters were harnessed in the shafts, and part of a shafter's harness was the breeching, heavy straps that were fastened to the shafts and passed around the hind quarters of the horse. When going downhill, shafters were trained to sit back in the breeching thus helping the brakes to steady the wagon. A wagonette had no shafters to augment the brakes so other methods had to be used. The most popular way was

A wagonette with the five-in-hand team.

to drag a heavy log behind the vehicle when going down a steep hill. On our journey to Retreat, a few days before we crossed the Barcoo, one of the team, Sam Albury and I caught a brumby stallion that had come into the horse plant looking for mares. Sam and I amused ourselves breaking in the stallion as we travelled. When we came to the Barcoo, the stallion had not yet been taught to lead. Sam had a bright idea: instead of a log why not tie the stallion on behind the wagonette. The horse would pull back and slow the wagonette down. We managed to get the stallion's halter rope fastened to the back axle before we crossed the first channel. The old cook, wanting no part in the proceedings, rode over with the horse plant. The main channel was my prime concern. It was dry but the banks were both high and steep. Everything went well as we crossed the first channel with the stallion hanging back on the rope as predicted. Unfortunately as I steered the team over the bank of the main Barcoo channel the stallion began to lead. The brake had no chance of holding the wagonette that was now threatening to overrun the team. I gave them their heads and cracked the whip over the backs of the five-in-hand.

We crossed the main channel like a Bondi tram—with the horses flat strap—and with the brumby leading like an old horse and Sam almost falling off with laughter. If Leichhardt crossed the Barcoo and he probably did, he no doubt made the crossing rather more sedately.

Early in 1848 the Darling Downs had experienced a very heavy wet. No one knows, of course, just how far west this rain extended. If the wet had been extensive, Leichhardt would have had little difficulty finding water; if however the rain had been restricted to the Downs, the explorer would have had to be careful. It must be remembered, however, that the inland waterholes in 1848 lasted far longer than they do today. Holes that were semi-permanent then, now last for only a few months; the cloven hooves of introduced animals have seen to that. The Australian environment has evolved over millions of years while being inhabited by soft-footed animals. The soft pads of marsupials did nothing to disturb or damage the fragile soil of the interior. This situation changed dramatically after settlement, when hard-footed stock, like sheep, cattle and to a lesser extent, horses, wrought havoc to the low-rainfall areas of the continent. Grassland around waterholes became denuded of all vegetation, and wind-blown dust ended up in creeks and rivers. Stock cut deep pads to waterholes, which after rain became gutters and gullies carrying silt into waterholes. As a result of this constant wind and water erosion, outback waterholes became silted up, greatly reducing both the water volume and the water retention of these holes.

It is true that the three years after Leichhardt's departure were drought years on the Downs and Maranoa, but by then the explorer would have been well out of the drought-affected area, or had already met whatever fate it was that overtook him and his party.

If, in fact, Leichhardt reached the Thomson, as I believe he did, he would have been delighted to discover a fine river containing many large permanent waterholes; he would have found game plentiful, and the travelling good. To the west there would have been no signs of Sturt's desert. It is possible that Leichhardt followed the

Thomson almost to its source, water permitting of course, and then crossed onto the headwaters of the Flinders somewhere near where Hughenden is.

However, on his way up the Thomson, Leichhardt would have seen in the distance a range of rough hills to the west, and I believe curiosity would have driven him to investigate whether creeks rose from the western side of this range. A tributary of the Thomson, now called Vergemont Creek, would have provided a safe route to a gap in the hills watered by a large rock hole. From the gap he would have seen the Mayne River running to the west. In 1959 I drove 1,350 head of Northern Territory bullocks up the Mayne and through the gap to Vergemont Station; Leichhardt would have had no trouble getting through. The Mayne would have led the expedition straight to the river now called the Diamantina.

Once again Leichhardt would have found himself on a major inland river running roughly from the north through good grazing land. The explorer would have seen no sign to the west of the desert country, and may well have believed there were still more rivers to be found in that direction. Creeks running into the Diamantina from the northwest could easily have led the expedition to the river we now know as the Hamilton. The Hamilton is not a major river, and Leichhardt would in all probability have noted its southwest course and followed it hoping to again pick up a larger stream. The river he would have met approximately 60 kilometres south of Boulia is now called the Georgina. It is the most westerly, and the most magnificent of all the major inland rivers in Queensland. Leichhardt would have found the creeks running into it from the west came from the desert, and I believe he would have realised that his only route now lay just west of north, up the shaded reaches of the Georgina.

The explorer may have reconnoitred further west to the Mulligan River, and if he had done so he would not have been impressed. I have worked on the Mulligan River and there must be few less inviting places in Australia; the area is semi-desert, the water is often brackish and the environment stark and unfriendly. Pituri Creek, a western tributary of the Georgina, is a far more attractive stream containing the two beautiful lakes on Glenormiston, however it has its source in the desert country, as do other western creeks higher up the Georgina. I see no reason why Leichhardt would have left the Georgina, a river that skirts the desert areas and has headwaters close to those of the Gulf rivers which were known to the explorer.

It is quite possible Leichhardt chose another route altogether. He may have followed the Thomson up further and turned west up the Darr, linking up with the Western and following that stream past where Winton now stands, down to the Diamantina. He may even have followed the Diamantina up to its source to run headlong into the ranges he had predicted would be found there. Crossing the Selwyn Range, however, would have been a formidable task. I think it more than likely Leichhardt would have swung southwest rather than attempt to tackle the rugged ramparts of the Selwyn Ranges. He would have seen good grazing land to the west as the expedition travelled up the Diamantina, and he was bushman enough to know that other south-flowing creeks rising in the ranges could well lead him to another major inland river. Had he done so he would have picked up the headwaters of the Hamilton.

It is possible, of course, that the explorer left the Diamantina somewhere in the vicinity of the present town of Kynuna and struck due north hoping to find the headwaters of rivers like the Cloncurry and the Flinders. There are, however, two factors against Leichhardt taking this route: the divide is not all that well watered, and by then the weather would have been very hot.

We know Leichhardt intended to make use of rivers flowing into the Gulf of Carpentaria in his journey west. Whatever route he took to reach these rivers, he would have been forced as far north as the Roper by the desert, by the poorly watered Barkly Tableland, and by the tangled scrubs of the Murranji. If Leichhardt and his party had reached the Roper they would have been travelling for over 12 months and would have covered in excess of 2,000 kilometres. It is logical to assume then, with Port Essington only some 500 kilometres away, the explorer would have called there to replenish his supplies and to send south a report on the country he had discovered so far. Leichhardt was not to know that the settlement of Victoria at Port Essington had been abandoned in 1849. In 1851 the government, after constant urging by men like Clarke, agreed that Leichhardt may indeed have gone to Port Essington for help after its closure. The barque *General Palmer*, commanded by Captain T. B. Simpson, left Sydney on 29 April 1851 and set out for Port Essington, escorted by the brig *Pioneer*. The voyage was not without incident, the *Pioneer* being wrecked in Torres Strait. The *General Palmer* reached Port Essington to find no evidence that Leichhardt had been there. On questioning the Aborigines, Captain Simpson was told no white men had been in the area since the demoralised garrison sailed away aboard HMS *Macander* in 1849.

Considering this, I believe it is reasonable to assume Leichhardt and his party lost their lives somewhere between the Barcoo and Port Essington. That is, of course, no horse paddock, but it does eliminate possible search areas west of the Georgina, the Barkly Tableland, and Leichhardt's old track to Port Essington. It also makes it very unlikely that the remains of the expedition will be found below a line running from Mount Abundance to the Georgina above Bedourie. It must be remembered that Leichhardt's stated plans were to head northwest, placing his route above this line. The natural barriers listed earlier would have steered him further north. As he did not call in at Port Essington, it is reasonable to assume his remains will not be found west of a line running between the Roper River and Port Essington. A. C. Gregory concluded that the remains of Leichhardt's expedition would be found between the Barcoo and the Gulf rivers. I believe he was right about this. Of the three possible routes, the Thomson, the Diamantina, and the Georgina, I personally favour the latter. Leichhardt's often-repeated plans were to skirt north of Sturt's desert, and with the interior of the continent completely unknown, only the Georgina could have shown the explorer the extent of the desert country.

WHEN, WHERE AND WHY?

As mentioned earlier in this book, there has been over the years a great deal of speculation regarding the cause of Leichhardt's disappearance. If the same factors I used in determining the possible route taken by the explorer in his last trip are applied, the fate of the expedition may become clearer. Let us look at each of the theories in turn and assess their likelihood.

Did Leichhardt and his companions die of thirst? There has been a long-established school of thought that claims the explorer simply led the expedition out into the desert, past the point of no return, and perished. To anyone who has studied Leichhardt's method of exploration this view is untenable. On his journey to Port Essington, Leichhardt never moved his main camp forward even when on a river, until he had reconnoitred ahead and established that there was adequate water for both stock and men as well as stock feed. He was far too experienced and cautious to be lured into arid country by a dubious water course. All I have discovered of Leichhardt and his methods virtually eliminates perishing from thirst as a possible fate.

Did the party meet its end simply by becoming lost? A person may be deemed to be lost if he or she does not know their position in relation to known geographical or man-made features. This situation never really applied to explorers, who were for the most part travelling through country previously unknown to whites. They knew where they had been, where they were going, and where they were, albeit roughly at times by calculating the latitude and longitude of their positions as mariners did at sea. Most explorers made slight errors at times in these calculations, as Leichhardt did in the Gulf on his trip to Port Essington; these small errors in position were of little consequence, and understandable, as a sextant carried in a saddle bag was not likely to remain in pristine condition. At times an explorer may have been prevented from reaching his goal by natural features, this happened to Eyre, who was turned back by salt lakes; to Charles Sturt, whose progress was thwarted by the desert; and to McDouall Stuart, who was twice defeated by the tangled barrier of the Murranji Scrub. These setbacks may at times have had fatal consequences, but none of the subsequent deaths could be attributed directly to the explorer simply becoming lost.

Did the party die of starvation? That fate overtook Burke and Wills, but Leichhardt was not Burke or Wills. As already related, on the trip to Port Essington, Leichhardt and his party lived off the land for a large part of the journey, and would have made full use of the game on the trip to the west. It is true that the wildlife of the inland is not as plentiful as on the explorer's earlier route; nevertheless Leichhardt would have dried the flesh of both emus and kangaroos to augment his meat supply. Every outback waterhole was a veritable cornucopia to the Aborigines; Leichhardt would have been quite happy to eat whatever the Aborigines ate, and would have made full use of the available food supplies at these waterholes. The explorer left the Darling Downs with 50 head of bullocks, the one he killed at his camp near Mount Abundance was estimated by the explorer to last until the party reached the Barcoo, about 300 kilometres away. Simple arithmetic plus Leichhardt's ability to live off the land should dispel any idea that the party died of starvation.

I believe the idea that lack of food was responsible for the demise of Leichhardt's party had its origins in the death of Burke and Wills, who, to be brutally honest, met their fate through Burke's poor leadership and lack of judgment. I find it difficult to understand how anyone could starve to death on Cooper Creek, particularly when one considers their erstwhile companion William Brahe had left the following stores at the abandoned depot when he returned to Menindee after waiting for the explorers for five months: 60 pounds (27 kilograms) of oatmeal, 50 pounds (23 kilograms) of flour, 60 pounds (27 kilograms) of sugar, 20 pounds (9 kilograms) of rice, 15 pounds (7 kilograms) of dried meat, as well as salt and ginger. When Burke, Wills and King arrived back at the depot on 21 April 1861, they were in a very weak condition and the expedition's remaining two camels were on their last legs. Instead of camping until both men and camels had regained their strength, Burke decided on a hurried and ill-advised dash to Mount Hopeless some 240 kilometres away, where Burke believed a cattle station had recently been established. It was a decision not endorsed by Wills or King and may well have been motivated by panic on finding Brahe had left the depot the same day they had arrived there. It was without doubt the real reason for the death of Burke and Wills. The party left the depot on 23 April. Before leaving the depot, Burke wrote a message saying that they had returned. He buried it in the 'dig' hole, then carefully filled the hole and raked the surface over so that the Aborigines would not disturb it. Nothing was left to indicate that the exhausted party had returned and buried a message except the broken bottle that had contained Brahe's letter to Burke.

By 6 May, both camels had thrown in the towel, and some of the stores had to be abandoned. On 27 May the three men started back to the depot on foot, carrying what they could manage in their weakened condition. In the meantime Brahe had met William Wright who was in charge of the main supply party at the Bulloo River. Both men returned to the Cooper Creek depot on 4 May in a last-ditch attempt to locate the explorers. But Brahe missed the significance of the broken bottle, and therefore seeing no sign of the missing party, departed, leaving Burke, Wills and King to their fate. It was a tragedy that should never have happened. The outback is an unforgiving place; it has never suffered fools gladly. I am quite convinced Leichhardt would have acted very differently, for he was as much at home in the bush as Burke had been in Melbourne.

Did Leichhardt and his companions drown in an inland flood? This is a much favoured theory. There is a possibility that the members of the expedition may have found themselves cut off by flooded channels. However, floodwaters in that area run very slowly, and I can see no reason why the expeditionary party could not have extricated itself together with stock and gear. Floodwaters do rise unexpectedly in the channel country when there has been no local rain for weeks, but because of the very slight fall in the country, flood crests do not roar down those rivers as they do on the coast. It is true that Leichhardt did once camp in a creek bed on his trip to Port Essington because the rough hills on either side of the water course offered no suitable camping site; but after Gilbert's death, the explorer made a firm decision never to camp close to water again because of the threat of attack from Aborigines. As Leichhardt's planned route would have taken him north of the main channel country, the chances of him and his party drowning in an inland flood are fairly remote.

Did the party succumb to fever? Fever certainly appears to have been a major factor in the abandonment of Leichhardt's first attempt to reach the west coast of Australia. Closer examination of that expedition, however, suggests that the effects of fever may have been exaggerated by men who wished only to return home. The route taken by the explorer on his final journey was one that would have avoided the fever-ridden coastal areas until he was in country bordering on the Gulf of Carpentaria. He had travelled the Gulf route before without health problems, and even if fever had struck,

I believe Leichhardt and his party would have managed to reach Port Essington.

Did the Leichhardt expedition perish in a bush fire? Since white settlement, there have been many bush fires that have taken a huge toll on both life and property. One of the reasons for these devastating fires is that the country is no longer burnt in a regular and systematic way as it was when the Aborigines used fire as a hunting technique. As a result of this regular burning off, there was no build-up of dry flammable material. It is a system that should be reintroduced into our national forests. Most of the outback does not have the tall eucalyptus forests so vulnerable to fire. It is comprised mainly of low scrub and open grasslands called downs. Despite the lack of tall timber, after a couple of good years, a fire on the downs can be a fearsome sight. The wind generated by these fires in open country has to be seen to be believed. I have seen these fires on the downs starting spot fires hundreds of metres ahead of the main fire front. In 1917, eleven men lost their lives in such a fire on Warenda Station, between Winton and Boulia. Tommy Reardon, a part-Aborigine, managed to survive by galloping his horse through the front of the inferno—only a top horseman could have done it. Tommy did not escape unscathed: the parts of his body burnt in his escape remained a pinkish white colour. From then on Tommy Reardon was known to his mates as the Piebald Pony.

Towards the end of 1946, I was involved in fighting a very bad fire on Morstone Station. Every available man was thrown into the attempt to save valuable grazing land. With the temperature over 100 degrees on the old scale, little could be done of a daytime other than burning back. The technique used then was to fight the fire at night and on foot, using wet bags or branches torn from trees. We battled to control the fire for two nights. Early on the second night we managed to steer the bushfire onto spinifex ridges. Spinifex is very poor cattle feed, so our job was to then prevent the fire from beating us back onto the good Mitchell-grass country. Spinifex, however, is the most difficult of all grasses to extinguish. It is rich in resin, which is used by Aborigines to fix spear heads to the shafts of their spears. The more you flog spinifex, the better it burns, at least that is the impression weary firefighters get. We had left the water truck miles behind us before we entered the rough hills. Our fire fighting bags were as dry as we were, so we had to resort to tearing branches from trees to battle the flames. An hour before dawn we had turned the fire well away from the good grazing land. The manager considered the situation safe for the time being and called a halt to the battle.

A count of heads showed everyone to be present and we started back to where we believed the truck to be. Now, after a night of fire fighting it is not hard to become a bit slewed, for nothing can be seen of the surroundings save the immediate area lit up by the flames. We had slogged along with our heads down for hours following wherever the fire had taken us. That morning, under those conditions it was impossible to know precisely where the truck was. We all started off in the same direction, but after a little while members of the party began to fan out, as each man headed for where he believed the truck to be. I found myself in the middle of the spreading group, and looking over I saw Paddy Doherty. Paddy had been on the station for years, and he had superb Aboriginal bush skills. As he seemed to be heading in the same direction, I decided to stick with him. It was a wise decision. We reached the truck just on daylight, well ahead of the others. We all managed to get one small drink from the depleted water bags. Just then Mrs Alford, the manager's wife, drove up with a huge billycan of iced coffee. I have never tasted anything as delicious as that coffee.

Leichhardt would have travelled through similar country in 1848. However, the Aborigines would have been carrying out regular burning then, greatly reducing the fire risk. That, coupled with Leichhardt's habit of following rivers, makes it rather unlikely that fire brought about the end of the expedition.

*   *   *

Did the expedition disintegrate after a mutiny by members of the party? This theory has been put forward by some so-called experts. However, the mutiny scenario depends largely on the word of Andrew Hume, and Hume was at best a very unreliable witness. There is no other evidence that a mutiny on this trip ever took place. The chances of a revolt occurring well into a journey like this are remote. Everyone would have realised that survival depended on the party sticking together, even if some were disenchanted. It is true that on Leichhardt's previous, failed expedition the men were close to rebellion, but the circumstances were quite different. That expedition had travelled no great distance from the Downs, and the way back was well watered. It is extremely unlikely that a mutiny was responsible for the disappearance of Leichhardt and his party.

Did the Aborigines wipe out Leichhardt's expedition? This is, I believe, the only logical explanation. It is a fact that very few of the tribes, including the fierce Kalkadoons, showed any hostility initially towards the whites; it was only after the overlanders and settlers moved into tribal lands with their flocks and herds that the guerilla war began. Nevertheless, if explorers gave cause or opened hostilities themselves, retaliation could occur, as evidenced by the death of Gilbert during Leichhardt's first expedition. It seems the likely cause of this tragedy was the contravention of the explorer's policies regarding Aborigines. So what could have triggered an attack on this last expedition? Leichhardt understood Aborigines, he was experienced in dealing with them, and had always gone out of his way to make friends with them. If the explorer followed his planned route he would have reached the Gulf rivers well west of the area where Gilbert was killed, thus avoiding any further trouble with that tribe. For the remainder of the Port Essington trip the Aborigines had been friendly, and if Leichhardt had succeeded in reaching the Gulf, the Aborigines he had met on his first trip would presumably have greeted him like a long-lost brother.

Shortly after Leichhardt set out on his final expedition, stories circulated that the party had been killed by Aborigines, and this finally led to Hovenden Hely's ineffectual attempt to find the remains of Leichhardt and his companions on the Maranoa. Very similar stories did the rounds after the explorer left on his first expedition, and may then, as later, have arisen from the questioning of local Aborigines by settlers. It has been my experience when questioning people of another culture that one has to be very careful not to lead. If one does, the answer is invariably influenced by the manner in which the question was asked. If Leichhardt and his men were indeed wiped out by Aborigines, I don't believe it was during the early part of the trip. Rather, their fate was, I believe, linked to the native drug pituri, which grew in a restricted location west of Boulia.

The late Dr Walter Roth was regarded as the greatest authority on the Aborigines of this area. He described pituri as a shrub or small tree growing on the headwaters of the Mulligan and west of Pituri Creek. To prepare the drug, Dr Roth said the Aborigines roasted the bark on coals, then moistened it and mixed it with ashes

Dried pituri. The plant was highly prized for its bark and was an important asset to the Aboriginal tribes on whose land it grew.

of gidgee leaves. The mixture was then moulded into quids for chewing. This is exactly the same preparation the Aborigines used for the plug tobacco issued to them by Europeans. Dr Roth claimed the pituri plant induced a strong craving; it was obviously a habit-forming drug.

The main tribe in the area was the Pitta Pitta of Boulia, but there were a number of other small, but powerful tribes in the district; the Wonkajera tribe, for example, controlled the Glenormiston area. The word 'pituri' is from their language; the Pitta Pitta called the drug ta-ram-bola. It was a prized commodity in trade, which played an important part in Aboriginal life. When working on Glenormiston, I often saw Aboriginal stone axe heads lying on the ground. These were of a hard green stone not found locally.

Roth showed in his research that Aboriginal trade routes crossed what are now stations in the Boulia district—Herbert Downs, Glenormiston, Marion Downs and others—trading in skins, spears, feathers, shells, stone knives and stone tomahawks. He discovered that the green stone was used by such groups as the Kalkadoon, and was found away from the area in the Leichhardt-Selwyn Ranges. Pituri, of course, was important to trade and there is no doubt that the Wonkajera would have guarded their tribal lands well, and would have been jealously protective of their prized plants.

Leichhardt's great love was botany, and it was his habit to obtain specimens of all new plants and trees he came across. If in reconnoitring west of the Georgina he had collected pituri and taken it back to his main camp, it may well have provoked an attack that ended Leichhardt's attempt to reach the west coast of the continent. The area around Glenormiston has figured largely in stories of massacres of whites by Aborigines. I believe there is a good chance that Leichhardt and his party met their fate on Glenormiston country.

LUDWIG LEICHHARDT:
A FINAL SUMMARY

The mystery that still surrounds the disappearance of Ludwig Leichhardt's last expedition has in many ways overshadowed the achievements of the man, and that is a great pity. For without doubt his journey to Port Essington was one of the greatest feats in the annals of exploration. When one considers that it was carried out without government assistance, the achievement assumes even greater significance. In his endeavours to reach the Swan River settlement in Western Australia, Leichhardt failed twice; failure, however, is no stranger to those who venture to the limits of what is possible.

There is little doubt that Leichhardt's early training proved advantageous to him in dealing with the rigours of exploration. He was better equipped both mentally and physically than many of his peers to handle the privations endured by the early explorers. From an early age in Europe, Leichhardt had embarked on a disciplined and Spartan diet and regime of physical training. His thirst for knowledge led him to study medicine, geology, zoology and botany. He went on long walking tours through Europe, collecting specimens and talking of overseas adventures with his friend William Nicholson. It was as though he was preparing himself for the challenges he was destined to meet.

Leichhardt added navigation to his fund of knowledge before leaving England. On arrival in the Colony of New South Wales, Leichhardt, disappointed by the lack of opportunity in Sydney, set out to learn everything he could about the new continent. He was determined to become familiar with the Australian bush, to examine the flora and fauna, and to discover all he could about the indigenous people. With little information available in Sydney, Leichhardt went into the bush and found the answers there.

Many armchair critics have decried Leichhardt's ability as a bushman. As an experienced bushman myself, I have found it difficult to fault him. Leichhardt usually did the reconnoitring himself. On a number of occasions he guided the party across the rough divide between the tributary of a river he had been following and the headwaters of another that better suited his purpose. Despite weak eyesight, he exhibited better bushmanship than he has ever been credited with. He was certainly a better bushman than Mitchell, who ventured nowhere without a compass. Unlike earlier explorers, such as Oxley and Sturt, who gained knowledge of the bush as they led expeditions, Leichhardt was a reasonably good bushman before setting out for Port Essington. The use of pack animals as a method of exploration was well established prior to 1844, and Leichhardt was not the first to pack bullocks. Nevertheless, and despite the fact that the use of pack bullocks slowed his progress, it is true to say Leichhardt pioneered the lightly equipped, highly mobile method of exploration—a style that was later adopted with success by other great explorers including A. C. Gregory and John McDouall Stuart.

Leichhardt's achievement in reaching Port Essington was made possible by two main factors. First, was his humane and commonsense approach to stock husbandry. Leichhardt's stock numbers were few; but to have nursed them for 14 months over a distance of almost 5,000 kilometres was a feat any drover could be justifiably proud of. Second, it was Leichhardt's knowledge of botany that enabled him to reach his goal without a case of scurvy. This debilitating condition, caused by a lack of vitamin C, wreaked havoc among the members of other expeditions. It was only the sound good health of Roper and Calvert that made it possible for them to recover from their wounds without holding up progress of the expedition.

As an explorer Leichhardt was cautious yet determined. Like McDouall Stuart, he hated to be thwarted in the realisation of his objective. His reluctance to accept defeat was, however, tempered by commonsense. In 1846 he bowed to the inevitable, and aborted his first attempt to reach the Swan River settlement. If Leichhardt made mistakes, as most explorers did, he was quick to learn from them.

A great deal of the initial antipathy towards Leichhardt can be attributed to the colony's predilection for all things British. The influence of Sir Thomas Mitchell and his followers was also a major factor. Mitchell was not only an anglophile, but also was extremely jealous of Leichhardt for stealing his thunder in reaching Port Essington. Later in the writings of Logan Jack and, in particular, Alec Chisholm, the tenor of the criticism against Leichhardt became blatantly anti-German. Leichhardt had his share of detractors, but few, if any, were of the calibre of the man they criticised.

Leichhardt did, of course, have faults. I'm not referring to the catalogue of transgressions levelled at him by members of his second expedition, but faults nevertheless. It appears he may have lacked motivational skills as a leader; this coupled with his own driving ambition caused problems when dealing with unpaid volunteers. Leichhardt was a man with a vision—his approach to exploration fell somewhere just short of missionary zeal. It is a sad fact of life that some men of real vision cannot always inspire others to embrace that vision, nor can they understand the indifference of others to it. Many explorers, of course, had no need for personnel management skills. Armed with government authority, their word was law and the men under their control accepted discipline as a way of life.

Ludwig Leichhardt made a significant contribution in the fields of both science and exploration. In examining the ongoing response of the establishment to his achievements, it is interesting to reflect on how differently he may have been treated, and remembered, had he been British-born. If the administrators of the young colony did not fully appreciate Leichhardt's work, the great scientific establishments were conscious of the contribution he had made. In 1847, as well as being awarded the Royal Geographical Society's Patron's Medal, Ludwig Leichhardt also received the Grand Prize of the Geographical Society in Paris.

PREPARATIONS FOR THE SEARCH

It was not until early 1995 that my thoughts turned again to the mystery of Ludwig Leichhardt's disappearance, and to those far-off days when we found the relics on Glenormiston Station.

After we left the Boulia area in 1948, Ross Ratcliffe, Bruce Hanson and I went our separate ways. In 1952 Bruce worked for me on the road droving; he then went to Korea with the Australian forces. I lost track of both him and Ross for many years, during which time the pressure of work and the responsibility of raising our families left little time to ponder the fate of Ludwig Leichhardt. I met Ross again in Rockhampton in 1974 and saw Bruce twice before his death in March 1992. The finding of the relics was all but forgotten and not spoken of during the brief time we spent together. Charley Trottman had died years before Bruce's death.

However, when I wrote of finding the Glenormiston relics in my book *Packhorse Drover*, published in 1996, it rekindled my interest in the significance of the site. (See Appendices, 'Explanatory Notes on Finding the Old Camp and the Loss of the Stirrup Irons'.) It is an accepted fact that metal objects will survive for a very long time in the low humidity and arid soils of the outback; in addition the position of the relics in the ground was consistent with them having been there for a very long time. After my research into the Leichhardt mystery, I was convinced of three things: first, contrary to popular belief, Leichhardt had been a competent explorer and a good bushman; second, nothing has been found that could throw any light on the fate of his expedition; and third, the Glenormiston site was worthy of investigation.

Late in 1995 I showed the manuscript of *Packhorse Drover* to my brother Jeff. He had spent a number of years droving with me, and now owned a stone-fruit orchard near Stanthorpe, in southeastern Queensland. He was appalled that I had told no one about finding the relics, and was adamant that something should be done before it was too late. Jeff pointed out rather forcibly that there was only Ross and me left of the original party and we were not getting any younger. I had to admit that what he said made sense. On my way back to Caboolture, where I live, I decided to give some serious thought to returning to Glenormiston.

Charley Trottman was with us when we turned up the relics on Glenormiston in 1948.

A few nights after returning from Stanthorpe I received a phone call from Alex Long. I knew Alex only slightly then, although he also lived in Caboolture. He told me he had been working for some time on a TV documentary on Ludwig Leichhardt. While in the Taroom district, he had heard from a mate of Ross Ratcliffe's of our finding the relics. He was obviously interested and asked if I was planning to investigate the site.

After talking to Alex, I gave Ross a ring. He agreed that we should investigate the relic site and was still convinced that it could hold the answer to the Leichhardt mystery. We further agreed any attempt to relocate the site would be a joint venture, and made a rather vague starting date of some time after the coming wet. Ross's availability would depend on sufficient rain falling on his drought-stricken property.

When I later met Alex in Caboolture, we found we shared similar views on Leichhardt's capabilities, and agreed the explorer had been the victim of a great deal of unfounded criticism. Alex was keen to join any expedition to investigate the site on Glenormiston, using the trip to add material to his documentary. Alex had been reared on a cattle property in the Taroom district, was an experienced bushman, and I had no qualms about including him in the proposed trip.

Having thus committed myself to returning to Glenormiston, I realised the decision meant I was responsible for organising the expedition. There were a number of matters to be considered: the make up of the party, the minimum number required and their qualifications; the four-wheel drive vehicles needed; the equipment required; whether it could attract sponsorship; and whether I could get permission to conduct a search on Glenormiston.

Ian Tinney, who works for the ABC rural radio in Brisbane, had, at his own expense, tidied up the manuscript of *Packhorse Drover* for me on his computer. Like most people he was intrigued by the story of our finding relics on Glenormiston. He is a four-wheel-drive enthusiast, whose job at times takes him over a lot of the outback. Ian had been to Glenormiston, and when he indicated he was keen to join the expedition I was happy to have him in the team. The party now had four potential members: Ross, Alex, Ian and myself. I thought my brother would be a starter if he could get away. At the time he was up to his elbows in stone fruit, so I merely outlined to him the progress that had been made. Soon after the remainder of his crop was wiped out by a late hail storm. My brother had nursed the crop through drought, frost and early storms; now he watched helplessly as peaches, plums and nectarines were destroyed. People on the land are a breed apart. Jeff took the loss philosophically, and after the festive season had a few days with my family and me in Caboolture.

We discussed preparations for the trip to Glenormiston and Jeff agreed to join us. I told him that transport could be a problem. At that time I had managed to obtain one four-wheel-drive search vehicle. When I told Jeff this, he suggested that Greg, his son, would greatly strengthen the party. Greg was a good mechanic and a jack-of-all-trades; moreover he was the proud owner of an eminently suitable vehicle, a Land-Rover. Greg had done a lot of outback travelling and had winches fitted to his vehicle. I agreed to Jeff's suggestion, and on contacting Greg, he said he was right, provided I could give him a month's notice. I made arrangements with both him and Jeff to meet for further discussions in March. Alex had advised me that he would be taking a soundman with him, so the group with Jeff and Greg now numbered seven. I considered that that was enough to do the job, but suitable vehicles were still a problem.

The wet finally came ensuring that Ross would be able to get away. I wrote to an oil company, asking if they would be prepared to help us with fuel sponsorship. Fuel was going to be the heaviest cost in attempting to solve the Leichhardt mystery. I also wrote to the North Australian Pastoral Company asking for permission to conduct the search on Glenormiston. Good relations with both the head office of the company and the manager of Glenormiston would be of the utmost importance if we were to be successful.

At our meeting in March we got down to discussing the equipment needed to carry out the search. I had a metal detector and

Ian had a global positioning device. We agreed that these items plus shovels, rakes, sieves, pegs and brickie's line to grid the site would all be required. We discussed the possibility of taking along an expert, possibly from the Queensland Museum; the others agreed to leave that in my hands.

When Greg asked me if I thought we would have any trouble finding the relics, I had to admit that after 48 years it would not be easy. We had found the site only by accident in the first place. Nevertheless, I felt confident that between Ross and me, we could locate it again.

Good communications would be vital during the search. I knew Ian had a two-way radio in his Toyota, and Greg assured me he could talk to anyone anywhere; glancing at the number of aerials on the Land-Rover parked outside I had to agree. Greg also had the answer to any minor medical problems; he always carried not one, but two first aid kits. Jeff sat back, 'Right', he said, 'now what about tucker?'.

I pulled out a list I'd been working on and read it aloud. My brother shook his head in mock dismay. 'You haven't changed have you? Here, give me that and I'll add a few extras.'

He and Greg worked on the list for a while, and when they had finished, it bore little resemblance to the original. I was happy enough though, I always welcomed input, and I certainly achieved that with the tucker list. While they were chuckling to themselves over my meagre shopping list, I gave some thought to a problem that was still worrying me. I wanted a well-organised camp and that sort of camp needs a cook. The thought of seven or eight men milling around the fire cooking for themselves filled me with dismay. I had asked Jeff to do the job, but he had politely declined. Greg must have been reading my mind, for, as Jeff passed the new list to me, he said, 'By the way, don't worry about the cooking. I'll do that.'

I knew Greg was an abseiling expert with the SES. I did not know that he also cooked for up to 30 men when in camp. He had a trailer fitted out as a field kitchen that he towed behind the Land-Rover.

The cooking problem was solved. If each of us took our own eating utensils, Greg would look after the rest of the camp gear. I was beginning to appreciate Jeff's keenness to have my nephew join the party. It was quickly becoming apparent how indispensable he would be on the trip.

I had to be in Winton in late April to help judge a poetry competition there, and then in Longreach on 4 May for the launch of *Packhorse Drover* at the Stockman's Hall of Fame. I knew Ian Tinney would also be involved there, so a firm date was set for the start of the expedition. We would gather at Longreach on 4 May and leave for Glenormiston on 5 May.

I had not heard from the fuel company regarding sponsorship so it seemed that fuel expenses would have to be borne by the individual members. This news caused them no concern; all were still as keen as mustard. (The company later advised us it was not in a position to sponsor the trip.) The shortage of suitable search vehicles was still a worry. We had only Ian's Toyota and Greg's Land-Rover, plus the two utilities belonging to Jeff and Alex. The last two would help to get us out to Glenormiston, but would be of little use on the search. In a few short days, however, our vehicle problem was solved. Ross rang to say a mate of his, Michael Percival, with a Jeep Cherokee would be visiting him and was keen to join the expedition. Next day Mark Poole, who worked with Alex Long, volunteered to drive the documentary team out in his Land-Rover Discovery. Mark is an effervescent character, who, although not a bushman, had gained some experience in bush driving. Within a week, Lloyd Linson-Smith had also joined the party and planned to take out his Nissan Navara twin cab, together with a three-wheel all-terrain bike. Lloyd had been in the Glenormiston stock camp when the relics were found, but had not seen them himself. I welcomed them all, although the group had now grown to 10, a few more than I had planned for. With so many vehicles on offer it was decided that Jeff would leave his utility behind and travel out with Greg.

Early in April, I received a letter from the North Australian Pastoral Company giving permission for the expedition to carry out the search on Glenormiston. Mr S. J. Millard, the Group Pastoral Manager, also advised me that a copy of his letter to me had been sent to Mr Mal Debney, the manager of Glenormiston.

I discarded the idea of including a historian in the team; if we found the site, there would be no shortage of interested people. On a visit to the Queensland Museum I had a yarn with Tom Baird, an expert in old weapons. Tom was most helpful, giving me the details of the type of guns Leichhardt would probably have taken on his last expedition. According to Tom, they would have been smooth bore muzzle-loading guns, using percussion caps to ignite the propellant. There could well be parts that had survived, in particular, the breechblocks, but these would have been left flat on the ground not at an angle to it like the pack and saddle plates. There would be a good chance that anything left of them would be under the surface.

I came away with the impression that Tom would have liked to join us had he been able to obtain leave.

My book *Packhorse Drover* had been on sale since mid-March 1996, and, as a result, interest in our expedition to Glenormiston was growing. There was no shortage of late volunteers but I wanted to keep the party as lean as possible. On 21 April I rang Mal Debney at Glenormiston to discuss our forthcoming trip. Mal seemed quite happy about our visit and advised me that the Georgina had run. It had not been a big flood but there was water in some of the outside channels. He also generously offered to supply the party with meat from the station if it was needed. I thanked Mal and told him we would probably see him on 6 May.

On Monday 22 April, Greg and I drove to a wholesaler he dealt with and purchased rations for the trip. When he dropped me off back in Caboolture, he picked up the metal detector, some camp stools, my swag and a small tent. Then with a 'See you in Longreach', he drove off.

Rations purchased and equipment already in Greg's keeping, on 24 April I boarded a coach at the Brisbane transit centre bound for Longreach. Once settled in my seat I went over the plans for the expedition again, then satisfied that everything had been properly organised, I sat back to enjoy the trip. Most of my companions would not be leaving for some days, but for me the adventure had already begun.

THE TRIP TO BOULIA

McCafferty's coach pulled into the rear of the company's depot in Longreach. I waited for the aisle to clear, then alighted and stretched my legs as I rolled a smoke. After a little while my battered green suitcase was dragged from the cavernous luggage compartment of the coach. I thanked the captain and made my way through the front office to Eagle Street, the main thoroughfare. Tossing my case on a bench I looked around. Longreach was beginning to liven up, the bushmen's muster was due to start on the morrow and already blokes in ringer's hats and 'laughing-side' (elastic-sided) boots were knocking about the street. I knew Jeff and Greg should be in the town somewhere and was considering my next move when Jeff stuck his head out of the bar next door to the bus office. He jerked his thumb over his shoulder and disappeared.

Inside Greg was sitting on a stool with his back to the bar. I ordered a rum and milk—it had been a long time since breakfast! Ted Fisher, who had joined the group looked at me as I took the glass: 'Christ what have you got there?'.

I shook hands with him and told him it was nourishment and punishment in the one glass. I had known Ted for 30 years or so. He was one of those quietly spoken chaps who had stayed on as a stockman through the ups and downs of the industry. Charley

Peacock was another who was drinking with us. Quite unlike Ted, it was often possible to hear Charley before you saw him. He was always lively company and took great pride in a hat so bedecked with metal badges that it was almost impossible to find an empty space. It must have been quite heavy but Charley was a nuggety character and the weight never seemed to bother him. Charley is from Blackall and is one of a very large family. There is an often-told story about his dad, who once took the whole family down to the Brisbane Exhibition. Peacock senior became very interested in the champion bull of the show and later took the kids around to the cattle stalls. He approached the owner and asked if he could have a closer look at the champion, the owner looked the family over and said, 'No you stay here and I'll bring the bloody bull out to have a closer look at you'.

I know that Charley, good sport that he is, will not mind the story being told once more.

After a few rounds of drinks, Jeff pushed his hat back, 'Well, we'd better get your gear up to the caravan park. They told us when we booked in that they had messages there for you.'

We had a meal at the cafe opposite then walked over to where Greg had parked. It was obvious that there was room for only one passenger in the front. Jeff and I eyed the laden back of the Land-Rover. Anyone riding there would be rather conspicuous and definitely in breach of the law. 'She's Jake', Jeff said. 'I'll find a possy up there somewhere.'

As he finished speaking, a police car cruised by. 'But I won't bloody well get in here. I'll go down that side street and you can pick me up on the way. The last thing we want is trouble with the cops at this stage.'

We finally made it to the Gunnadoo Caravan Park and Greg pulled up in his allocated site on the back fence where he had left his trailer.

After a couple of hours' rest, I was aroused by Greg's call of 'Tea or coffee here if you want it'. I sat up and looked over to where he had a billy boiling on a small gas burner and, beside him, a small metal box. He flipped open the hinged lid, and, like a magician pulling rabbits from a hat, he proceeded to take out three pannikins, a bottle of coffee, a packet of tea, a tin of sugar, a small carton of long-life milk, a tube of condensed milk and spoons. How the blazes he got the contents in there I'll never know but it was typical of the methodical and economical way Greg had packed his Land-Rover and trailer. During the trip he never ceased to amaze me with the ease with which he could produce items that were required. I sometimes had the feeling that if someone had asked for a set of bagpipes, Greg would have given his usual laconic 'no problem' and produced the instrument from some hidden compartment.

As I sat drinking my tea, Greg told me Lloyd Smith was also in a cabin at the caravan park. Lloyd's proper surname was Linson-Smith, something of a mouthful, but he'd always been plain Lloyd Smith to his bush mates.

Just then Lloyd came over towards us. Lloyd had left the bush earlier than the rest of the Glenormiston group, and, apart from a few grey hairs and glasses, he looked little different to the dapper young stockman I had known so many years before. We greeted each other warmly and after shaking hands I introduced him to Jeff and Greg. Lloyd was overflowing with enthusiasm and delighted at the prospect of going back to Glenormiston. But there would be some delay. Because of some business both Ian Tinney and Mark Poole had to attend to, it appeared we wouldn't be able to start out from Longreach until the following Monday—in three days' time, I knew the team was impatient to begin the search and as everyone had jobs to get back to, our time was limited. Every day we stayed in Longreach meant one day less we could spend on Glenormiston. The delay was frustrating for me too, but I was under an obligation to the people at the Hall of Fame, as they were launching my book the next day. I also owed a debt of gratitude to Tim Butler, the manager of the ABC in Longreach. Above all I wanted to keep the party together.

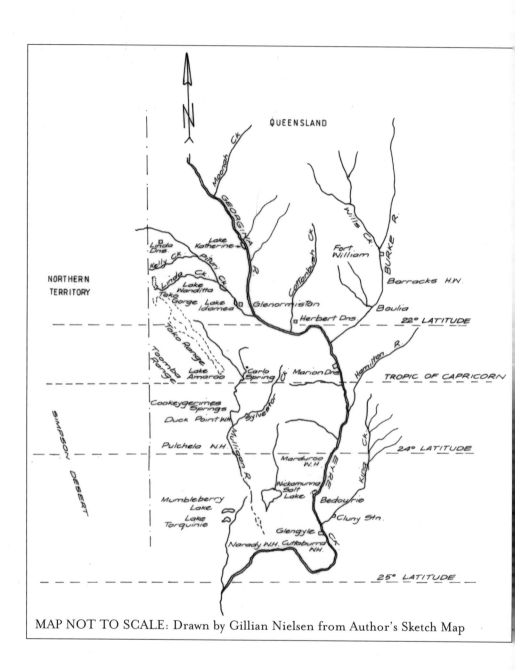

QUEENSLAND

NORTHERN
TERRITORY

Moonah Ck.

GEORGINA R.

Wills Ck.

BURKE R.

Lake
Katherine

Linda
Dns

Kelly Ck.

Pitur Ck.

Linda Ck.

Lake
Wanditta

Toko
Gorge

Lake
Idamea

Glenormiston

Cattonbah Ck.

Fort
William

Barracks H.W.

Boulia

Herbert Dns.

22° LATITUDE

Toko Range

Toomba Range

Lake
Amaroo

Carlo
Spring

Marion Dns.

Hamilton R.

TROPIC OF CAPRICORN

Cookeygerimes
Springs

Duck Point W.H.

Sylvester

SIMPSON DESERT

Mulligan R.

Pulchela W.H.

24° LATITUDE

Marduroo
W.H.

EYRE CK.

King Ck.

Nickamunna
Salt
Lake

Bedowrie

Mumbleberry
Lake

Lake
Torquinie

Cluny Stn.

Glengyle

Narady W.H.

Cuttaburra
W.H.

25° LATITUDE

MAP NOT TO SCALE: Drawn by Gillian Nielsen from Author's Sketch Map

146

'Well I hope you and Ross can locate the site quickly', Jeff said as we discussed the schedule. 'A lot is going to depend on that.'

Later after a clean-up we made our way to the business centre of Longreach. In the cafe where we had eaten lunch earlier, we ran into Billy Moore, a Wintonite I had known for many years. He had also been on the road droving with Jeff. After a lively conversation over a good meal, we drifted over to the poetry on the lawn at the Hall of Fame. We stayed until half time, had a drink of coffee then headed back to the camp and our swags.

Next morning we rolled up to breakfast at the stone building at the Hall of Fame, registered for the ringers' muster and were given a name tag. As we ate, we were entertained by the bush poets, many of whom I knew through my visits to other poetry gatherings. After lunch I was leaning on the fence watching the bronco branding competition when someone behind me said, 'No, that can't be Bruce Simpson. He looks too bloody old'. I turned around to see Ross Ratcliffe grinning at me. We shook hands, while I noted that he too had changed a little. In place of the stripling I had known on Glenormiston was a seventeen-stone senior citizen. We talked for a while then Ross said, 'Come and meet this mate of mine'. He led me over to where a relatively young chap was standing with two small children. Ross introduced me to Michael Percival and his children, Jesse and Camille. I was rather nonplussed to hear that Michael's two children of primary-school age would be accompanying us. I had deliberately restricted membership of the party to men with a knowledge of the bush. However Michael was a sensible sort of chap, and, as things turned out, the children enjoyed themselves during their short stay with us.

I spent an entertaining day at the Hall of Fame yarning with Ross and other old mates, going through the Hall and talking to other authors. Jim Laffin, a 92-year-old ex-Kidman drover, was to have his autobiography launched the following morning, and I made a mental note not to miss it.

Later that afternoon I met the rest of the party and we decided that we would return to our favourite cafe for the evening meal and

At the Stockman's Hall of Fame, Longreach, with Lloyd Linson-Smith (centre) and Ross Ratcliffe (right).

be back at the Hall for the book launch at seven-thirty. As usual the meal was top class and we smoked and yarned for some time afterwards. When Greg looked at his watch and asked me when my book was being launched, I told him casually seven-thirty, but they are launching four and I doubt if mine will be the first cab off the rank. Soon after we decided to return to the Hall and I found to my dismay that *Packhorse Drover* had already been launched. I felt I had let a lot of people down, who had promoted the book and made my apologies. My brother, who thought the whole episode hilarious, quipped, 'You must be the first bloody author who has ever missed the launching of one of his books! The shame of it all!' I told him as cheerfully as possible to get stuffed and headed to the bar for a rum.

Early on Sunday morning on my way to the ablution block, I met Mark Poole by his vehicle tucking his shirt in. He told me he, Alex Long and Alex's son Joshua, who was to be his soundman, had pulled in at about three o'clock that morning. The whole party was now together for the first time but it was a situation that would not last long. I returned to the camp and had just got myself a drink of tea, when Ross and Lloyd announced that they would be going ahead with Michael and the kids, as they wanted to look up some old mates at Middleton. We agreed that we would meet up in Boulia on Monday night. As Lloyd had plenty of room in his car fridge, I gave him $15 to buy bread for the whole party and wished them luck. My plan to have the party remain together was shot to pieces, but no real harm was done. If the team had to split, it was better to have the splinter group ahead rather than behind.

Jim Laffin's book was to be launched at the Hall of Fame at ten-thirty. Having missed the launch of my own book I was determined not to miss seeing the introduction of the autobiography of the old-time Kidman drover. During the launch I was invited to say a few words and was happy to comply. I was extremely pleased to see Jim honoured by being made an honorary life member of the Hall of Fame.

On the way back to camp I could not help reflecting on the changes that had taken place in Longreach in the last few years. The town was established in the latter part of the nineteenth century to cater for the needs of the growing pastoral industry. Longreach is situated on what was once part of Mount Cornish, an outstation of Bowen Downs. Together these two properties were regarded as the largest pastoral holding in Australia. In addition to Longreach, the huge run took in the site of Aramac and ran east almost to Clermont. The properties were taken up in 1862 by a syndicate that included Nat Buchanan and William Landsborough, two giants of Australian pastoral development. Bowen Downs ran sheep, while Mount Cornish had a large herd of cattle. It was from Mount Cornish that Harry Redford lifted the mob of cattle that made him famous. In 1870, Mount Cornish ran a herd of some 60,000 head, all branded with the 'LC5' of Bowen Downs. Redford was employed on the station as a bullocky. During the wet, he and four accomplices built a holding yard on the Thomson River, not far from where Longreach now stands. Under the guise of looking for lost working bullocks, Redford mustered 1,000 head. He then started on his marathon droving trip to South Australia, where the Bowen Downs brand was not known.

A white stud bull found its way into the mob, and whether it was from carelessness or greed Redford allowed it to remain. Not long purchased from Gracemere, a property just west of Rockhampton, the bull was clearly out of place *in* Redford's stolen mob. The bull finally brought about his downfall when he swapped it for rations soon after reaching South Australia. The trip was not without tragedy. On the way down the Cooper the mob rushed, killing an Aboriginal stockman. Soon after, two men, MacKenzie and McPherson, pulled out. The canny Scots may have had some Celtic foreboding of disaster; on the other hand they may have just had a gutful of Redford's ambitious plan. Redford battled on with his remaining two men. He continued on down the Cooper, then followed Strzelecki Creek across the border. At Blanchewater, Redford sold the mob for £5,000, a fortune in those days. The cattle duffer was apprehended after some little time. Redford was later found not guilty on the charge of cattle duffing. The decision appears to have been based more on the jury's belief that stealing from a big station was not a crime, rather than any regard for the evidence or legal argument.

Like that of most outback towns the economy of Longreach has always been subject to the vagaries of market prices and weather. The opening of the Pastoral College helped a little, but it was the establishment of the Hall of Fame, with the resulting rise in tourism, that has at last given Longreach some small but nevertheless significant protection against rural recession. River cruises on the Thomson River now add to the town's attractions. Like many larger western towns, however, Longreach has prospered to the detriment of other smaller towns. The air-conditioned MidLander passenger train from Rockhampton that until recently ran to Winton has been replaced by a modern tourist train that terminates at Longreach.

Tourism is of growing importance these days to all towns in western Queensland. Businesses and local authorities are turning to it to offset the slump in the pastoral industry. Blackall is promoting its wool scour, while Barcaldine has established a fine tourist attraction and a lasting monument to outback toilers with its Workers' Heritage Centre.

As some of the western towns became established, the streets were named in a rather original way: Winton was given the names of early settlers and stations for its streets, while Barcaldine's streets were named after trees; in Longreach the founding fathers had favoured birds.

We were up early Monday morning and had a quick breakfast of toast and coffee. Ian, who had been staying elsewhere joined us at the caravan park, and after a last look around to see nothing had been forgotten our three vehicles drove off. At long last the expedition had begun. As we drove over the bridge on the Thomson, I noticed the discoloration of the water. It had not rained for some time but the Thomson River was still turbid with suspended sediment particles.

After a couple of hours' driving, our convoy arrived in Winton, the first western Queensland town to realise the potential of tourism. Winton was quick to capitalise on the 'Waltzing Matilda' connection—Banjo Paterson wrote the song on a nearby station in 1895—and it has other attractions such as the dinosaur footprints at Lark Quarry and the Mayneside opal fields. The town also has an excellent historical museum.

Like most western towns, Winton was established to service the rapidly expanding pastoral industry. In Winton's case love was also to play a part. The publication in 1862 of reports of good land by explorers who had been searching for Burke and Wills led to a race to acquire land. In the late 1860s and early 1870s stations were established on the Diamantina and other inland rivers. A great deal of the land was taken up long before grazing licences were issued. One of the first runs in the Winton area was Elderslie. The first owner, William Forsayth, made application to the Lands Department for a grazing lease in 1873. The following year he sold out to Donald

Wallace who built a crude homestead near Pelican waterhole on the Western River below the present site of the town.

The first mail run in the district was from Aramac to Old Cork Station, a run on the Diamantina taken up by Thomas McIlwraith. Wallace's camp was a regular stop on the mail run. The next step in the development of the future town was due entirely to cupid. In 1875 Robert Allen, sergeant of police at Aramac, fell in love with and proposed to a widow by the name of Mrs O'Toole. Now Mrs O'Toole must have been a woman of strong character and even stronger opinions for she advised the love-lorn sergeant that if she ever remarried it would not be to a copper. Robert Allen, like many men before and since, allowed his heart to rule his head and promptly resigned from the force. Later that year, Allen and his bride moved to Pelican hole and opened a store-cum-grog shanty. By then Wallace had built elsewhere and the place became known as Pelican waterhole rather than Wallace's camp. In 1876 a flood swept down the Western River, and Allen and his wife were forced to take refuge in the timbers of their roof. The founder of Winton—Allen—later moved his business to the present site of the National Bank. When W. H. Corfield built beside Allen in 1878, Elderslie Street was established. Later, Robert Allen was to take his own life, a tragic end for a man who could rightly be called the father of Winton.

After stopping in Winton to refuel ourselves and our vehicles, we set off for Boulia, 354 kilometres away. Much of the country we had travelled through since leaving Longreach had been declared drought-affected. In places it was obvious that over-stocking was as much to blame as the drought. In some paddocks, although the grass was eaten down, the Mitchell grass stools were still healthy. There were areas, however, where the stools had disappeared completely and the earth was bare. I mused on how different the country must have looked to the early explorers.

While drought and over-stocking had damaged the country, the root cause of the problem is the way the country was cut up originally. Many of the holdings were made too small to be viable. In times of low prices graziers are forced to over-stock to survive, and when wool prices lift they look to obtain maximum returns. This strategy is all right when the seasons are good but there are more bad seasons than good ones out here. With no reserve country to act as a buffer against drought, land degradation is inevitable. Graziers can and often do get additional land, but usually they have to put their original holding into hock to finance the purchase of a neighbouring block; later if they are hit with spiralling interest rates and low prices or drought, they are back where they started.

In due course, we crossed the channels of the Diamantina; a few small muddy holes were the only visible signs of water. Alex, Mark and Joshua filmed us crossing, then quickly caught up and went ahead again.

The road to Boulia is a historic one, first opened as a rough bush track in the late 1870s to service the numerous runs taken up in the district. Soon slow-moving wagon teams, dashing coaches and mobs of cattle and sheep followed the dusty route between Winton and Boulia. In those days there was a mail change with fresh coach-horses every 40 kilometres or so, and the now-lonely road boasted eight hotels that catered for the needs of travellers. Of the eight, only one, the Middleton Hotel still survives. Motorised transport, fast cars and sealed roads have put paid to the rest. Progress often wields a double-edged sword. We crossed Britcher's Creek where one of the wayside pubs once stood. It was built by a man named Britcher, an early settler. Later he was murdered by the Kalkadoon on a run he had taken up over the Swords Range.

We travelled on past Woodstock Station, once the site of another hotel on the road to Boulia. Alex and his crew were waiting to film our two vehicles as we travelled through the Woodstock hills. I had travelled the road years before with Territory bullocks and retained few pleasant memories of the area. It was almost mid-afternoon when our three vehicles pulled up at Middleton. Stopping a while at

Middleton is an unwritten law—no one drives past the lonely outpost. Mrs Clauson, the wife of the licensee, made us welcome. The members of our party who were visiting Middleton for the first time listened with interest as Mrs Clauson gave us a brief history of the place.

Although Middleton is just a few kilometres short of halfway between Winton and Boulia, it did not acquire its name from its geographical position. The place gets its name from Middleton Creek, just west of the outpost. John McKinlay was a well-known explorer who was commissioned by the South Australian Government to look for the missing Burke and Wills. On 10 April 1862 he named Middleton Creek after W. Middleton, a member of his expeditionary party. In 1876 a hotel was built at Middleton by a teamster named Wiggans. However, records show that the first hotel licence was not issued until 1889, when Frederick Henderson made an application. Over the next 107 years the hotel has had a total of 25 licensees.

Middleton was proclaimed a township on 9 May 1908 and became a small but important business centre for the district. The town then had a hotel, a school, a police station, a store, a blacksmith's shop and a market garden. In those days it was also home to a number of teamsters and drovers. Now sadly only the hotel and a small community hall remain. In the early days Middleton got its water from Gymbie Gymbie waterhole, a once permanent hole in Saville Creek. The junction of Saville Creek and Middleton Creek is just to the west of the township. For many years now Middleton has depended on an artesian bore for its water supply. The hotel still plays an important part in the social life of the district; long may it prosper.

The road west from Middleton is almost completely sealed now, with only 20 kilometres or so of dirt between Middleton and Boulia, our destination for the night. We travelled past many historic station properties on the way to Boulia, many of them taken up in the nineteenth century. We had seen the Llanrheidol turn-off just before arriving at Middleton. Now along the way there were signs to

Chiltern Hills, Mackunda Downs and Lilleyvale. The first man to take up the last station was a man named Lilley, who later built the legendary Min Min Hotel. It was one pub that did not fall victim to progress; it later burnt to the ground.

Between Lilleyvale and Lucknow Station there is a line of hills called the Cornpore Hills. It seems obvious that at least one of the early settlers in the area had some connection with India. Leaving Lucknow, on the right the road passes the site of the old Min Min Hotel then goes on over Min Min Creek. The only evidence of the hotel's existence today is a heap of broken bottles. It was on station properties in this area that the mysterious min min light was often seen; the source of the light has baffled both bushmen and scientists to this day. The same phenomenon has been seen in many places across the outback, but because of the name and the early sightings, the min min light has always been closely associated with the country around the old Min Min Hotel. A number of stories regarding the light have emanated from the area. One describes how a min min light panicked a coach team, resulting in the coach over-turning; another yarn tells of the death of a man who broke his neck when his horse cartwheeled over a sheep fence while he was chasing the light. I was first told these stories over 50 years ago by Jack Britt who had worked on Warenda Station, another of the district's historic runs. I have not authenticated either story but include them here as typical examples of the folklore surrounding the mysterious min min light.

Some 30 kilometres after crossing Min Min Creek our convoy came to the channels of the Hamilton River. If one alights from a vehicle and stands by the channels, it is not hard, in the ensuing silence, to imagine how different things once were. In those days straining horse teams negotiated the river channels, travelling west with station loading, and back east with wool. Back then coach drivers eased their sweating five-in-hand teams as the coach wheels rattled across the rough corduroy crossings. Once clear of the channels, the drivers would blow a blast on their bugles to herald the eminent arrival of the mail to the Hamilton Hotel. Passengers would prepare to board the coach and grooms would be waiting ready with five fresh horses for the next stage of the journey.

Not far from the crossing is the spot where the old hotel once stood. The Boulia Shire Council has erected a barbecue shelter for tourists there and marked the spot with a fitting memorial. The pub was once a popular drinking spot for the young bloods of Boulia. There were no police stationed there, so some of the lads made the short trip for a weekend carouse. In 1918, Mrs Hasted, a highly respected pioneer woman, purchased the hotel from a Mrs Darge. Mrs Hasted, with the help of her daughter Mrs Britten, ran the hotel for over 50 years. After her death, the hotel licence passed from the family, and some years later, the hotel closed its doors.

We arrived in Boulia about 4.30 pm, and in the time-honoured tradition of outback travellers we made straight for the pub. Being a public holiday the bar was crowded with road workers, ringers, council workers and a few townspeople. Boulia has had only the one hotel for many years but obviously there was no danger of it going broke.

I left to ring Mal Debney and tell him we would be at Glenormiston the following morning, then after some more drinks at the pub we retired to a cafe for something to eat. Ian had invited Kase Connole, a relieving sister at the hospital he knew, to eat with us. Remembering the hospital as it once was, I asked how many were on staff. Kase gave me a bright smile: 'You're looking at the staff: I'm it'.

I was surprised and looked it. Kase explained she was on-call 24 hours a day. In case of an emergency she had to leave a contact phone number whenever she went anywhere. The hospital was now staffed by relieving sisters on a rotational basis. Kase hastened to add that she could, of course, contact the flying doctor if there was a problem she could not handle. It was quite obvious to us all that Kase was coping with the situation and enjoying her stay in Boulia. Nevertheless, I could not help thinking that it was a heavy responsibility for one person and a sad reflection on the state of outback medical services.

The expedition party at the Boulia Caravan Park. From left to right:
Ross Ratcliffe, Michael Percival, Ian Tinney, Lloyd Linson-Smith,
Jeff Simpson, Greg Simpson, Bruce Simpson, Alex Long. Front:
Jesse Percival, Camille Percival, Joshua Long.

We were about to leave the cafe when Ross, Lloyd and Michael
strolled in. After camping near Middleton the previous night, they
had looked over Boulia and had booked in at the caravan park just
over the Burke River from the town. After paying for the meal, we
said goodbye to Kase and followed Ross and company over the
bridge to the caravan park. It was, as Lloyd had said, a top spot. Ian
and Greg parked near a grassed area and after unloading our swags
we walked over to where the others were camped by the bank of the
river. There was a cheery fire burning and at long last the whole
expedition was in camp together.

Seeing Boulia again after so many years brought back memories
of my youth, I was sure it had much the same effect on Ross and
Lloyd. My only regret was that Bruce Hanson was not with us.

Boulia on the Burke

Boulia is a typical outback town, its buildings sprawl unpretentiously on the slope of a ridge on the western side of the Burke River. The town has always had a fearsome reputation for summer heat and dust. I have seen the mercury hover around 119 degrees Fahrenheit [48 degrees Celsius] in the shade, for over a week. I have also seen dust storms so intense that it is difficult to see across the street. Mind you, the width of Boulia's streets are generous indeed—I'm sure the main thoroughfare could easily accommodate a six-lane highway. The district once suffered a seven-year drought, and it was in Boulia that the story originated about the six-year-old boy who fainted when he first saw rain—to revive him his mother had to throw a bucket of dust over him! Many years ago a wag once said that Boulia was not at the end of the earth, but if one climbed a tree there, the end of the earth was clearly visible. Today, modern communications and advances in transportation have largely overcome the tyranny of distance that once isolated the little outpost.

The population of Boulia has retained its sense of humour, self-reliance and independence from the days when it was sometimes easier to travel to London then to reach Boulia. It is also the friendliest town I have ever been in.

The first white men known to be in the Boulia area were without doubt the four members of Burke's ill-fated expedition. The party must have passed the present site of the town in mid-January 1861 on their way to the Gulf of Carpentaria. If my theory is correct Ludwig Leichhardt would have passed within 40 kilometres of the present town in 1848.

The first white man to settle where Boulia now stands was a character whose surname was Vallis. He camped on the Burke River at a waterhole the local Pitta Pitta tribe called Bulzoo. Vallis was still camped there when Ernest Henry arrived in 1877 with two wagon loads of supplies and set up a crude store to cater for the rapidly expanding pastoral industry. It is believed that the name Boulia is a corruption of the Aborigine word Bulzoo.

Settlers who were rapidly developing stations in the area met little serious resistance from the local Pitta Pitta and allied tribes. Further north, however, the war-like Kalkadoon tribe resented the intrusion into their tribal lands by white settlers. Based in the natural fortresses of the rugged Selwyn and Argylla ranges, the Kalkadoon proved to be a serious threat to pastoral expansion. In 1878, the government built police barracks at Boulia and sent Sub-inspector Eglington with a squad of native mounted police to the town. Eglington and his small force soon had their hands full. In December 1878, a man named Molvo and three others left Boulia with cattle to take up a selection on Sulieman Creek, some 100 kilometres north of the town. The local Kalkadoon, who had their own ideas about ownership of the land, wiped out the party at Woonamo waterhole. When word of the massacre reached Boulia, Eglington set out with his mounted troopers, and with the help of settlers dispersed the hostile Kalkadoon.

As the years passed, the town flourished. The power of the fierce Kalkadoon was finally broken at Battle Mountain. It was there that the native police under Sub-inspector Fredrick C. Urquhart, together with Alexander Kennedy and other settlers, inflicted a crushing defeat on the Kalkadoon that ended their resistance. From then on peace reigned on the frontier. The native police, no longer needed, were disbanded and the only reminder of their presence in Boulia is the heap of broken stones where the barracks once stood.

When Ross Ratcliffe, Bruce Hanson and I left Glenormiston back in 1948, we caught Sid Jones's mail truck to Boulia and decided to have a break before looking for other jobs. We took a shared room at the pub and proceeded to live it up a little. Tim Howard, a great old character, owned the hotel. Tim had very poor eyesight—he wore glasses at least a half centimetre in thickness. To see Tim inspect a cheque that had been put over the bar was an unforgettable sight. Holding the cheque up to his face he would pass it back and forward in front of his eyes. Despite his handicap I doubt if Tim ever cashed a dud cheque.

Most outback towns have their hard cases; Boulia seemed to be over-endowed with larger-than-life characters. Many were old bushmen who drank and played crib in Tim's bar. At other times they sat and yarned in Walter ('Pop') Lloyd's saddler's shop—their presence gave the town an aura of stability and continuity.

Jimmy Cardno was one great character, a kangaroo shooter, who'd had little or no schooling, but was a straight shooter in more ways than one and a master at his trade. It was said that Jimmy could shoot and skin a 'roo in under one minute. There are always doubters, of course, and money was put up to prove the feat was impossible. Jimmy quietly agreed to meet the challenge. A referee was appointed and given a stopwatch to time the attempt. Kangaroo shooters shoot at night, when the 'roos are out feeding in the open. On the night chosen the party left Boulia in Jimmy's old truck that had a spotlight attached. They cruised around until the spotlight picked up a 'roo about 30 metres away and Jimmy signalled the driver to stop. Jimmy took careful aim and fired as the stopwatch started running. He then vaulted out of the vehicle and raced to the fallen 'roo, pulling out his skinning knife as he ran. The blade glinted in the spotlight like quicksilver as the 'roo shooter cut around the neck, down the belly and tail, then up and around each leg. It was done in seconds. Then Jimmy stood up placed his boot on the 'roo's head and pulled the skin off like peeling a banana. He held the skin up as the time-keeper stopped the watch on 58 seconds. Jimmy walked over to the group and held up the hide. 'There y'are', he said. 'There's yer 'roo, kilt an skint as clean as a whistle.'

While Ross, Bruce and I were relaxing in Boulia, having a few beers each day and looking forward to the dance on the coming Saturday night, the idea of work was the last thing on my mind. On the third morning Tim Howard told me that Pop Lloyd wanted to see me. I had no idea why, but strolled to the saddler's shop, situated on a side street past Donahue's store.

I walked in to find a solidly built man of about 60 working on a saddle. He turned as I entered and glanced at me over the top of his glasses. There are times when people meet and an instant rapport is established, I liked Pop instantly. We talked for a while, then he offered me a job off-siding for him. After a moment's thought, I agreed.

'You can sleep in there', Pop said, nodding towards a half-partitioned room full of broken packs, busted saddles, partly used sides of leather and other junk. 'I'll pay you station wages and you can eat with the family. The house is just over the street. You'll have to clean the room up, of course. You can throw your swag on the veranda for a night or two if you like.'

I went back to the pub and told my mates I had a job and would see them later. I then rolled my swag and returned to do battle with the junk room. It took me two days to clean the place out. During the process I found saddler's tools that Pop hadn't seen for years. His delight at seeing them again was rather amusing.

Pop was quite a character. He was the shire chairman, a great wit, and was totally devoid of pretence. Pop had been a stockman in his youth and later a drover on the Birdsville and Strzelecki tracks. He often spoke of how his first wife, a part-Aboriginal girl, had saved their young family from perishing when a waterhole was found to be dry. She drove the wagonette all night to a rock hole she knew and averted what could easily have been a tragedy. Sadly, his eldest son, Walter, was later killed while serving with the Australian army in New Guinea. After the death of his first wife, Pop married again, and when I worked for him his second family was quite young.

My first job in the shop was to put new padding and lining on pack saddles. The packs belonged to 'Crying Jimmy', a well-known drover in the district. The base of the padding on packs used to be made up of the oaten-straw envelopes or open-ended cylinders that were once slipped over bottles to prevent the bottles breaking in transit. Held together with light thread, the cylinders kept their resilience and were ideal for the job. During the great drought in Boulia, a Chinese market gardener caused a minor mystery in the town when his old horse remained in prime condition. The wily gardener was later found to be feeding the horse on the oaten cylinders, after removing the ties.

Pop and I yarned a lot while we were working, and one day I told him about finding the remains of the old camp. Pop stopped stitching, and turning, looked over his glasses at me. He told me that years before an old Aboriginal had told him that the blacks had killed a camp of white men somewhere on the Georgina River. It was food for thought and I regretted again that the others and I had not been able to investigate the site thoroughly.

Soon after I started in the saddle shop, Bruce Hanson got a job with Fred Deim, a tank sinker, while Ross went out to Marion Downs. I saw more of Bruce, as he came into Boulia at the weekends. We drank a little and danced a lot; every Saturday night saw us at the hall. The girls were friendly, the floor was fast and the music of waltzes, barn dances and gypsy taps transported us to a world far removed from the dust and sweat of the cattle camps.

My association with Eric Beaumont, the common ranger at Boulia, was responsible for getting me back in the saddle. A common ranger's job is to control and look after stock, including drovers' horses grazing on the town common. The date of Boulia's annual race meeting was fast approaching and Eric asked me to ride the two horses he had entered. One of them was a gelding he called Bullarooka, and the other a filly whose name escapes me. I galloped them both every morning at the track. I thought entering the gelding in a race was a waste of time, but I believed the filly stood a good chance in the maiden. I also rode Jimmy Cardno's gallopers until his jockey arrived from Townsville. Jimmy took the race game very seriously. At the track I met an old mate of mine from my Territory days, Barney Smyth, who was training an imported horse called Summer Bachelor for the local sergeant.

A week before the races Eric had a blue with the race committee and scratched his horses. On race day I stood at the fence and watched Barney win the Boulia Cup on Summer Bachelor. It was a bit of a disappointment to me not to have ridden at the meeting, but knowing Eric, it was not entirely unexpected.

The knowledge I gained while working with Pop Lloyd was to stand me in good stead later when I became a drover. I stayed with Pop until the end of the year.

Boulia today is a progressive town with an eye to developing the tourist trade. Cliff Donahue, an ex-shire chairman and the third Donahue to run the family business in Boulia, has plans to erect a replica of the min min light in the town's main street. An early prototype failed, but Cliff is determined to get the min min light up and running. Boulia has other unique attractions. Opposite the school, the Boulia Council has preserved a belar tree that was of great significance to the local Pitta Pitta tribe. Called the Corroboree Tree, it has tragically outlived the tribe. Near the town there is a stand of another unique tree. The waddy tree, *Acacia peuce*, is one of the rarest and most remarkable trees in the world. It is estimated to live for over 1,000 years, and its timber is the hardest in Australia, possibly in the world. There are so few waddy trees in existence that it would be possible to actually count their number. There are only three stands known; the one near Boulia;

Known as the 'Corroboree Tree', this belar tree at Boulia had great
significance for the local Pitta Pitta tribe.

one north of Birdsville, and another north of Andado in the Northern Territory. Truly a fabulous tree.

Boulia looks much the same as it did when I first saw it in 1947. The Saturday night dances have gone, alas; television and videos have changed the social life in places as remote as Boulia. However, the ethos of the community remains unchanged.

THE GEORGINA

Tuesday 7 May dawned fine and clear. The whole camp was up before sunrise with everyone keen to start the search. After breakfast we waited impatiently for the shops to open. We made a last-minute purchase of perishables then we were on our way to Glenormiston.

The road is almost all dirt, but in good order. The expeditionary vehicles formed a convoy with Ian Tinney's diesel Land Cruiser (where I sat) leading, Greg Simpson's Land-Rover and trailer at the end. Both front and rear vehicles were equipped with two-way radios enabling us to quickly deal with any problems that arose en route. Greg and Ian kept in touch from time to time and often indulged in good humoured chiacking, most of these exchanges touching on the relative performance of their vehicles. It was a habit that was continued throughout the search and was often to lend some light relief when things were going badly.

Ian had told me he was bringing a GPS (global positioning system) with him. I had no idea what a GPS looked like, and knew only that the device could establish where you were. Ian and I got on very well, but I hesitated to show my ignorance and ask him about it. The world of technology is completely alien to me. In 1995 I was dragged kicking and screaming into the twentieth century by the purchase of a second-hand word processor. The strife caused by galloping bullocks and buckjumping horses was nothing compared with the misery visited on me by that cursed machine. I finally mastered the word processor to the point where it would grudgingly perform the limited tasks I set it. Despite this I always felt that it was merely biding its time before gleefully mutilating beyond recognition every word I had painstakingly entrusted to it.

Curiosity finally got the better of me, and I asked him about the GPS. Ian looked at me and nodded towards the dashboard. I looked, but could see nothing that resembled the mental image I had of the equipment. Seeing my bewilderment, Ian laughed and pointed to the corner of the windscreen, 'That's it there'.

I shook my head in disbelief. The GPS was smaller than a mobile phone. Ian assured me that the device would do any job we asked of it. To prove his point he fiddled with it for a second or two, then read out our position from the tiny screen. I could not help thinking how different it had been for the early explorers, who depended on sextants and the accuracy of chronometers to establish their position. Despite the fact that early government surveyors did not always achieve complete accuracy, there have been writers who have criticised explorers for minor mistakes in calculating their position.

We made excellent time along the Glenormiston road, now called the Donahue Highway in honour of the highly respected Boulia family. The first time I had travelled over this road was with Sid Jones, who ran the Boulia–Glenormiston mail in those days in an ancient Overland utility that left a lot to be desired regarding comfort. The road then was little more than a bush track. It was often said then that a bullock urinating on the Glenormiston road was enough to close it.

The mail road from Selwyn to Boulia was little better. It wound its way down the Mort River, then down the Burke River to Boulia. The Norris brothers ran the Selwyn-to-Boulia mail back then. I remember that it was with a great sense of relief that I climbed from the goods train at Selwyn and found Lou Norris loading supplies onto his mail truck. There were a number of stations en route and plenty of gates; no doubt Lou was happy to have a gate opener with him. The first station we came to was Chatsworth, a cattle property running Shorthorns, an English breed of beef cattle, where I met Mick O'Neal the manager, a well-known cattle man. Seven years later I was to take a mob off Chatsworth and spend one of my worst nights on the road as a result.

I had delivered a mob of Territory bullocks to Brighton Downs. On the way back with the plant I was in Boulia when Mick O'Neal contacted me. He needed a drover to take a mixed mob of 1,000 head to Butru; the money was good so I accepted the job. With me were Kevin Ryan and Ron Condren. I picked up a young lad in Boulia, then headed up the Burke River to Chatsworth with a team of three men and myself. I was still two men short of a full camp, but I knew it would only be a short trip and there was always the chance of obtaining a man from Chatsworth. Butru is on the Wills River, some 80 kilometres northwest of Chatsworth homestead, as the crow flies. Situated on the railway line to Dajarra, it boasts no more than a droving reserve and a trucking yard. There is no stock route to Butru from Chatsworth; we would head across through the bush.

We arrived at Chatsworth two days before the mob was ready to be delivered to me. I made use of the time to check the gear and to ensure no horses needed re-shoeing. I also bought seven young horses from Noel Primas, the head stockman. They were O'Hara Gap brumbies, but nevertheless were good types. Four of them had not long been broken in. The stock camp was mustering the mob I was to take on the western side of the run. I would take delivery there, thus shortening the trip to just two rather long days. We would truck the mob on the third day at Butru.

Mick O'Neal lent me an Aboriginal stockman to help guide us through the trackless bush. I took delivery of the mob, gave them an early drink and headed for Butru. There were now three men and myself with the cattle, and Ron would bring the horse plant along. Before leaving, I urged Ron not to be too far behind us with the plant. I was riding one of the newly broken-in horses, a filly I called Charm. I intended changing to a seasoned mount when Ron caught up. I had another reason for wanting the plant horses at hand—the cattle I had were fresh, had never been watched at night before and were still close to home. I knew we would have our hands full when darkness fell. We would need fresh horses and two men on watch all night. The four of us had a bit of tucker in the saddle bags and full water bags slung around our horses' necks. There would be no water until we got to Butru.

At noon I pulled the mob up at a dry dinner camp. We had covered about six kilometres so far and everything was going to plan. Filling our quarts up from our water bags we boiled up and snatched a bite to eat between turning straying cattle back onto the camp. I had expected Ron to catch up with the horse plant before we left the dinner camp, but at two o'clock there was still no sign of him. A little annoyed at his tardiness I started the mob walking again. By half past three my annoyance had become concern, something was wrong. Pulling the mob up I asked the Chatsworth stockman to go back and see what the problem was. I impressed on him the need to have all hands and fresh horses to hold the cattle that night.

Telling Kevin and the other lad that everything would be right, I started the mob moving again. Every step the cattle took put their feeding grounds further behind them and sapped their energy a little more. At sundown there was still no sign of the horses. I decided to put the mob on camp and try to settle them down before dark. The prospect of watching cattle not broken in to droving with only two men besides myself was a daunting one, particularly as our horses were far from fresh. I advised the lads to use their remaining water sparingly, as there was no guarantee now that the plant would turn up before morning. We were in timber country so I got the lad from Boulia to gather wood to fuel a circle of fires around the cattle. I knew we would need luck and all the skill we could muster if we were to hold them. As darkness descended, Kevin and I took up positions where trouble was most likely to occur. I sent the other lad to the front of the mob. Charm was tired but still showed plenty of spirit, the other two were better mounted, having ridden seasoned horses used to long days. The night became a constant struggle between us and cattle determined to return to their home run. As soon as we had turned one lead back into the mob, another lot was off. The little respite we got was spent stoking the fires, they proved to be of some help. My main concern was the fitness of the horses. If they threw in the towel, then the game was up. I nursed Charm as much as was possible, but towards morning, when galloping after a flying lead, she put me up a tree. I didn't blame the mare: she was leg weary and not used to night work. I escaped with no more that a gashed forehead and together the mare and I wheeled the cattle back into the mob. I was never more glad to see the blush of daylight in the eastern sky. The night was over. We had held the mob but our troubles were far from over. We hastily boiled our quarts in the dying fires and snatched a quick drink of tea. I knew the easiest way to control the cattle now was to keep them moving. I had no idea what had happened to the horse plant and could do nothing about it. My immediate problems were the the bawling, recalcitrant mob and a trucking date in Butru. I sponged Charm's nostrils with a damp handkerchief and emptied the rest of my water into the crown of my hat to give her a few mouthfuls of life-giving fluid.

Both Kevin and the other lad were also out of water. I started the mob off and silently prayed for the sound of jingling hobbles that would herald the approach of the horse plant. We made slow progress, for our horses were close to exhaustion. At ten o'clock Kevin rode around to me and told me that the lad from Boulia was about to ride away in search of water. I rode over to the young fellow and found him in a state of abject panic. I tried to reason with him—unsuccessfully. The cattle were beginning to stop and look back. Drastic situations call for drastic actions. I grabbed his reins and told him to get off his horse and look for water on foot. If he wanted to perish that was his choice, but I wasn't going to lose a good horse and saddle as well. That seemed to shock him into some semblance of rational thought. I directed him to go back to the tail of the mob and wait for the horses.

With our horses on their last legs the horse plant finally caught up. Ron had left it too late to start and had lost our tracks. It had taken the Chatsworth man nearly all night to find him and the horses. I was too relieved to say much. We caught fresh mounts and sent the plant ahead to Butru. We finally trucked the Chatsworth cattle and I was never more relieved to see the last of a mob.

Our expedition, led by Ian's vehicle, had travelled through sheep places for quite a while after leaving Boulia, but now we were in cattle country. About two-thirds of the way to Glenormiston we passed the Herbert Downs turn-off. Herbert Downs was taken up by a man named Kirwin in 1876 on behalf of a New South Wales grazier. Like all pioneers, Kirwin was a courageous and enterprising man who saw the potential of the district. He was not, however, a young man and his acquisition of the run was to have tragic consequences. Soon after taking possession Kirwin sent a man with a horse team and dray to Burketown for supplies. Burketown was over 800 kilometres away without a crossing or causeway built over the many creeks and rivers en route. It is not surprising that Kirwin died of privation before the man returned, the trip having taken over 12 months. It is doubtful if the arrival of the dray would have helped Kirwin even if he had survived the long wait—the driver had consumed almost all the rations on the return trip.

Kirwin, or Kirwan as he is sometimes referred to, had, before he died, taken up leases on three blocks west of Herbert Downs. These blocks later became known as Glenormiston. On Kirwin's death these three leases were acquired by Walter Douglas, who appointed Henry Skuthorpe, 'Jack Dick's' brother, to look after his interests. In 1884 James Tyson bought Glenormiston. After the death of Tyson, the Glenormiston leases passed into the hands of Collins White. Collins White and Company retained ownership of Glenormiston until 1968. The property was then sold to the North Australian Pastoral Company, a major shareholder in Collins White. The two pastoral companies had, in fact, enjoyed a long and involved business relationship. This relationship had been strengthened by marriage and cross-share holdings resulting in dual directorships of the respective boards.

Early settlement of the Georgina suffered many major setbacks. Runs on the top end of the river were pioneered and later abandoned by pastoralists from north Queensland. Initially pioneers from the south fared little better. John Costello, a pioneer of the Cooper, came to grief on the Georgina. A company formed by Charles Rome, Sydney Donner and Oscar De Satge took up a large parcel of land above Glenormiston. The company, called the Carandotta Pastoral Company, planned to run sheep. De Satge was no new chum. On the morning of 18 October 1861, he and a man named Sandeman were camped two days out from Peak Downs. Their horse tailer, an Aborigine, came back to the camp in a panic, reporting seeing a large group of tribesmen streaming past loaded with loot. Later De Satge learned that the Aborigines seen by his horse tailer had come from Cullin-la-Ringa. Nineteen people including children had been massacred there the day before. De Satge's venture on the Georgina was to fail, but the name is still well known through the descendants of the pioneer and his Aboriginal partner. Because of De Satge's noble-sounding name, she became known as 'the Duchess'. It is said that the Duchess copper mine and Duchess township were named after her.

We had agreed to pull up at the Georgina for a midday meal before going in to pay our respects to Glenormiston manager Mal Debney. As we approached the river, we saw great dust clouds ahead indicating that the Department of Main Roads' gang was hard at work near the crossing. The bull dust thrown up by passing trucks became a real hazard as we got closer to the work site, forcing Ian to quickly switch to their radio channel to advise them of our approaching vehicles. At the main channel of the Georgina we turned left and drove to Midginger waterhole. The track was in quite good, as Main Roads' water trucks had been filling up there. One by one the other four dust covered vehicles joined us. Jeff alighted and slapped his hat on his thigh, causing a small cloud of dust to arise. 'Dust and flies! Flies and dust!', he remarked, with wry humour. 'I'm beginning to remember why I left the bloody outback!'

I grinned at him. 'You'll be right mate, a few days of this and you won't want to go back to where the monkeys sing soprano.'

'I don't know about that, some of the coldest nights I've experienced have been out here, and anyway you don't have to ride around fruit trees in the freezing cold singing to the bastards', Jeff retorted, taking off his coat and giving Greg a hand to unload.

Keeping the cook happy is always top priority. Ross picked up a bucket and went down the bank for water while the rest of us gathered wood and got a fire going. He came back, saying to Joshua, 'You won't get water as pure as this out of any tap young feller'.

Ross was right. It was no exaggeration. I was delighted to find the river water the same as it had been nearly 50 years before—just a slight milky tinge to it. Water in the Georgina has always seemed clearer than that of other inland rivers. The reason must be because there are fewer close settlements to it than other rivers. The Georgina River runs through large cattle properties for its whole length. The river's upper tributaries, the Buckley, the Ranken, the James and Lorne Creek, all have their sources in lightly stocked rough country. Lower down, the Templeton River and Moonah Creek carry a lot of sand from the ranges between Duchess and Mount Isa. There are certainly creeks running into the Georgina from the east in the Boulia area that flow through sheep holdings, but I doubt if the influence they have on the river is significant.

Telling the group this, I added that closer settlement and the introduction of hard-hoofed animals had just about ruined the environment of much of Australia.

My brother threw a cigarette butt into the fire and said, 'It's very easy to be a conservationist if you don't have to depend on the land for a living, and if I had a dollar for every bullock you've watered at a hole I dare say I wouldn't have to depend on it either!'.

I had to admit he had a point.

'Perhaps', said Lloyd, 'we should have farmed native animals from the start'.

'Perhaps we should have', Alex said. 'But I doubt if it would have been successful. There were plenty of settlers who ate bush tucker, but setting up wider markets then for 'roo meat would have been the problem.'

'That wouldn't have been the only problem', Jeff said, clearing his throat. 'Droving the bloody things would have been murder.'

During lunch I had a chance to have a discussion with Ross about the best way to conduct the search. Ross and I both had a vivid recollection of the relic site, but neither of us could remember where we were camped at the time. Ross could recall more than me of events just prior to the finding of the relics. According to him we had just ridden up a 'jump-up', or steep rise. He was also sure we had a mob of bullocks in hand almost ready to hand over to a drover. As the rail head was north of Glenormiston at Dajarra, it was logical to assume the stock camp would be mustering on the northern part of the run. We ended the talk with the decision that we would commence the search up near the Roxborough Downs boundary.

I mentioned to the group we should keep it in mind that we were on the property as guests of the North Australian Pastoral Company. Our activities should not give the manager cause for concern. It was probably unnecessary for me to do so, as every one of us was bush-wise, nevertheless, I felt it had to be said.

'I think we should ask Mal Debney about the "L" tree, don't you?' Ross said.

I nodded. 'Yes, he should know if it is still standing or not.' At this time we did not know the tree had been burnt down.

'I've heard there was a Durack tree somewhere on the place too', Ross said.

A very early photograph of road cattle watering along the old river route down the Georgina.

I nodded, 'Yes, I've heard that'. The Georgina was one of the most important routes to the north during early settlement. Later the river became one of the busiest stock routes in Queensland. Each year thousands of cattle were walked down the Georgina to the fattening properties in the channel country. In the droving season of 1950 alone, 120,000 head walked down the river past Urandangi. Over the years literally millions of cattle travelled the old river route. I have always been a little proud that, for a while, I played a small part in those stirring days.

During the time of early settlement the river road had its tragedies. In *Tales of the Overland*, an old manuscript by Barney Lamond published in 1986, the author tells of two tragedies that occurred on the Georgina. In the 1880s a bullock wagon pulled up at dinner camp on the river between its junction with the Burke and its junction with Pituri Creek. The wagon was loaded with explosives for Cloncurry, then a fast-developing mining town. No one knows what went wrong, but the load exploded killing three men and the bullock team. Barney stated that the resulting crater could be seen for many years. A little further up the Georgina the same author wrote of finding a dead man propped up against the wheel of a dray he had been driving. The man had scratched a message on a blackened billy that said he had been bitten by a snake. The unfortunate victim had unharnessed his horses and sat against the wheel to await a lonely and inevitable end. Just one of the many men who died lonely deaths in the outback.

After we finished lunch, we set off to pay a visit to the homestead. We would then head north and select a suitable camp. The station complex had changed quite a bit over the years. The homestead was now surrounded by a fine garden. In my day the manager, who was a bachelor, did not place a very high priority on lawns and shrubs. Mal and Liz Debney greeted us cordially. Both were interested in our quest and offered to help us in whatever way they could. The Debneys are a relatively young couple. We were later to meet their daughter, Megan, at a branding yard west of the Georgina. Mal Debney is a typical cattle man and the epitome of the modern station manager—a lot of his time these days is spent on a motorbike or flying the station aeroplane. Liz does the station books and generally looks after the homestead complex when Mal is out on the run. After an interesting three-quarters of an hour, we left with their best wishes for success, some corned beef, rib bones and a station map showing the new roads that motorisation had made necessary. To our disappointment Mal told us about the 'L'-marked tree being burnt. We thanked them both for their hospitality, waved our farewells and headed up the river to start the search. The serious business of locating the relics was about to begin.

THE FIRST CAMP

We drove north from the river taking a short cut out to a seldom-used track that was heading in the right direction. Lloyd's twin cab heavily loaded with the all-terrain trike found the going difficult at first, but as the track improved driving became easier. Three wheel, all-terrain trikes are normally farm or pleasure machines. Despite early tyre trouble the trike proved to be a valuable addition to the search vehicles. A number of times on the way I saw places that had a strong resemblance to the site we were looking for. I made a mental note to return later and search the areas thoroughly. After travelling for about an hour, Ian and I drove into an outer channel of the Georgina near Rabbit Hole. I jumped out and saw that there was a fair supply of water in the channel. The spot looked like a good camp site with a huge coolabah tree for shade. As the other vehicles arrived, I told Greg we would at least be staying for the night.

There was a plentiful supply of dead gidgee close to the camp site, and by the time the camp was set up I was convinced the place would be an ideal base for our operations in the top end of Glenormiston. Ross agreed with me and the party was advised of our decision. As we sat around the fire, we outlined our plans for the next day's search. Because Ross and I could not remember just where we were camped at the time we found the relics, a careful search would have to be carried out in any area that looked promising. Greg had indicated that despite his cooking duties he would be available to give a hand each morning. As a result, it would be possible to split the party in two, each group with a radio set, and each group including either Ross or me.

'Just what do you expect will be still visible on top of the ground?' Jeff asked.

'Well the steel work from the saddle and pack trees should be much as we found them. They should not have deteriorated to any great extent—it was in light gidgee country.'

'You don't think they could be buried by now?'

Ross replied that the ground was fairly stable, and that the things had been there a hell of a long time and there were still metal buttons on the surface.

'If you do find anything that fits the picture', I added, 'don't disturb the site. Get back to us as soon as possible and we'll use the metal detectors to determine the extent of the site then grid and photograph it.'

The weather had become unseasonally hot since leaving Boulia. The bush flies were a real menace and it was essential to maintain hygiene about the camp. Greg had set up a flyproof plastic bag for all food scraps, which would later be buried. Toilet arrangements were simple but effective. A shovel and paper were placed in a tree at the camp, each party member was asked to go a reasonable distance from the camp, to then dig a hole and when finished to make sure everything was completely covered.

Lloyd, with some help, unloaded from his twin cab the all-terrain three-wheeler bike he had brought. It became the centre of attention for a while as members of the party inspected it and discussed its role in the search. Some time later, Lloyd and Ross said they were going for a look around on the three-wheeler. It was then about five o'clock, and I advised them not to go too far, as Greg would have rib bones cooked on the coals for the evening meal. I watched them go out onto the track then head south.

A little later Alex asked me to do an in-depth interview on how the relics were found in 1948. He then got me to discuss my theories regarding Leichhardt's last route on his last expedition. By the time we had finished the sun was down, and an enticing aroma coming from the fire indicated that the cook was grilling the rib bones on the gidgee coals. Rib bones on the coals are great tucker and highly regarded by bushmen. I was surprised but not worried that Lloyd and Ross would risk being late for the feast, but as yet there was no sign of their return.

We ate our meal of rib bones and vegetables, the enjoyment tempered by the absence of Lloyd and Ross. It was now dark and I was cursing inwardly; looking for missing party members on the first night was not part of my plans. By this time Michael, Ross's friend, was rather upset by our inaction. I had explained to him that they were experienced bushmen who had been in the area before and knew where the camp was. If we had to search, I had no idea where they may have gone other than seeing them head off south.

After talking it over and hoping they had only got a flat tyre, we gave them a few more minutes, then Ian and I drove out to where I had seen them turn south onto the track we had travelled up from the station homestead. Every few hundred metres Ian stopped and blew the horn while I got as high as I could on the vehicle and flashed a torch. We continued for some seven kilometres in this fashion without success. I could find no trace of the trike's tyre marks so we decided to return to where I last saw the pair. Although we would have been over the road twice I believed I still had a chance of picking up the tracks of the trike.

Ian checked in with Greg as we drove back. The pair was still missing. Ian stopped the Toyota, turned around when I gave him the nod, and shone the vehicle lights on the rough track. I alighted and managed to pick up the trike's tyre marks, then with Ian driving just behind me I began the tortuous task of tracking. We continued in this vein for about one and a half kilometres, then I realised I had lost the tracks of the trike. We went back a hundred metres or so and after a few minutes searching I found where the pair had turned off the track at right angles to follow an old cattle pad, the deeply trodden cattle tracks usually leading to water. There was little moon and in the shadows cast by the vehicle on the pad the tracking became even harder. After about half a kilometre, the trike's tracks left the pad and headed north up along a stony ridge. The ground there was littered with Turkey Bush stakes, the sharp broken stems of the bush, and tracking would have been almost impossible in that light. To continue along the ridge would risk staking a tyre. So Ian and I agreed nothing further could be done until the moon came up. It was now nine-thirty. Ian called the camp over the radio and advised Greg we were returning for a council of war.

Back at the camp I explained that tracking was too slow just at that time. It would have taken Lloyd and Ross only fifteen minutes to get to where we left the tracks. It was possible they had driven kilometres past there before running into trouble. Jeff was of the opinion that they may have turned back south and gone into the river channels where they could have possibly overturned or bogged the trike. He and Greg were keen to cross the channel we were on and drive down between channels to try to find the missing pair. I agreed it was worth a go and they set off in the Land-Rover. Ian and I got ourselves a drink of coffee, lit smokes and waited.

Half an hour later they radioed in to say they had seen nothing of Lloyd and Ross and were heading slowly back to camp. At ten-fifteen the Land-Rover was almost back in camp when we saw a faint light in the north. Greg waved to us to indicate he had seen it and drove off to investigate. They found Lloyd and Ross pushing the trike that had indeed had a puncture. All returned to camp in due course. The pair had gone further than they had initially intended and were apologetic about the trouble they had caused. All's well that ends well I told them, and the party finally settled in their swags on the right side of eleven o'clock. I settled down and gazed upwards at the star-spangled sky; the outback heavens at night have never ceased to be a source of wonder to me. The brilliance of the western stars have to be seen to be believed. Compared with them, the tawdry glitter of big city lights fades into insignificance.

To have unrolled my swag beside a waterhole where once I had watered road mobs stirred half-forgotten memories. Droving back then was a tough life, but one usually tends to think only of the good times. Lying there it all came back to me—the wild rushes, the cold wet nights, the dry stages and the hassles with station managers en route. Some of them were understanding and would give a drover a fair go, but there were others who hounded a drover for doing exactly what they expected their own drovers to do. I remembered one instance when I had just put my bullocks on dinner camp through a boundary gate, the manager roared up in a motor car and accused me of picking up station cattle. I looked at him incredulously and told him I wasn't stupid, as fresh cattle would stand out like country toilets in the dusty, road-weary mob I had. He persisted, however, then demanded I give him a horse to better inspect the mob. Not content with calling me a liar and a thief, he now wanted me to help him to prove his wild allegations. I decided I'd had enough of the officious bastard and told him to go back to his bloody station and get his own bloody horse. After a few more heated words, he disappeared in a cloud of dust and did not bother me again.

One of the most unusual altercations I had with a station manager was after I delivered a mob of Territory bullocks to a channel country station. The manager was a rather erratic character who was known as the 'Black Ant'. He and I had agreed on the count, and I had left the mob where he requested after drafting out some of the weaker bullocks. Next day I settled the mob down then rode up to the homestead to pick up the cheque for the trip. I walked into the station office to find the Black Ant seated behind his desk with a revolver in front of him. Ignoring the hand gun, I gave him the mileage I had travelled and produced my droving contract that stipulated the contract price. 'Hang on', said the Black Ant, 'your mileage is out. I'm paying you for 80 miles [130 kilometres] less.' As he spoke, he glanced at the revolver. It had been a long and difficult trip. I was not going to be cheated out of what was rightly mine. Pushing back my chair I got up, as I reached the door I turned and gave him a hard look.

'I've got a thirty-eight Smith and Wesson in my saddle bag. If we're going to have an argument, I'd prefer it to be on even terms.'

The Black Ant's hand shot out, but it was for the cheque book not the revolver. Happy to be paid in full, I rode back to the camp.

There had been good times too, of course—the balmy autumn days and nights when the bush seemed to be a place of magic—the wild times in the drovers' towns after a successful trip. If I had my time over I would not change one day of it. I stretched out in my swag feeling at peace with the world. As sleep overcame me, I had the distinct feeling that I was back where I belonged.

Hazards of the Search

Wednesday morning broke warm and fine, although a bank of clouds was looming on the northern horizon. We were up at daylight but beat the flies out of bed by only a few minutes. Greg put on a breakfast of cereal, toast and coffee. The flies made eating the cereal something of a challenge, even those of us who in the past had become inured to their presence cursed the sticky little pests. Firewood would be needed if we were to stay at the camp for some days. Lloyd had space in his vehicle, so I commissioned him to do the job and asked Michael to give him a hand, as I thought it would be easier for his children around the camp when they returned and unloaded it.

The three-wheeler was recovered and the tyre mended. At eight o'clock the two search parties left camp. Ian and I, together with the documentary team, would cover an area out from and to the north of the camp; Greg with Jeff in the Land-Rover, and Ross mounted on the three-wheeler, would search country to the south. After checking through patches of gidgee close to the camp, Ian headed further south, and at nine o'clock, a walking search was started on a likely patch of gidgee. When nothing was found there, we continued searching gidgee clumps out from the channels for the rest of the morning. Just before noon we marked the extent of our search

Repairing the three-wheeler. This vehicle was very useful when it was operational.

with a bag placed out on the track. We then headed back to camp searching as we went. The other team had also been unsuccessful, but spirits were high nevertheless.

Back in camp we found that Jesse, Michael's young son, had an upset stomach, no doubt due to the bush flies. Both he and his sister were now wearing mosquito-net fly veils. Bush flies are a real menace. Smaller and darker than their domestic cousins, they are responsible for what bushmen call the 'Barcoo spews'. They also inflict bung eyes on their victims, particularly children. The little tormentors gave horses hell. When I was following stock work, I saw horses virtually driven mad by bush flies during that period following the wet. Those months were often called 'fly time', with good reason. Flies would cluster around horses' eyes and sooner or later the skin would be broken by the tormented animal rubbing to dislodge the sticky pests. Once that happened the flies would eat away at the wound until it was as big as a saucer. Horses could escape the attentions of the flies when not feeding by pairing off head to tail, each horse using its tail to keep the insects out of its mate's eyes. When the flies were bad, it was simple to keep plant horses on camp when they were needed, a smoke fire would be lit and the horses would stand with their heads almost in the fire to escape the continual harassment. But this was a luxury not afforded to horses running in paddocks. We made fly veils for the horses we rode by suspending strips of leather from the forehead band of our bridles, and treated any sign of fly wounds with a mixture of stock tar and fat.

Stockmen did not escape the vexatious attention of the winged plague. Despite the constant annoyance, I never saw a bushman wear a fly veil. The idea of hanging corks from a hat is a practice, I believe, restricted to fancy dress balls in the south. There is, of course, an exception to every rule and the one in the field of fly veils was a cook on the Georgina who invented and wore the 'Boulia fly veil'. Like most great inventions, the idea was a simple one. He merely cut a hole in the seat of his trousers and claimed it was most effective in keeping the flies out of his eyes!

The Australian bush fly, *Musca vetusyissima*, breeds in soft dung. Ideal conditions for the rapid completion of its life cycle occur after the wet, when green grass is plentiful and cattle dung stays soft for some time. Although smaller than the house fly, the bush fly lays larger eggs, many flies depositing eggs in the same pat of bovine dung. In temperatures of around 32 degrees Celsius, the eggs will hatch in as little as seven hours. The complete life cycle from egg to adult fly, can, in the right conditions, take no more than a week.

In an attempt to control the bush fly, dung beetles were introduced into Australia. The most successful, *Onthophagus gazella*, is having an effect on bush flies in some areas. Its ability to control the pest in the inland is yet to be established. Because of the large cattle numbers introduced into Australia, it is reasonable to assume that the bush fly population today is far greater than in 1848. Leichhardt's party and his livestock should not have suffered quite so badly from the ravages of the bush fly.

There are, however, reports of many early explorers being tormented by bush flies. The wind will carry the sticky little pests many miles, and it is possible that because of their slow progress some explorers contributed to the problem.

After a lunch of cold corned meat and bread, we planned the afternoon's search. Greg would stay in camp and prepare the evening meal, while Lloyd in the twin cab would take his place in the team. Michael unfortunately had to stay in camp due to his son's illness. Both search parties would concentrate on areas beyond those covered in the morning. Numerous likely patches of gidgee were gone over. I walked through any I thought promising without result. We marked the limit of the extended search and arrived back in camp at half-past five, after travelling a total of 20 kilometres. The party working the other side of our camp had also drawn a blank.

The prospect of finding the relics quickly, was becoming unlikely. It looked as if we were in for a long haul. The three-wheeler had again suffered a puncture and had been left out in the search area. However, after the flies had gone to bed, a first-rate meal of steak, potatoes, pumpkin and onion gravy did a lot to lift our spirits. It was the first time in 48 years that Ross, Lloyd and I had had the opportunity to have a good talk together. Soon the talk turned to the past, and the yarns began to flow as we relived our time on Glenormiston.

The next day Michael Percival and his children headed back to Port Macquarie. Despite Jesse's illness, I think the children had enjoyed the trip. We farewelled the family, then all went out and repaired the trike. Resuming the search with three vehicles, plus Lloyd and Joshua on the trike, we all concentrated on an area out from Longreach waterhole, carefully checking gidgee clumps wherever we found them. I was with Greg in the Land-Rover at this time and at ten o'clock we got a call from Ian that his group was on a large and promising patch of gidgee. He thought it would be better if the whole party investigated the area, so we headed over to where he was. For the next hour the party conducted a thorough walking search of this area at times using the metal detectors. Nothing was found, however. It was a disappointing result, as both Ross and I agreed the spot looked familiar.

Greg had brought along the smoko gear and a fruit cake. It was a welcome break before resuming the search. The remainder of the morning was spent searching to the south through more-open country containing sparse areas of gidgee. Again unsuccessful, we returned to camp for lunch. Over the meal it was decided to concentrate the afternoon search in the area up to and around the Roxborough boundary.

The party split up, covering areas north of the camp up to the boundary, but by sundown we were all back in camp after another fruitless search. The only success was reported by Mark, who had photographed a perentie, Australia's largest goanna. The flesh and kidney fat of the perentie was greatly prized by the Aborigines. When ringing on Glenormiston, we had often witnessed the ritualistic cooking of these large goannas.

After a hearty meal (the importance of having a competent cook on this type of expedition cannot be overemphasised!), we sat around the fire and analysed our progress—or rather our lack of it.

Jeff, who had not spoken much, looked at me, 'You and Ross have got to try and remember where you were camped otherwise finding the site could take a hell of a long time'.

I knew that, I assured them—'And don't think I haven't tried to remember'.

'Well the information is hidden away in your subconscious', Jeff persisted. 'Why don't you let me hypnotise you?'

'Like bloody hell!' All Jeff's knowledge, I suspected came from Max Walker's *How to Hypnotise Chooks*!

But Jeff was not finished. 'There are other ways', he announced, and walked over to the wood heap, where he selected a metre-long stick of gidgee. 'This', he said, tapping the stick on the ground in front of me, 'is known to us in the profession as a total memory

187

recall stimulator. Your subconscious has 24 hours, then crack go the knee caps.'

I don't suppose it was all that funny but strangely enough, just prior to lunch next day I did remember another detail about the camp although, sadly, it would only be of any use if we found the site. When Jeff heard, the amateur shrink crowed, 'Ha! You don't need psychiatrists to unlock the subconscious. All you need is a bloody big stick!'.

While we had been yarning around the fire, the cloud cover had increased, rain, it seemed, was not too far away.

Around midnight I awoke to the patter of rain, I pulled the swag cover over me hoping it was only a short shower. But the rain persisted and grew heavier, so rather than risk a wet swag I rolled it up and carried it over to the vehicles. Ian was throwing his bedding into the covered back of his Toyota and quickly followed it into shelter.

Stoking the fire, I noticed that both Jeff and Greg were on the move as well. Greg dragged a large tarpaulin over close to where I was, threw his swag on it as a pillow and invited Jeff and me to do the same. When we were all settled, the balance of the tarp was pulled over the three of us. I lay there listening to the rain falling on the tarp hoping to Christ that it was not going to set in. After a fitful sleep, I awoke at daylight on Friday morning to see Greg putting the billy on. Thankfully the rain had cleared, although the sky was still overcast. After a breakfast of hot porridge, we held another council of war.

During the morning Alex advised me that he, Mark and Joshua, his sound-man son, would be leaving us after lunch. It was a pity to lose them, but I had known from the outset that their time with us was limited. Alex and Joshua had missed no opportunity in recording the activities of the expedition to date. Mark, as their driver, had done yeoman service, as well as joining the search party when required. We were going to miss them for they had been excellent company.

For that morning, we decided to search an area closer to the homestead while Lloyd and a crew got another supply of meat. Just as we started, a Main Roads' utility pulled up. I recognised Barry Sorenson at once; I had known him quite well in Winton some 30 years before. He was interested in what we were doing and I saw no virtue in being evasive. Eventually Barry asked, 'Have you found that old post yet?'.

'What old post?' I asked, interested at once.

'Well, it was shown to me by a manager here years ago. I found it again just the other day. It's very old and must have been put there by a white man. If you're interested I can run you out to it now', Barry volunteered.

Were we interested? The words were hardly out of his mouth when I had the utility door open. Alex, who had not yet left, grabbed his camera and climbed in beside me.

'We shouldn't be too long', I told the others. 'Have an early smoko if you want to.'

After about 20 minutes, Barry turned off the road. He drove for a little way then stopped the ute. We walked a couple of hundred metres and there it was. The post had obviously been placed there with a definite purpose in mind. It stood slightly over one metre in height, a little of the top having rotted away. The post had been placed in the ground with stones built up for about 40 centimetres. Half of the exposed post was rounded bush timber, with the top half squared truly with an adze. On two sides of the post were straight lines of stones going out for about two metres; each line of stones appeared to be in true alignment with the other through the centre of the post. The post was weathered but still solid, apart from the top. No inscription could be seen on the squared portion. I was intrigued but at the same time disappointed, for it was unlikely the post had any connection with the missing explorer.

'What do you think?' asked Barry after my inspection.

'Well, I doubt if it has anything to do with Leichhardt, but there is a mystery here just the same.'

We hoped this weathered post had had some connection with Leichhardt. We discovered its real significance later that day.

Alex shot some film of the post and the area it was in, then we walked back to the vehicle and drove back to where the rest of the party was waiting. Barry dropped us off and returned to the Main Roads' camp near the river. Alex and I described the old post to the others and voiced our doubts about it having any bearing on Leichhardt's disappearance. It seemed we were uncovering mysteries rather than solving them.

As we worked through the country back to the north, I became convinced we were in the right area, however, we returned to the camp for lunch with nothing to show for our morning's efforts. Over lunch I decided to shift the camp further south to avoid wasting time in travelling to and fro. Rain was threatening, so as soon as the meal was over I told the team to start packing up. Before leaving, Alex and Mark promised they would fly back as soon as they got word of any find.

It did not take long to unpack at our new site and after Lloyd had erected his tent, he strolled over to where we were having a drink of tea and announced he was 66 that day. 'I never thought I'd have another birthday on the bank of the Georgina.'

We all wished him a happy birthday, Ian, true to his name, produced some cold tinnies, and Greg dug out a bottle of rum from some hidden niche in his trailer. We drank Lloyd's health and to the success of our quest. That night we settled down to a serious review of our efforts. There were now six of us left in the party; Ian, Ross, Lloyd, Jeff, Greg and myself. No one saw this as a problem, as we had always been the hard core of the expedition. Most importantly, we all got on well together. As far as transport went, we still had the two main search vehicles, Lloyd's twin cab, and the all-terrain trike. Ross had taken over the trike, and on it he had scouted far and wide covering a lot of ground. The trike's only drawback was its lack of a radio. The search had been frustrating to date, and I knew Jeff, for one, thought that progress had been too slow. Unfortunately, without knowing where Ross and I had been camped at the time, we had little option other than to check everything as we went. We all agreed that we should be able to give our full attention to field work in future and sought our swags in good spirits.

Saturday morning broke fine and warm, and we again set off on the search. The method we used was simple but effective. The driver of each vehicle would drop walkers off at one likely spot then go onto the next, searching that until the groundmen caught up. In this fashion the team could cover quite a lot of country. The vehicles gave some relief from the flies, but once on foot they were hard to put up with. When Jeff alighted from the Land-Rover to search a line of gidgee, he set off cursing the pests. But unknowingly my brother was on a collision course with a creature far more dangerous than bush flies: one of the outback's deadliest snakes. When Jeff told us the story at smoko, I had little trouble in identifying the snake as a western brown or gwardar, a close relative of the dugite of Western Australia.

Some time before our search began, the gwardar, aroused by the warm weather, must have edged out of its hole at the base of a fallen gidgee tree. The gwardar, like all reptiles is cold-blooded, so it must have been seeking the heat of the sun to warm the blood pulsing sluggishly through its slender body. This gwardar was a big snake, longer than the 1.5 metres acknowledged by herpetologists to be the maximum length of the species. It must have crawled slowly to the nearby spot where small stones would help concentrate the heat of the sun and where the tall, thin grass would offer some protection.

By the time Jeff was in the vicinity, the gwardar would have regained the lightning-fast reflexes typical of all brown snakes. Like most browns when confronted with a large intruder, it usually strikes high and with incredible speed. The snake would have been alerted to Jeff's presence by the faint ground tremors generated by his footsteps. In one fluid motion the snake adopted the strike pose, neck and upper body forming the 'S' conformation that would propel it forward. Jeff saw the snake just in time and froze. For what must have seemed an eternity to Jeff both he and the gwardar remained immobile, then the snake whipped around and made back to its hole. Jeff snatched up a rock and hurled it after the retreating reptile, cursing as he did so to relieve the tension. Had he hit the snake, he probably would have killed it and I can't say I would have blamed him. It is of course unlawful now in this mainly urban society of ours to kill snakes, but I doubt if any of the high-minded politicians who drafted the legislation have ever had a close encounter with the business end of a dangerous reptile.

Most bushmen have had their close calls with snakes but few are too worried about them. Jeff and I were raised on a property that was lousy with snakes. One of our favourite sports was snake killing, aided by very clever dogs. Being 11 years older than my brother, I was away before Jeff took up the challenge. However, in turn, he and my other brother Alan did their share of ridding the place of venomous reptiles. Our mother was terrified of the snakes that turned up regularly in and around the house, so we regarded the dispatch of the wrigglers as a family duty.

Unbeknown to us, the property was within the habitat of the taipan, Australia's largest venomous snake. Once thought to inhabit the far north only, the great snake was later found as far south as northern New South Wales. The taipan's venom is eight times more potent than that of the Indian cobra, and over 100 times more lethal than that of the American diamond back rattler. The taipan's venom, together with its huge fangs, make it the world's deadliest snake. My brothers and I grew up good mates with Bob and Joe Nash of Pinnacle, west of Mackay. In 1988 Bob took up a contract to clear a paddock for Laurie Neilsen of Dunwold. The spot was approximately four miles (six kilometres) as the crow flies from our old property. Laurie told Bob that he had seen big snakes in the area, an observation that was verified when Bob dozed out a large paper-bark tree. A huge taipan had made its home among the roots of the tree, and as Laurie stepped down into the hole, the great snake struck at his chest from the top of the excavation. Luckily for Laurie the taipan had been injured, its fangs stopped just short of striking him over the heart.

Bob Nash and the enormous—and extremely deadly—taipan.

The taipan was dispatched just as ambulance bearer Nev Schaper of Mackay was passing by. Nev positively identified the snake and officially measured it at 8 feet, 3½ inches, or 2.53 metres. The taipan was then photographed by Charles Preston. It remains one of the largest taipans ever to be officially identified, measured and photographed. The legendary Ram Chandra of Mackay is recognised as one of Australia's greatest authorities on the taipan. He was shown the photo and stated it was the largest taipan he knew of. The fangs of the huge killer were 2.1 centimetres apart and 1.9 centimetres long.

The taipan's reputation as the world's most dangerous snake is well earned. For sheer potency of venom, however, the inland taipan, or fierce snake, takes the belt. The venom of this little-known snake is 50 times more potent than that of the Indian cobra. Fortunately its fangs are less than half the length of its coastal cousin. (Our search area was within the habitat of this recently discovered and deadly reptile!)

The biggest venomous snake I've ever seen was killed at Alexandria Station in the Northern Territory during the summer of 1945—a king brown, or mulga snake, just on 8 feet (2.5 metres) long, its body as thick as a man's forearm. A formidable snake indeed. On one occasion I was camped at a waterhole called Bellyabba with a plant of horses. The mosquitoes were bad, so I rigged my bush net and settled down for the night. Some hours later I awoke with a start to find a large brown snake racing up and down my swag in an attempt to get out of the net. Somehow it had crawled under the net before being disturbed by my movements. Thankfully it tried to escape rather than sink its fangs into me. It took me no more than a split second to show that snake a short cut out of the mosquito net. Most snakes will try to get out of your way as that one did, but not death adders. These stumpy little reptiles will lie half hidden in leaf litter or dust until touched. They then strike like a released spring. Death adders have very efficient biting equipment, and before the introduction of death adder antivenene in 1959, 50 per cent of death adder bites were fatal.

Death adders are usually nocturnal, and there is an erroneous belief that they cannot climb. However, one morning the cook in the Avon Downs, Northern Territory, stock camp found a death adder coiled up in the cutlery box on the camp's trestle table. Jack Daily, an old bushman, was my neighbour in Camooweal, and one night he called me over to show me a death adder lying on a beam in his laundry. A hurricane lamp was swung below and the snake seemed to be interested in the large moths attracted to the light. Death adders are not insectivorous, so what it was doing there is a bit of a mystery. One thing is certain, no one lifted it up there.

When I was working on Morstone, a cattle station between Camooweal and Burketown, another stockman told me a rather amusing story about the victim of a death adder bite. This chap had been a member of a scrub-clearing gang near Chinchilla during the Depression. In those days Chinchilla was lousy with prickly pear— the home of thousands of death adders. On returning to the camp one evening, a member of the gang sat down on his swag and was promptly bitten on the cheek of the bottom by a death adder. Another member of the gang, who had just sharpened a butcher's knife to cut up meat raced over to the victim and told him to drop his tweeds. Then pinching the fang marks between finger and thumb, he pulled hard and slashed down with the knife, removing about half a kilo of prime rump. At the Chinchilla hospital the victim was advised that the adder bite was not a problem, but recovering from the wound in his backside might take some time.

Later that day, while working to the west of the others, Ian and I found a small pile of rocks that appeared to have been human-made. We ran the metal detector over adjacent areas but found nothing except two bottle tops. It was at least a good test of the value of the detector. A little time later, we found a post set in the ground close to a small excavation that had obviously been dug with a horse-drawn scoop. The metal detector picked up an old horseshoe and one stirrup iron nearby. The work had been done many years before, but its purpose eluded us, as the excavation was miles from anywhere. The other party and Ross had nothing to report when we met back in the camp for lunch.

The afternoon's search was also disappointing, so we all agreed we had to find some method of pinpointing the area the stock camp was mustering in when the relics were found in 1948. Ian asked whether the head stockman would have kept a diary. Neither Ross nor I could say, but we all thought it was worth a try to find out. Ian and I would go to the station on Sunday afternoon. If the diaries were still in existence, we would ask Mal Debney if we could look through them for clues. The prospect of obtaining information from the station diaries lifted the spirits of all the party and the talk reflected renewed hope and confidence.

At seven-thirty on Sunday morning, we set off to search an area just north of the Donahue Highway. On the way out we ran into Barry Sorenson again and he generously invited us to use the hot showers at the Main Roads' camp. The gesture was appreciated as cooler weather made the prospect of a dip in the river far less attractive than before. The area we were now searching looked promising and I walked over a lot of it until satisfied it held nothing of importance. At about nine-forty, a light plane flew overhead, and on rejoining Ian he told me the plane was piloted by Mal Debney. Ian had changed the radio to the station channel and talked to the manager, advising him we would visit the station that afternoon.

At smoko Ross produced an old sauce bottle and an empty fruit tin he had picked up.

'They're a bit after Leichhardt's day I'd say', Greg observed.

'I know', said Ross. 'But I once knew a drover who was tight with tucker and he used to pick up things like these and toss them around his own camp so people would think he fed his men well.'

Ian laughed, 'His name wasn't Simpson was it?'

'No', Jeff replied. 'Our esteemed leader ran a tough camp all right, but he didn't give a stuff who knew it. I remember once', he added, cutting himself a large slice of fruit cake, 'he bought a tin of sliced peaches at the Ranken—one bloody tin mind you—you'd have thought he was bloody Santa Claus the way he produced it.'

I grinned at my brother. 'Well I must admit we didn't have bacon and eggs for breakfast, or for that matter fruit cake like the one you're hoeing into at the moment, but I always reckoned you worked better after you'd lost a bit of weight.'

My nephew looked at his father then at me. He shook his head and started packing up the smoko gear.

We had the metal detectors working in a number of places until lunch but turned up nothing more than a .22 bullet. The search continued further southeast and at twelve-thirty we headed back to camp. Ian was keen to see the mysterious post shown to Alex and me by Barry Sorenson, so before going to the station after lunch, we made our way to it. Ian took a reading from the GPS and got compass bearings on the two lines of stones. He was as intrigued as I was as to its origin and ventured the opinion that the accurate compass bearings of the two lines of rock indicated survey work.

Ian took a couple of snaps of the post then we headed for Glenormiston homestead. Both Mal and Liz Debney were keen to know how the search was going and seemed only too happy to assist us with the station diaries. Liz looked through the records and finally turned up the manager's diary for the period in question. With their approval we copied a number of pages we believed would help, then Ian mentioned the post we had seen. Mal had apparently done some research himself, for he told us it was placed there in about 1880 by a government surveyor named Bedford. Bedford was apparently surveying a traverse line through to Tobermorey, a station further northwest, over the Northern Territory border. We both thanked Mal and Liz for their help, then returned to camp. Ian, who has contacts in the Lands Department, declared that he would later investigate the early survey work in the area and find out as much as he could about Bedford, a true pioneer in this field.

CONTINUING THE SEARCH

Ian and I got back to the camp just as a spectacular sunset turned the western sky into a panorama of brilliant colours. We found the others waiting expectantly, keen to know what we had learnt. As Greg had dinner almost ready, we decided to leave closer examination of the data until later. Over dinner we discussed the story of Bedford's survey post. I thought it supported my belief that the steel relics we found would still be in reasonable order. We just had to find the bloody things!

I had harboured a vain hope that the diary may have recorded our finding the relics. It did not, however, for Martin Hayward, the manager at that time must have regarded brevity as a virtue. The entries for most days were limited to four or five lines, and I realised that the diary was not going to be as helpful as I'd hoped. During the two months prior to our departure, the stock camp had mustered over much of the station. Entries ranged from the Roxborough boundary to Bottle and Glass waterhole on Marion Downs and the old Herbert Downs homestead; from Lake Wanditta to the Twenty Mile camp. During the first part of May there were stockmen from Linda Downs, Tobermorey and Roxborough attending the muster. According to the diary, the men left on 21 May taking 370 head back to their respective stations. On 25 May the stock camp handed over 708 fat bullocks to drover Andy Collins to drove to Dajarra. This dove-tailed with Ross's recollections. I thought that it was unlikely we had located the relics during the time the men attending the muster (the attenders) were with the stock camp.

According to the manager's diary, half the stock camp went to Lake Wanditta on 26 May, while the rest of the ringers picked up fresh horses. After shoeing the plant at Wanditta, the stock camp began mustering a mob of cows. Most of the country mustered for this mob was south of the station. The cows were inoculated and on 23 June, drover Collins returned and joined the stock camp. On 26 June, the mob was handed over to Collins at the Twenty Mile.

'I'm afraid it doesn't help all that much', I said. 'It seems we were all over the flaming run. But I doubt if we found the site while attenders were in the camp. If it was during the bullock muster it must have been after they left.' Ross agreed, but Lloyd seemed rather puzzled.

'It must be right about the ringers from Roxborough and those other places', he said, 'but I don't remember them being in the camp'.

'It's a wonder you don't remember that bloke from Linda Downs', I said. 'At times he was more interested in galloping after dingoes than he was in mustering cattle. He was bloody good with a stirrup iron—I forget how many he skittled, but it was a fair number.'

To me the memory was quite vivid, but Lloyd still could not recall the dingo hunter. A stirrup pulled free of its bar on a saddle can be a deadly weapon in the hands of a man who knows how to use it. On the other hand, if swung by a novice, it can inflict injury on both the user and his horse. I once worked for an old drover with the nickname of 'Stirrup Iron'. He no doubt earned the title in the wild days of his youth.

Not long after Rocklands Station (near Camooweal on the Queensland–Northern Territory border) was taken up, the manager there was bludgeoned to death with a stirrup iron. According to the story, an Aboriginal stockman had apparently done something to greatly upset the manager. Both men were mounted at the time, and pulling out a revolver, the manager galloped his horse after the fleeing stockman, firing without result as he rode. The stockman was no fool, for he was able to count the shots, and after the sixth he wheeled his horse around, pulled the stirrup leather from the stirrup bar and brained his pursuer with the iron.

After reading the diary, I thought we probably needed to re-check where we gave delivery of the bullocks later, but for now we needed to concentrate on the southern end of the run for a while, as it seemed to offer the best chance.

Ian shuffled through the diary pages. 'It says here that the camp was split for a lot of that particular muster, and as there was only four of you who found the relics, it seems likely that the camp was split up at the time.'

I knew both time and resources were limited. Our fuel supplies were half exhausted and the days we could afford to spend on the search were numbered. Shifting the camp further south was one option and it would save some fuel. But the present site was an excellent one, with plenty of good water, plenty of shade and the cook had things set up to his liking. And it would mean losing the best part of a day moving and setting up again. After a lengthy discussion, we agreed that the camp should remain where it was. In the swag that night I tried to objectively review our efforts to date. Our inability to find the site as yet was a worry. When organising the expedition without backing or sponsorship, I had gambled on locating the spot quickly. I had to admit to myself that in doing so without knowing where Ross and I had been camped had been overly optimistic. I had retained a vivid recollection of the relic site, but it was the memory of one isolated spot. There were literally hundreds of likely sites that could not be ruled out until properly investigated. We still had the southern half of Glenormiston to cover plus parts of Herbert Downs and Marion Downs. The task ahead of us was a formidable one indeed. I finally went to sleep determined to keep my concerns to myself as much as possible.

Monday morning was cool and clear with a fairly strong southeasterly blowing. Just as we finished breakfast a couple of dingoes started howling down the river from the camp. Lloyd, who had taken over the filming, ran for his camera to record the dingoes on the sound track. Camera in hand, he burst out of his tent and the howling stopped as if on cue. This pantomime was to be repeated every morning until we left the spot. I don't think Lloyd got as much as a whimper on the tape.

By smoko our search was again proving unsuccessful. I had probably walked a total distance of 4 or 5 kilometres, this time south, near the Marion Downs border, searching through areas that at times showed little promise. None of the others had anything to report. The gidgees were scattered and the country very hard. Ross and I both agreed we would be better to continue the search further north, where the country looked more promising. In the new area Ian and I found the remains of what appeared to be a fencer's old

The metal detectors were essential equipment.

Waiting for the billy to boil: Ross Ratcliffe, Lloyd Linson-Smith and Bruce Simpson.

camp. More out of interest than anything else we put the metal detector to work and found some iron scraps and a number of old .303 cartridge cases. Ian, who had taken readings of all points of interest during the search took a bearing on the old camp from the GPS (global positioning system) before continuing. Again the morning proved to be unproductive, so we changed direction to towards Mark Tree waterhole in the Georgina in the afternoon. The country towards Mark Tree was more like my recollections of the relic site. We investigated every possible area, kicking at the ground to see if we could turn up burnt earth in case the relics had become buried. But it turned out to be another disappointing day. The diary pages, as I suspected, had been helpful only in a general way. We discussed the possibility that the gidgee cover may have changed— after all, 48 years is a long time. Perhaps the site no longer looked anything like it did then.

'I don't agree', Jeff said. 'Gidgee grows very slowly. After 25 years, I went back to that opal mine we had on Woodstock. There were gidgees there I remembered around the camp that hadn't grown an inch in that time. No, I'm sure you'll both know the place again when you see it.'

On Tuesday, the next day, we searched along the channels back towards the station. We ran into a number of gullies and small creeks in the area and driving became quite difficult. It did not, however, deter Greg who charged into gullies and channels while radioing advice to Ian who was a little more circumspect. The two vehicles were travelling close together when we came to two steep channels only a few metres apart. Ian pulled up and inspected the spot, then drove up the channels to a place where we crossed without much difficulty. Greg, scornful of such caution, backed up and prepared to charge as we waited on the other side. Jeff was standing right at the back of the Land-Rover, arms stretched wide, each hand gripping a stanchion on the back corner of the tray. The Land-Rover bucked and swayed through the rough going; at times it was almost perpendicular. We watched in amazement as Jeff was tossed backwards and forwards like a monkey on a stick. As Greg pulled up beside us in triumph, Jeff got down stiffly and spoke to his grinning son.

'You're a lunatic! What do you think you're driving, a bloody tank?' He dropped his arms to his sides. 'Look at that. By the time we leave here my knuckles will be dragging on the ground like a bloody chimpanzee!'

'That won't be so bad', Greg grinned. 'At least you'll be able to pick your fruit without a ladder.'

From the gullies and creeks, we split up to go through light ridge country with areas of gidgee further north. But it proved again to be a frustrating end to the morning's search, for although we saw a number of places that aroused our expectations we went back to camp for lunch disappointed. As the vehicles pulled up in camp, Greg made straight for the trailer to get things ready. We were startled to hear him utter a burst of profanity that was quite out of character. 'A bloody great goanna', he roared. 'The bastard has eaten all the bloody eggs.'

On investigation we found it to be true. Every egg Greg had been saving for another slap up breakfast of bacon and eggs was gone. Eggs were not the only things the perentie had devoured: every cake of toilet soap we had left by our towels was gone as well! We cursed the greedy reptile in unison and hoped the marauder might suffer a terminal gut ache as payment. Greg looked about the camp and growled, 'You blokes should track the bastard and we'll bloody well eat it!'.

I grinned at him, 'I'll track a bullock or a horse for you but not a goanna. That's a job for the Aborigines, or rather for their womenfolk'.

What I said was accurate. The Aboriginal women have historically done the tracking of small game, such as lizards. As a result of this demanding pursuit, they have always been regarded as better trackers than the men, who were normally involved in the hunting of larger game. It was the women who also had a greater knowledge of plants, knowing where to look for yams and winkling out the witchety grubs from the roots and trunks of their favourite hosts. In the very early days of pastoral development in the Northern Territory, Aboriginal women were employed in stock camps in preference to the men. They dressed as stockmen and were regarded as being the more reliable of the sexes. Perenties, smaller goannas, shinglebacks, blue tongue lizards and 'carneys' formed an important part of Aboriginal diet. The carneys, so called by the inland tribes, are a ground-dwelling, thick-set lizard of the genus *Tymanocyptis*. They were quite common on the Barkly Tableland when I worked there, and we often rode over them when mustering. It was a common sight to see a carney hanging by the head from an Aborigine's saddle dee. I once saw a top buckjumping exhibition when a carney, thought to be dead, made an unexpected recovery and dug its claws into the flank of a stock horse. The rest of the musterers thought it a great joke.

After we had eaten, I talked to Ross for a while then discussed with the others the idea of spending a day searching in Marion Downs. We had mustered and tailed cattle there while we were putting the mob of cows together and we could not ignore the possibility that the site was through the boundary. I explained that I would have to visit Glenormiston homestead early next morning as our tobacco was almost exhausted and while there I would ring Marion Downs regarding our plans.

The remainder of the afternoon proved to be just as fruitless as the morning. We got back to the camp just before sundown and consoled ourselves with a drink before demolishing the sausages and vegetables Greg had prepared.

Going over the events of the day both Ross and I began to question the accuracy of our memories of the country around the relic site. 'Forget your doubts. You have to trust those memories, after all we've nothing else to rely on. I still think you'll both recognise the spot at once when we find it', said Jeff reassuringly.

Ian changed the subject: 'You must have brought cattle down the Georgina. Was it a good route?'

I nodded. To be one of the first drovers to go down the Georgina after a big wet was a picnic. However, even in a fairly good season, if you happened to be in charge of one of the last mobs to travel the river, grass could be scarce. Those of us who brought in mobs from the far west generally found the Georgina route tough going, for we were usually among the last of the drovers to go down the river. In a very dry year, the Georgina, like most routes, was difficult for any drover. To get good horse feed, horse tailers sometimes had to camp out with the horses some distance from the route. Getting grass for the cattle was always a problem in a bad year. One year I was forced to leave the Georgina and cross over onto the Wills River, which joins the Burke above Boulia, in an effort to keep the mob in reasonable condition.

Lucky Blackman, an old bushman and drover, tells the story of a Kidman drover who was caught in a drought year back around 1900. He was forced to ride away from a mob of cattle too weak to travel. The driest stretch of stock route I ever travelled was up the Mayne River. The grass was so scarce we had to watch the horses as well as the bullocks, but despite being short-handed, we got through all right.

Next morning, Ian and I headed for the homestead, leaving the others to their own devices. At Glenormiston, Liz Debney greeted us cheerfully and asked about our progress. She listened sympathetically to our problems. To our request for tobacco Liz looked doubtful, saying she wasn't sure if there was any in the store. Smokers were apparently pretty thin on the ground at Glenormiston. After diligently rummaging through the shelves, Liz, to our great delight, produced three packets of Drum ready-rubbed tobacco. They must have been there for a very long time for the contents were as dry as chips. We assured Liz that a bit of potato peel would make the tobacco as moist as when packed. We thanked her for the trouble and asked if we could talk to Marion Downs. Liz quickly agreed, indicating the telephone on the table and telling me the number to ring. I got through and gave advice of our plans, mentioning that the expedition had permission from head office to conduct the search.

We paid Liz for the tobacco and for meat we had got earlier, then yarned for a while. I was interested to learn that Liz shared our interest in Australian history. When asked, I was only too happy to sign a copy of *Packhorse Drover* that she and Mal had bought. After tending our thanks for all the help, Ian and I returned to the camp.

While waiting for Greg to heat up the leftover sausages, I went through the diary pages again. I was amused to see the last entry in the pages we had, dated 30 June. It was terse and to the point, reading: 'Simpson, Ratcliffe and Hanson off books from tonight'. The blue I'd had with Martin Hayward related to the Aboriginal stockmen. Hayward was a good manager but I could not agree with his policy of putting the interests of the Aboriginal stockmen before those of the four young Brisbane lads, wanting, for example, to take the indigenous stockmen back to the station for a break, while leaving the rest of the hardworking men back out at the Twenty Mile. I showed the entry to Ross and we had a good chuckle over it. The entry had been scored out—as we had no means of leaving the station, Martin had relented and kept us on the books until the Boulia mail arrived. Had we stayed on Glenormiston we may have solved the mystery long ago and the present expedition would not have been necessary. Despite my shared amusement over the scratched out entry, I was keenly aware that it had been a disappointing end to my association with the North Australian Pastoral Company and the Collins White group. It was an association that had lasted for over three years, during which time I had worked as a stockman on both Alexandria in the Northern Territory and on Glenormiston.

The sausages disposed of, we left camp and by one-thirty we were on Marion Downs. We had split up as usual looking through ridges out from the river. The country did not impress neither Ross nor me, but we continued the search without result until five o'clock, then headed for camp. After talking matters over, we decided to abandon the search there and to concentrate on a couple of other areas mentioned in the diary. Time was now of the essence, as I knew Greg had made business sacrifices to join us. Over the evening meal he advised me that he would have to return on Saturday. It was a blow but not altogether unexpected. The next two days would be crucial in determining the success of the expedition.

After breakfast on Thursday, we loaded the trike on to Lloyd's twin cab and proceeded north to the area where delivery of the bullocks had taken place. We unloaded the three-wheeler at our first camp site, then split up as usual to search carefully through gidgee country. The area had a familiar appearance to me that augured well for success, there were old pads in evidence and the whole scene encapsulated the features Ross and I had remembered. But at the end of an hour I had to admit defeat; it was just one more disappointment. Working back towards our first camp, the feeling of déjà vu I had experienced earlier did not return; another promising area had been thoroughly searched without result and time was running out.

A little excitement erupted during the afternoon's search when I heard a cooee from Ian. I just about broke even time dashing through the gidgee to where I could see his parked Toyota.

'Hang on, don't get excited!', he exclaimed. 'I just thought you would want to see this. I think it's part of a harness from a wagon team.'

He indicated the item he had found, and I saw at once that he was correct in his assessment of the relic. I leaned against a tree and caught my breath. Ian looked at me. 'Leichhardt only had packs didn't he?'

I nodded. 'Yes, this could have belonged to anyone. It's possible it may be early stock camp gear.' Deflation again.

We continued searching every possible site as we moved south, but again it was a fruitless day.

The general feeling now was that our chances of success were greatly diminished. Discussion back at camp turned to the morrow, our last day in the field. We agreed that there were places that warranted another more thorough inspection on foot. Against that proposal was the fact that in the diary there was a mention of at least two areas we had not looked at at all; these places were well within

Examining the map to decide which sector to search next.

the parameters we had set for the search. It was finally agreed that to leave without checking them would be untenable.

During breakfast next morning the dingoes serenaded us as they had been doing most mornings. Lloyd, to his chagrin again missed recording their performance. 'I think the bludgers have a lookout posted', he grumbled as he returned to his bowl of porridge.

'Perhaps they aren't dingoes at all', Ross speculated. 'Perhaps they are the spirits of the old Aborigines who are worried we will uncover evidence of their attack on Leichhardt.'

Ross's flights of fancy had always proved a source of entertainment to us when we were together on Glenormiston. He was blessed with a vivid imagination and became enthusiastic about some of the most outlandish schemes. Tommy Green, an old-timer on Marion Downs, once gave Ross a piece of opal potch (worthless opal). That was enough for Ross. He invited me to go opal gouging with him. There was nothing to it, we would make our fortunes. According to Ross, the fiery gemstones were there for the taking. On another occasion my mate declared he was going to build a boat and sail to South America.

There he would work on cattle ranches, and after making his fortune, would return in his trusty boat. Ross was a great mate and usually included me in his wild plans.

Lloyd interrupted these memories, saying he wanted a final photo of the group. As we posed for the shot, Ross commented: 'Well, I've heard of the Ragged Thirteen and the Dirty Dozen; I reckon we'd qualify as the Horrible Half Dozen'.

We left the camp in good humour at a little after seven o'clock next morning—the final day of the search had begun. We met for smoko empty-handed at a station yard. Greg and Jeff had, however, seen an area that they believed warranted a thorough search. As we still had a fair bit of country to go over, I asked them to handle it on their own. In hindsight it was the wrong decision, for during the day we were to search through far less promising places. After smoko, Ian, Lloyd and I went on to the next area mentioned in the diary. Ross, on the trike covered sites wide of us. When we met for lunch, we had found nothing but for an old wire yard containing what looked to be a rough branding panel. It was somewhat of a mystery, for it was kilometres from anywhere and fairly well screened by gidgees. Greg and Jeff turned up eventually, saying the area they were to search had turned out to be too large. They had given most of it no more than a perfunctory going over. It was regrettable and no fault of theirs. We would not, I decided, go back to the area.

With lunch finished we moved north to cover areas out from the river. Some of the ground we had already looked at but according to the diary there were places that needed checking. We walked on foot through kilometres of country containing creeks and patches of gidgee without result. The last day was proving to be as frustrating as those before.

At about three o'clock, Ian dropped Lloyd and I off at a long patch of gidgee. Lloyd, who had left his twin cab on a station road, planned to search through the eastern side, while I worked the opposite fringe. It took me some time to complete my search of the big gidgee patch. When I got to the far end, I looked around expecting to see Lloyd. As there was no sign of him, I rolled a smoke and sat down to wait. When I had finished the cigarette, I thought I might as well inspect another isolated spot ahead of me. That done I returned to where I should have met Lloyd. There was still no sign of him and I could not hear the sound of any motor at all.

I sat down, rolled another smoke and waited, wondering where the hell everyone was. Finally, I heard the sound of Ian's Toyota and walked across to intercept him. One look at his face and I knew he was not the bearer of good news. Ross had punctured a tyre on the three-wheeler and it had been loaded on to Lloyd's twin cab and taken back to the camp. That was not all the bad news that Ian had to convey. Greg and Jeff had seen a patch that they were sure held the key to the search and in getting to it, they had punctured a tyre on the Land-Rover. I looked at Ian in disbelief. 'Where are they now?'

'They put on the spare and have gone back to the camp to repair the damaged tyre.'

I cursed inwardly. Instead of ending in triumph the search was ending in disarray. Ian got out of the vehicle and had a leak.

'I've got a fair idea where this spot is', he said over his shoulder. 'It's pretty rough getting in to it, but we'll have a go if you want to.'

My watch was on the blink. 'Thanks mate, what's the time?'

'Just after four.'

I thought for a minute. 'No Ian. We'd run out of time even if we managed to get there without trouble. I'm afraid we'll have to call it quits—it's a bugger of a way to finish up but there's nothing more we can do.'

It was a bitterly disappointing end to our search. We had slogged in vain through gidgee, over ridges and across dry creeks. It had been for the most part monotonous and painstaking work, through country as starkly beautiful as it is unforgiving. Many times I had marvelled at the courage and fortitude of Leichhardt, and at the magnitude of the task he had set himself.

The End of the Search
and Beyond

Beginning our final evening in the camp, the mood was morose. Ian got up, scratched his stubbly beard and announced, 'There's some beer left in the fridge. Who'd like a tinny?'

The suggestion received general approval. Suddenly I remembered it was 17 May. I looked over at the cook and asked, 'Hey Greg, is there any rum left?'

'Yes, there's a bit left in the bottle.'

'Well I'm going to hit myself with a rum. Tomorrow is my birthday, so at least we have something to celebrate.'

The mood of the camp changed perceptibly. Lloyd grinned at me. 'To think, after 48 years we've both come back to the Georgina to celebrate our birthdays. I was 66 the other day, but you'd be older than that wouldn't you?'

I nodded. 'I'm 73 and at the moment I feel like it, but after a rum or two I'll be as fit as a mallee bull.'

We had a few drinks before sampling the expedition's last dinner. Greg's reputation as a camp cook remained unblemished with a meal of sausages with four vegetables plus onion gravy, followed by fruit salad and custard. After the plates were cleaned up, we sat around the fire replete. Despite our hopes, the failure of the expedition to find the relics was not entirely unexpected. Over the last few days we had come to accept the fact that we might be unsuccessful. I took the opportunity to review the work of the expedition and to thank everyone for their wholehearted efforts. The talk soon turned to whether we would try again and if so when.

'You're still convinced it's worth it?' Jeff asked.

'Well nothing has changed really, apart from our failure to locate the relics, and with more time I'm certain they will be found. Ross and I both know the bloody things are here and the spade work we've done will be a big help if another attempt is made.'

The matter of another expedition was kicked around for a while. In the end it was the general opinion of the party that we should try again.

As organiser and leader of the expedition, the responsibility for the failure rested squarely on my shoulders. It had been my decision alone to proceed without adequate backing. Responsibility had never troubled me. In one capacity or another I had been making decisions for myself and for others since the early 1950s. Failure, however, was new to me and something I would have to come to terms with. Before going to sleep, my thoughts turned to Ludwig Leichhardt, the man whose fate we had been attempting to discover. Perhaps in 1848 he had camped close to the spot where I had unrolled my swag.

Jeff and Greg wanted to get away early on Saturday. It had been agreed then that after saying goodbye to them, the four of us left would attempt to find the Leichhardt tree. After that, if we had the time, we would also have a last look around Lake Wanditta.

After farewelling Jeff and Greg the next morning, we set off in the two vehicles for the Marion Downs boundary. The 'L'-marked tree was reported to be on the western side of the river. We reached the boundary and the four of us climbed through the fence. After some time, we found two trees that had been marked years before—both only a few metres from the boundary fence. One tree was still

Marked trees on the boundary
between Glenormiston and
Marion Downs. Ross and I
investigate one that has been felled.

The coolibah tree at the Mark
Tree Waterhole was deliberately
scarred.

standing and was probably an early boundary marker. Lloyd took a photo of Ross and me standing beside it. The other tree looked as if it could have been marked earlier, but like the first one I doubted that it was the work of an explorer. The tree was dead and had been on the ground for some time, the scar on the trunk was overgrown in a similar manner to the other one. Before we left, Ian took photos of the scar in the fallen tree.

We ruefully agreed that the tree known as the Leichhardt tree had indeed been destroyed by fire. Climbing back through the boundary fence into Glenormiston we drove to the station. Mal and Liz listened sympathetically as we told them of our lack of success. We said we would keep in touch, thanked them for their help and support, then headed for Lake Wanditta.

The four of us had lunch at the lake, then after a look around we decided it was time to head back. Ian rejected the idea of striking out through the scrub to pick up the Donahue Highway and we returned via a station road. Ross and Lloyd planned to drive into Herbert Downs to have a yarn to Bobby Kirk. Ian and I headed straight for Boulia, arriving there a little after five o'clock.

We found the hotel bar crowded. Saturday afternoon is prime drinking time in all outback towns. Ian ordered our drinks while I managed to find seats facing the street. Donahue's store is opposite the pub. I saw Cliff Donahue over the road and, asking Ian to hold the fort, I went over to see him. I had known the family for many years. Cliff greeted me cordially and we settled down to have a yarn. Cliff was keen to hear the result of our search on Glenormiston and commiserated with me on our lack of success. He then told me an interesting story regarding the Durack tree, reported to be at Pump Hole on Glenormiston. Dame Mary Durack had made arrangements to visit Boulia when Cliff was shire chairman. The plan was for the council to remove the tree and with Dame Mary's permission to preserve it in Boulia. Unfortunately, negotiations with Glenormiston

The Durack Tree (marked by a 'D' and the date) that stood near Pump Hole on Glenormiston Station.

to remove the tree broke down and the tree was left where it was. The next year it was completely destroyed by fire.

We spent a very enjoyable hour or two in the pub, then adjourned to the cafe to put the nose bags on. Ross advised us that when at Herbert Downs, Bob Kirk had confirmed that the Leichhardt tree on the Glenormiston boundary had indeed been destroyed by fire. The news had a sobering effect on the company, two historically important trees had disappeared from adjoining properties within a few short years.

The four of us camped that night at the Boulia caravan park. Next morning we got a daylight start, stopping for breakfast at the ruins of the Hamilton Hotel. After some steady driving, we reached Longreach for a late lunch. As Ian planned to stay there for a few days, I transferred to Lloyd's vehicle. We reached the Ratcliffe home at the Willows shortly after dark. Kathleen, Ross's wife, made us welcome, gave us a good dinner and organised beds for the night.

The Ratcliffes are a very hospitable family. Lloyd and I did manage to get away next morning, but it was by no means an early start. At ten o'clock that night Lloyd dropped me off in Caboolture and went on to Brisbane. The expedition was over.

I knew that a German-based expedition that was shooting a documentary on Leichhardt had been in the field while we were on Glenormiston. I had also heard that historian and Leichhardt researcher Dr Glen McLaren had accompanied them as they retraced part of Leichhardt's route to Port Essington. I managed to obtain Glen McLaren's phone number in Western Australia and had a yarn with him. He had followed Leichhardt's route to Port Essington identifying a large number of the explorer's camp sites and river crossings. His book, *Beyond Leichhardt*, had just been published, so we had a common interest in the lost explorer. Glen gave me the phone number of the leaders of the party he had travelled with, who had by then returned to Germany. I later rang Martina and Hans

Gally, who were then making a documentary of their trip to Australia. They were interested to hear of our search and asked me to keep them advised of any developments. They told me that they had visited Wantata waterhole on Durrie Station, but had found no new evidence of Leichhardt's fate. Both appeared to have an open mind regarding their countryman's final resting place. One interesting thing they did say was that with new DNA matching techniques, it would now be possible to identify Leichhardt's remains if found. DNA extracted from teeth, for example, could be matched with the DNA from a great-grand-nephew. The name of this family descendant, aptly enough, is Ludwig.

To establish if the Glenormiston tree cover had changed, I decided to do some overdue research on the humble gidgee. In this I was greatly assisted by John Reynolds of the Queensland Department of Primary Industry in Longreach. The gidgee of the Georgina basin is called *Acacia georginae*, and is restricted to that particular area. The growth of gidgee in far western areas is very slow (see report on expedition). Invasion of Mitchell-grass country by other gidgee species has been recorded further east and it is possible that some invasion has occurred on Glenormiston where *Acacia georginae* is growing on black soil. The gidgee we saw there were far healthier than those trees growing on harder ridges.

Ian Tinney also managed to unearth some information regarding the surveyor, Bedford. As a government employee, Bedford had been engaged in geodesic traverse surveying at the time. This is a method used to fix permanent points of reference, quite different to cadastral survey work that establishes property boundaries. The two lines of stones out from the survey peg were called 'lock spits' and were then in common use. I later spoke to Mr Bill Kitson of the Queensland Landscentre at Woolloongabba in Brisbane. Bill told me that the purpose of Bedford's survey in 1886 was to check the position of the Queensland–Northern Territory border which had been surveyed earlier by South Australia. In his diary, Bedford wrote that he had buried bottles containing data beneath the stone cairns that surrounded his survey posts, and he expressed the hope that if in 100 years' time the posts had disappeared, the bottles might be found.

While Bedford was engaged in his survey work, his wife contracted typhoid and died before he could return to Roma, Queensland, to see her. It must have been a hard life for Bedford and other surveyors back then. There is no doubt that the early surveyors stand tall among the unsung heroes of the outback.

The time we spent on Glenormiston had been interesting and at times enjoyable. The expedition had failed, however, to solve the mystery of Ludwig Leichhardt's disappearance. Despite this, my conviction that the Glenormiston relics are of vital importance remains as strong as ever.

THE SECOND SEARCH

In January 1998, I received a phone call from Cecil Jensen. I had not met Cecil, but he told me he had read my book *In Leichhardt's Footsteps* and had discussed it with Russell Cooper, the then Queensland Minister for Police in the Borbridge Government. Cecil added that I should contact the Minister as he might be able to help in a further investigation of the Glenormiston site.

I was still thinking over what he'd said when I was rather surprised to get a call from Russell Cooper himself. He seemed very

The Leichhardt search expedition sign for attachment to the vehicles.

Search members at Banjo Paterson Memorial at Winton. Left to right: Bruce Simpson, Kerry Kendell, Gary Kennedy, Greg Simpson, Keith Arnold, Ross Ratcliffe, Lloyd Linson-Smith and Jeff Simpson.

interested in the Leichhardt story and asked what funding I'd need to undertake a further search. I told him I thought $10,000 would be sufficient and he told me he would discuss the matter with Premier Borbridge. Then on 16 February I received a letter from the Premier's Department enclosing a cheque for $10,000; and the next day, I opened an account with Westpac in the name of Leichhardt Expeditionary Account, with myself as signatory.

The following day I rang the members of the first expedition and told them the news that the search for the old camp was on again. During the next week, I rang Steve Millard of the North Australian Pastoral Company to obtain permission to return to Glenormiston. I also rang Mal Debney, manager of the station, to advise him of our plans.

On 3 March I travelled to Brisbane and had a long discussion with Russell Cooper and met Premier Rob Borbridge. A further meeting was held on 18 March. Present were Russell Cooper; the

Police Commissioner, Jim O'Sullivan; and Helen Gregory and Mike Rowling from the Department of Environment.

The Queensland Police Service was very generous in its help, giving the expedition a vehicle, a generator, a satellite phone and hand-held radios for contact between searchers.

As I was leaving the meeting, a young Senior Constable called Gary Kennedy approached me and asked could he join the expedition. I told him if he could get leave he'd be welcome. He joined the expedition and took control of the police vehicle. Three other new members also joined.

The full team now included myself, Ian Tinney, Ross Radcliffe, Jeff Simpson, his son Greg, Lloyd Linson-Smith; and the new members Gary Kennedy, Keith Arnold, who was on Glenormiston when we found the old camp in 1948, Kerry Kendall, an ex-stockman, and Lloyd Radcliffe, Ross' son.

Greg Simpson organised the catering. I with half the team left Brisbane on 10 June; the rest were to join us en route. I had organised fuel from the Shell Service Station in Boulia, and Kerry Kendall had also got a donation of $400 for fuel from Capricorn Coal.

The whole team arrived in Boulia on 13 June. After fuelling up, at Jim O'Sullivan's request, I saw the local police and advised them of our plans. We camped overnight at Boulia. The next morning after picking up some perishable food stuff, we set out for Glenormiston. We called in on the way at Herbert Downs to see Bob Kirk. Bob had been in the area for many years, and offered to assist us if he could.

We arrived at Glenormiston and saw Liz Debney, the manager's wife, then we travelled on with all four vehicles to Mark Tree Waterhole on the Georgina River, and set up camp on the western side.

We had decided to start the search at Mark Tree Waterhole for two reasons. First, from there we could search any area of Marion Downs we wanted to look at and then search further north throughout the whole area. Second, Keith Arnold, who back in 1948 had joined the stock camp during the second muster at Mark Tree waterhole, clearly remembered us talking about the old campsite we had found. This led us to think that perhaps the old camp was closer to Mark Tree than we had previously thought.

We had gathered some firewood on the way into Mark Tree camp, so Greg soon had a fire going and in no time our multi-talented cook had a slap-up meal of steak and vegetables ready.

After we had eaten and cleaned up, we settled down to a team meeting, discussing search methods, who would drive what vehicles to the search areas and which foot searchers would be allocated to each vehicle.

Ross's memory of a jump-up or steep hill before we came across the old camp was still an important factor in looking at search areas, but knowing that memories are fallible, I was keen to do a complete search of every possible area as we went, in that way we could be fairly confident that the old campsite was not behind us.

The team we had was an excellent one. With the exception of one man, all of us had extensive bush experience. The exception, of course, was Gary Kennedy but he'd had experience with police searches and his cheerful enthusiasm made him a great asset to the team.

Bobby Kirk from Herbert Downs said he would join us and had in mind an area in Marion Downs that he considered to be very likely, so we hoped he would join us before we left the Mark Tree area.

Most of us were sleeping in our swags out on the flat, but at about 12 o'clock that night, driving rain and a very cold wind put a scatter in us. Most went to their vehicles for shelter but Kerry and I went to the fire, stirred it up and put a billy on. By the time we had a billy of coffee ready, the whole team had gathered, so we sat around drinking coffee and cursing the rain. We finally dispersed, most of the chaps going to their vehicles, and I sat up with the fire for the rest of the night.

It was still raining next morning, so after breakfast we got together and erected a very large tent we had fortunately brought with us. Greg, Jeff and Ian were pretty well equipped with their own tents, but the rest of us threw our swags into the newly erected tent, and we all settled down for the day as we certainly could not do any searching. I filled in part of the time by bringing up to date my expense ledger and petty cash book. I had assured both Russell Cooper and the Police Commissioner that a full financial report on the trip would be made available to them at the end of the expedition.

By the next morning the weather had cleared and we started doing some field work. We looked at an area on Marion Downs we were interested in (not the area Bob had mentioned), also part of Herbert Downs and did a wide search to the west of the Georgina River. Over the next four days we continued searching the area around the Mark Tree Waterhole moving up the river to the east and to the west. However, the only trophy we found was a pair of shoeing pinchers that a stock camp must have lost some time ago.

The hand-held radios proved to be a great success, enabling the foot searchers to keep in touch with one another while spread out

Waterhole in the Georgina River.

over quite a large area. When we felt we had searched the area around the Mark Tree Waterhole thoroughly we moved camp up to Maginga Waterhole on the Georgina and fairly close to Glenormiston Station.

I had arranged for fuel to be sent out to Glenormiston from Boulia. So while the rest of us set up camp, the drivers took the vehicles into Glenormiston to fuel up. The flow in the river that year had not been good, so the water in the waterhole was low and very muddy to get to so we set up a camp shower at the base of a big paperbark tree on the bank. I had toyed with the idea of getting a camp toilet or portable toilet before leaving Brisbane, but abandoned the idea, so we resorted to the time honoured method of a walk down wind with a shovel on the shoulder.

When the drivers returned with the vehicles, Ian told me that we would have a visit the next day, which was Sunday the 21st, from a couple of Boulia policemen. No doubt they would report back to Commissioner Jim O'Sullivan on our progress.

Ian had also brought back a copy of Martin Hayward's diaries covering the period when we accidentally found the old camp in 1948, Hayward was then the manager. Mal Debney had given him the diary; he and his wife were a wonderful help over the whole period of the search. Though some of us from the first expedition two years previously had already carefully read the diary covering the relevant period, it was worth another shot. Who knows, perhaps one of the new blokes might find something of significance? But unfortunately it wasn't to be. All Hayward mentioned was where the stock camp was on any particular day without saying what we were doing or who was doing it. Although the diary was a disappointment, we still pored over it for weeks afterwards hoping to glean some clue.

That afternoon a group went out to get a load of firewood for the camp. There was gidgee available, the best cooking timber in the outback. Before leaving, Kerry Kendall showed me his prized axe he was going to use to chop gidgee. It was a very fine axe with a very fine blade. I warned him that gidgee was a very tough wood and he needed to be careful with the axe. The group returned with a load of firewood and a very rueful Kerry showed me the half-moon piece that had come out of the blade of his axe—he agreed gidgee is a very, very tough timber.

That night after tea, we discussed at length Martin Hayward's diary and its lack of information; we also went back over our progress to date and tried to reconstruct the circumstances surrounding the finding of the old camp in 1948. We knew that the three of us who found the old camp were musterers not tailers. Tailors are men who look after the main mob of cattle gathered throughout the muster. So if Ross's memory of us having cattle in-hand was correct, it could have only been right at the end of the muster when we were looking after bullocks prior to handing them over to the drover, or at the end of a day's muster when we took freshly drafted bullocks out to the main mob. After some discussion, we agreed that the second scenario was the most likely of the two. However, this meant that the old camp could then be on any one of a large number of locations in the area. We further agreed that while keeping Ross's memory of a jump-up prior to finding the camp in our minds, we could not afford to ignore any likely spot in any of the searches.

Bobby Kirk had not yet joined us but when he did we would have to go back to Mark Tree. We were keen to see the spot on Marion Downs that Bobby said might hold the answer to our search. When Bobby Kirk did eventually join the team, we journeyed down to the spot on Marion Downs that he had told us was so promising. Unfortunately, it did not live up to our expectations. However, while we were down there we took the opportunity of photographing the tree that gave the nearby waterhole its name. This tree believed to be marked by Leichhardt is now just a large stump and the blaze cut by the explorer is completely burnt out. In 1947, I had ridden past this coolabah tree and it was evident now that the ravages of time and weather had taken their toll.

Search vehicle crossing a rough gully.

Despite the shortcomings of Martin Hayward's diaries, the team was still in good spirits. We were all enjoying the challenge of the search and we all got on well together. There were a couple of humorists in the team and their dry wit usually brought comic relief to any situation.

At about midnight that night, rain and a mini cyclone hit the camp causing mild confusion and dislodging a ridge pole that hit a team member on the head. Fortunately he suffered no ill effects and after sorting things out we resumed our sleep hoping that the rain would not last.

Sunday morning dawned cloudy and with a bitter wind but fortunately the rain had ceased. We were soon sitting down to a traditional Sunday breakfast of bacon and eggs prepared by Greg. Apart from ordering the rations and doing the catering, Greg was also in charge of the metal detector with which he religiously scanned every likely spot we found.

After breakfast we decided to have a short search up along the top of Yallumbah Creek and across to the Herbert Downs boundary.

Although the Georgina had been running well in 1948, there had been little local rain. So we may well have held the main mob of bullocks out in that area to get good grass.

We returned to the camp to greet Gary and Dave from the Boulia Police. They were doubly welcome for they brought a fresh supply of bread and tobacco. Half the team were smokers, so the supply of tobacco was fairly high on our priority list. Most of the rest of the day was spent in yarning with Gary and Dave, and talking about the search. I made a point of informing them on how the search was going and what progress we had made. If they were to report back to the people who had backed us, I wanted them to know that we were on the job and not enjoying a grand bender on the banks of the Georgina River. After a fine dinner, a bottle of rum was produced and we had a very convivial evening around the camp fire.

After breakfast the next morning, we farewelled Dave and Gary who had spent the night and started doing some serious searching. Most of the team continued the search down Yallumbah Creek, throwing a wide net across the country on either side of the creek all the way down to its junction with the Georgina. Ian, Gary and I went up the Georgina—we badly wanted to locate a waterhole by the same name as the creek that was in the outside channel but not shown on our maps. Later in the morning we found the waterhole and Ian added it to our maps.

We met the rest of the team for a midday meal and after a short break, the team started to do a wide search to the east. Jeff, however, was keen to go and have a look at a feature he had noticed earlier. My brother was a fine bushman. He had done a lot of prospecting and at times during our search he delighted in being given a 'wandering' brief. He had earlier stuck two large feathers in his hatband, and Ian Tinney immediately dubbed him 'Two Feathers, the Indian Scout'. The Indian Scout part was later dropped but the name of Two Feathers stuck.

We arrived back at camp that night with nothing to show for our efforts save an old, heavy six-ring hobble chain used for hobbling draught horses. It had probably been lost by a teamster back in the days when horse-drawn wagons brought supplies out to the isolated stations of the inland.

That night after tea we sat around talking about our progress; we knew that the search for the old camp was a formidable one. It had only been found by accident back in 1948, and even then most of the relics were buried, so we had no idea what nature had done to the site since. I lit a smoke and looked over at Ross who was idly turning the pages of a copy of Martin's diaries, 'What do you think mate?' I asked him. He answered without looking up, 'Well,' he said slowly, 'if the pen is mightier than the sword then Martin's pen would hardly be mightier than a pocket knife.'

During the following weeks we searched a large area from below Glenormiston Station to the Roxborough boundary, and from the hills at the black mountain on the east out to the west and along Pituri Creek. We scanned every likely spot with the metal detector but with no success. We did find places where drovers had camped and where the Glenormiston stock camp had been, but these sites bore no resemblance to the burnt out old campsite with its half buried relics we were looking for. Near the black mountain we found the remains of a well set out tent camp. It may have been the camp of some people from a university, for when I was mustering there in the past, I had seen the odd fossil or two. We estimated that the camp site was about 60 years old.

During this time work commitments were beginning to have an effect on our numbers. On 25 June, Ross's son Lloyd had to return to the family property. Ross ran him up to Boulia to catch a bus, he also took Keith Arnold on to Mount Isa to see a doctor. Keith had been suffering from a chest infection, and the inclement weather had not helped. He saw the doctor and both he and Ross returned the following day to resume the search.

On 8 July we also farewelled Kerry Kendall. Both he and young Lloyd had done a great job while they were with us and we were sorry to lose them, but I knew they had thoroughly enjoyed the time they spent out there with us. But we also knew time was running out for Lloyd Linson-Smith and Ross. Lloyd had a business to run and Ross was worried about his property in the Arcadia Valley. On 10 July they shook hands with us, wished us luck and drove out to the Boulia Road to head off home.

Back at Maginga that night I got Ian to put a new dressing on a finger of mine that I had injured a week before when Ian and I were taking a shortcut back to his vehicle. The vehicle had been parked at the bottom of a very steep incline with large rough limestone boulders from top to bottom, three quarters of the way down an untied bootlace resulted in a dramatic increase in the speed of my descent. After bouncing and skidding off the remainder of the boulders, I landed at the bottom with a thud and minus a fair bit of skin. Ian, who was our photographer and cartographer, was also our first-aid man. He produced the first-aid kit from his vehicle and soon had me patched up, and the search went on. The only lasting damage was a deep jagged tear to one of my fingers and an even bigger jagged tear to one leg of a good pair of moleskin trousers.

The satellite phone that the police had lent us had been set up at Maginga but had been used very little as we knew it was for emergencies only. I had rung Russell Cooper's office once and left a message telling him of our progress. However, a new government had been elected in our absence, so I decided to leave any reporting until I got back to Caboolture.

That day we concentrated in searching an area to the east of Pituri Creek and returned to it the following day, as some of the areas looked quite promising. On the afternoon of 16 July we asked Mal and Liz Debney over for a few drinks, they had both been a wonderful help to us during the search and we wanted to thank them both for their assistance. On the night of the 17th we had our final team meeting. We had been almost five-and-a-half weeks in the field and our budget was getting low. Keith Arnold was not a well man, and we reluctantly came to the conclusion that although we had given it our best shot, the mysterious old campsite had again eluded us.

Breaking for lunch in typical search country.

Next morning we packed up with mixed feelings, went in and farewelled Mal and Liz Debney and headed for home. Ian left us at Longreach and on the night of the 21st we rolled our swags out on the lawn of the caravan park at Roma. Cold wet changes had often made it difficult for us when we were in the field but the weather gods had not done with us yet.

At 4 o'clock in the morning, an unexpected deluge hit the caravan park, we hastily rolled our swags, threw them in the vehicles and jumped in ourselves. The rain did not look like stopping, so we decided to make an early start for home. Gary Kennedy and I arrived in Caboolture before midday. We had a drink of tea and I said goodbye to Gary who took the police vehicle back to Brisbane. He had done a sterling job during the search. Over the next two days I compiled a written and full financial report on the search, and closed another chapter in our attempts to solve the mystery of the old camp.

APPENDICES

REPORT ON THE GLENORMISTON
EXPEDITION 1996

A copy of the following report was sent to all members of the expedition party.

I would like to express my appreciation to the members of the expedition, all of whom were unstinting in their endeavours to make the search successful. Unfortunately, we were not able to identify the site where the relics were found. Despite this failure I believe the trip will provide valuable information for future searches.

The main problem was that neither Ross nor I could remember just where we were working at the time. Sadly, the station diary did not help in this regard. It may have been felt at times we were covering unlikely terrain. Nevertheless it was imperative, I believe, that all areas containing possible sites were explored. To leave Glenormiston with some areas uninspected would have resulted in lingering doubts on the thoroughness of the operation. In the ten days we spent in the field the party covered all likely areas on the station. What we did not have time for was to go back to places that warranted a detailed search by the whole party on foot. Two of these areas were seen on the last day in the field. However, the groundwork that has been done and the knowledge gained will be invaluable in the future.

Both Ian and Greg did yeoman service in their vehicles. The work they carried out in difficult terrain was outstanding. Lloyd's twin cab and the three-wheeler also did a fine job. It was a pity we had to lose the documentary team so early in the search. They were a big help while they were with us. The expedition owes a lot to all the drivers who volunteered to use their vehicles at their own expense.

I had some concerns about the changes that may have occurred to the country in the 48 years that have elapsed since we found the relics. Since returning I have done research on gidgee with the help of John Reynolds of the Department of Primary Industry in Barcaldine. His advice is that gidgee has a life span of up to 200 years. The growth of the tree is very slow, indeed, and largely dependent on a succession of good seasons. During the 1950s and 1970s it is believed the seasons would have stimulated some growth. The bushy regrowth we saw of up to half a metre, could, in John's opinion, be over 20 years old. This regrowth normally shows little change until nearby trees die.

The many dead gidgee trees we saw may have been the result of an infestation of wingless 'hoppers during a very dry period. Such an infestation killed many trees in the Quilpie district some time after World War II. In short, apart from the cutting down of a few trees and the possible death of others, the changes to the gidgee stands would have been minimal. There were, however, a lot more stock in the search area back in 1948; the Mitchell-grass areas may have changed a little.

I believe to continue the search we will have to attract financial support. This could be achieved by either a government grant, or by commercial interests. Obtaining finance without having too many strings attached will be of the utmost importance. Although the search was unsuccessful, the fact remains—the relics are there.

I have written a short note to Mal and Liz Debney to thank them for their help and support.

In conclusion I would like to thank each and every member of the expedition. Ross and I could not have wished for more able and agreeable companions.

THE LEICHHARDT NAMEPLATE

On 23 November 2006, Senator the Hon. Rod Kemp issued a media release announcing that the National Museum of Australia had acquired the brass plate stamped 'Ludwig Leichhardt 1848'. The plate had been found by Charles Harding in Western Australia around the year 1900. The Director of the National Museum of Australia, Craddock Morton, stated that the nameplate was an authentic Leichhardt relic, which indicated that Leichhardt and his party had travelled two thirds across the continent.

The main character in the saga of the Leichhardt nameplate was Charles Harding, born at Kanmantoo, South Australia on 1 August 1862. Like many of his peers, Harding grew up without any education, but this was not such a big handicap in the pioneering days as one might suppose. Harding was later to become a drover and part-time prospector.

At the turn of the nineteenth century, Harding and an Aboriginal named Jacky were in the southeastern Kimberley region of Western Australia. Jacky gave Harding a partly burnt gun butt that he had found in the fork of a boab tree. The exact site of the boab tree was subject to a great deal of confusion and debate, it was finally determined that the location was approximately within a 100 kilometres of the Northern Territory border and a day's ride from the Musgrave Range.

On the partly burnt gun butt, Harding found a brass plate with 'Ludwig Leichhardt 1848' stamped on it. Harding removed the plate and kept it in his possession for some 17 years obviously believing it to be of some importance.

In 1917, Charles Harding gave the plate to Reginald Bristow-Smith, then a lad of 14, Harding also told the lad the story of how the plate was found. Though unable to read or write, Harding must have realised the significance of the plate, but why he did not tell the authorities before 1917 is a mystery. The reason could have been due to his lack of education and deep suspicion of anyone in authority. I have worked with men of similar limited learning, and found them to be deeply suspicious of those with higher education and in positions of authority.

On 24 July 1920, Bristow-Smith lent the plate to the South Australian Museum. The museum was interested but returned the plate to Bristow-Smith on 27 April 1921, when Bristow-Smith refused an offer of purchase by the Museum.

In 1934 Bristow-Smith wrote to the explorer L. A. Wells telling him the details of Harding's find, including Harding's habit of polishing the plate with ash from a fire and that Harding had told him there was a single 'L' on the boab tree in which the gun butt was found. Bristow-Smith was at the time District Clerk of Laura, South Australia. Laura was also where Charles Harding had died in March 1926.

During this time a number of people became interested in the story of the nameplate, including J. D. Somerville of the South Australian Branch of the Royal Geographical Society of Australasia. Somerville initiated a number of investigations into the history of the nameplate and the boab tree. He was later to compile a report for the proceedings in the Royal Geographical Society of Australasia in Volume 37.

Bristow-Smith loaned the plate to L. A. Wells. When Wells died, the plate was in the possession of J. M. Maugham who worked in the South Australian Lands Department. On his death in 1940, the plate became lost in the bureaucracy until it was finally returned to Bristow-Smith in 1964. The plate then passed to Jeffery Bristow-Smith several years later on his father's death. When Jeffery died in 2004, his widow Catherine and four children inherited the Leichhardt plate.

It was from Catherine and her family that the Australian National Museum purchased the plate. I congratulate the Australian National Museum on its acquisition of such an historical relic and believe the Bristow-Smith family received a just reward for their careful preservation of the Leichhardt nameplate.

The National Museum carried exhaustive tests on the plate which proved beyond doubt that it was a genuine Leichhardt relic. Further tests showed that the plate had been subject to mild heat and that it had been polished with wood ash, thus confirming Harding's story about the partly burnt gun butt together with his habit of polishing the plate with wood ash. In conversation with Matthew Higgins, the Senior Curator of the Australian National Museum, he told me that as two aspects of Harding's story were scientifically proven, it was reasonable to assume that the rest of the story was also correct, giving rise to the belief that Leichhardt and his party had reached Western Australia.

There can be no doubt that the 'Leichhardt plate' is a genuine relic, however, the circumstances surrounding the discovery of the plate are not so clear cut and pose a number of interesting questions. None of the stories about the finding of the plate suggest that Jacky had any problem in removing the gun butt from the boab tree. This raises the following questions.

So, who had put the gun butt in the tree and when?

Could Leichhardt or one of his party have placed the gun butt in the fork so firmly that it withstood half a century of top-end weather and not become so firmly jammed and overgrown that it would need an axe to free it?

Was the gun butt given to Jacky by local Aborigines?

Had the gun butt been carried from elsewhere along the well-established Aboriginal trade routes, as described in Dr A. Grenfell Price's report on the proceedings of the Royal Geographical Society of Australasia, South Australian Branch, Volume 39? If this is correct, then it was the Leichhardt nameplate not the Leichhardt expedition that reached Western Australia.

Did Harding ever see the boab tree, and if so was it marked with an 'L'?

Harding said there was an 'L' in the boab tree, or more accurately Bristow-Smith wrote in 1934 that Harding told him in 1917 there was an 'L' in the tree. I have no doubt that Harding and Bristow-Smith were honest men, but verbal communications over a period of years can become confused and corrupted with no intent to deceive. The single 'L' is also interesting. Leichhardt may have marked trees with a single 'L' but the trees that we can definitely attribute to him are marked with a double 'L' above the year.

The key to the story is the boab tree; boabs live to a great age and if it is still standing the 'L' will still be visible. Boab trees initialled by A. C. Gregory's party in the Victoria River District can still be clearly seen after 150 years.

Mr Matthew Higgins advised me that an expedition is going to be formed to try and locate the boab tree. I wish them every success. If it is found, it will prove Harding's story is true in every detail and vindicate the Museum's faith in him. If it is not found however, we will never know with any certainty if Leichhardt or members of his party ever reached Western Australia.

The Leichhardt nameplate.

'L' MARKED TREES IN QUEENSLAND

The following is not a complete list of 'L' marked trees in Queensland but it does includes a number of marked trees attributed to Ludwig Leichhardt and three trees which were definitely marked by William Landsborough.

The debate regarding which of the two explorers marked certain trees is ongoing. Old photos are seldom conclusive, and official documents and the journals of other explorers can only provide some of the answers.

When the markings of a tree are in doubt there has been a tendency to attribute the mark to Leichhardt. This is understandable considering the disappearance of the explorer and the natural desire of people to play a part in solving the mystery. The tree on the Paroo River appears to be an example of this tendency. It was seen by an early manager of Yarronvale Station on the Paroo who sketched the tree and attributed the tree to Leichhardt. There is no evidence that Leichhardt was ever on the Paroo River, to have made a radical change south from the Barcoo so early in his trip is highly unlikely. There is a possibility, however, that Landsborough marked this tree. He did mark a tree at Charleville but his journal makes no mention of the Paroo River. He did make an entry, however, that he had seen trees marked by other explorers, including Kennedy and Walker. J. D. Somerville in the proceedings of the Royal Geographical Society of Australasia in Volume 37 quoted the following from Favene's *Australian Explorers 1788–1888*: 'Luff the man mentioned here, was with Kennedy on his Barcoo expedition, and some of the trees on the Warrego marked "L" and ascribed to Leichhardt were probably some of his markings.'

It is quite likely then that it was Luff who marked the tree on the Paroo River.

'L' TREES ON THE FLINDERS RIVER

In 1861 William Landsborough joined the search for the missing Burke and Wills. He took his expedition by ship to the Gulf of Carpentaria, landing on Sweers Island off the Gulf Coast on 23 September. He later moved his base camp to the Albert River on 22 December. From there he searched the Gregory River and the upper Georgina River. Landsborough then headed to the Flinders River, reaching there on 19 February 1862.

Landsborough was renowned for marking trees; there are entries in his journal of his marking two trees in one day on that trip. Landsborough makes it plain in his journal that he searched both sides of the Flinders. He had two Aborigines with him who would have been excellent trackers. They found no evidence of Burke and Wills or of Leichhardt on the Flinders River. Landsborough's party certainly would not have missed marked trees, for these are usually close to a waterhole, and waterholes are prime search areas. What Landsborough did note in his diary, however, was that he had seen trees marked by himself on a previous trip on the Flinders with Nat Buchanan in 1859, a trip that could account for the tracks Walker saw while searching for Burke and Wills.

At the end of 1864 the citizens of Melbourne received news that marked trees on the Flinders River had been found that might solve the mystery of Ludwig Leichhardt's disappearance. The bearer of these tidings was Duncan McIntyre, an aspiring pastoralist. McIntyre was born at Argyll in Scotland in 1831. Raised by foster parents, he came to Australia with them, disembarking at Port Phillip in 1849. McIntyre worked on pastoral properties in Victoria for some years but he was a man with visions of wider horizons.

Duncan McIntyre and his brother Donald left Victoria in mid-1863 to select a property in the Gulf Country of Queensland. Before entering Queensland, he found the state government required a permit to bring stock into Queensland. He spent some time exploring the western rivers, then took a small party to Cooper Creek. As the permit had still not arrived, most of the party returned to Victoria but Duncan went ahead with a small party, and by 1864, they had reached the headwaters of Gulf Rivers in what was to become the Julia Creek and Cloncurry districts. By that time, stations were being established on the Cloncurry and Flinders Rivers. Duncan McIntyre is reported to have spoken with the manager of Lara Station and was told by the manager that he had seen trees marked with an 'L' on the Flinders River. McIntyre was at once interested, he set out and found the trees mentioned with the aid of an Aborigine who had been with

Landsborough. He also found two fat horses, older than McIntyre's oldest horses. Believing the 'L' marked trees and the horses were related to the missing Leichhardt expedition, he set off back to Melbourne with the news.

Although some people cautioned him that Landsborough could be responsible for what he had seen, he found an ally and supporter in Ferdinand Mueller. Mueller began to publicise McIntyre's claims and to raise support for an expedition to support those claims. In a letter to *The Age* newspaper of 23 December 1864, David Wilkie and Ferdinand Mueller gave details of McIntyre's discovery. They wrote that McIntyre had an Aborigine with him who had been with William Landsborough when he found the trees. The Aborigine had told McIntyre that it was not a Landsborough camp, as the explorer had been on the other side of the river.

The letter further pointed out that Landsborough marked his trees with a camp number, while the trees McIntyre found were just plain 'L's, the letter further stated that the horses found by McIntyre must be Leichhardt's as no other explorer had been in the area.

On 3 January 1865, *The Age* newspaper printed an interview with McIntyre taken from the *Riverine Herald*, 31 December 1864. In the interview McIntyre said the 'L's were quite different in size, one being very large and the other quite small.

The above information sounds convincing, however, it does not stand up too well under scrutiny. Despite what the Aborigine said, Landsborough made it quite plain in his journal that he searched both sides of the river. As pointed out earlier in the book, when questioned the answers given by unsophisticated Aborigines are often couched in terms to please rather than to inform.

It is true Landsborough usually added the camp numbers to his marked trees, and it is true that Leichhardt it seems marked his trees with two Ls. An explanation, however, can be found in Landsborough's journal. In it he wrote that his Aborigines sometimes marked trees and this could explain the discrepancy in the size of the 'L's. With regard to the bark growth on the blazes, the rate of growth varies with different trees, and is influenced by regional conditions, McIntyre was new to the Gulf Country and his opinion that the growth was of 15 years duration, not five, was not that of an expert.

With regard to the two fat horses, it is highly unlikely they belonged to Leichhardt. When Leichhardt put his horse plant together at the beginning of 1848, he would have chosen strong mature horses, as the trip to Swan River would have taken at least 18 months. By the end of 1864, his youngest horse, if still alive, would have been 21 years of age, their manes would have been matted, their tails knotted and reaching the ground, and they certainly wouldn't have been fat. As horses get older, the sharp ridges of their back teeth need to be filed down with a tooth rasp. If this is not done fairly regularly, they cannot process their food properly and quickly lose condition.

In Wilkie and Mueller's letter of the 23 December 1864, they stated 'on the Flinders McIntyre saw two old horses where no other explorer had been'. It was absurd to believe that the horses were Leichhardt's considering McIntyre knew Landsborough had been on the Flinders before him. In the same *Age* article on page 6 Duncan McIntyre is reported as saying, 'The Flinders was settled from its head to within 280 miles of the sea and one station had been established 100 miles further down the river.' McIntyre must have known all of these pioneer settlers would have taken a number of horses with them to start their stations: in fact anyone of a number of people could have owned the horses McIntyre saw.

McIntyre's backers were successful in gaining public support, a committee was formed of wealthy ladies and money raised for an expedition to go to the Flinders River. Duncan McIntyre led the expedition and was given a fee of £1500. The expedition was somewhat of a disaster and was finally abandoned when funds ran out. Early in 1866 Duncan McIntyre had left the expedition and went on ahead. He spent sometime around Burketown and died of gulf fever on 4 June 1866. He was buried on his brother's property later called Dalgonally Station. With McIntyre's death and the disintegration of the expedition interest in the trees on the Flinders River seemed to wane. It appears no further attempt was made to investigate McIntyre's claims, this may signify that his story was not taken too seriously by the general public.

The Flinders River is a long way from Leichhardt's intended plan to skirt the desert before picking up the headwaters of the northern flowing rivers. No one knows at this point just where Leichhardt went, but we do have documented proof that Landsborough was on the Flinders River on two occasions some years apart. The overwhelming odds, therefore, are that it was Landsborough and not Leichhardt who marked the trees there.

TREES ATTRIBUTED TO LEICHHARDT'S FIRST TRIP

LEFT: The Taroom Tree, photograph taken in 1908. On his trip to Port Essington, Leichhardt marked this tree with 'LL' over 1844.

BELOW: The Taroom Tree today. This coolibah aged over 300 years old by the experts, stands in the main street of Taroom. The blaze higher than a lot of the explorer's marks has now grown over. This tree is one of the few living trees marked by the explorer. The people of Taroom and district are justifiably proud of their connection with the long lost explorer.

Suttor Creek Tree. This tree is a blue gum that once stood on the banks of the 9-mile lagoon on Suttor Creek Station. It is almost certain Leichhardt marked it on his first trip. Ray Gilham, owner of Suttor Creek Station, first saw it around 1946, by then the blaze had rotted away. In recent years a mining company knocked the tree over but Ray Gilham salvaged the blazed area. Ray now has the salvaged part of the tree in a glass case in his home.

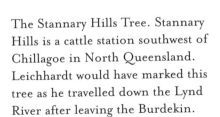

The Stannary Hills Tree. Stannary Hills is a cattle station southwest of Chillagoe in North Queensland. Leichhardt would have marked this tree as he travelled down the Lynd River after leaving the Burdekin.

MARKED TREES ATTRIBUTED TO LEICHHARDT'S SECOND TRIP

ABOVE: The Sugar Loaf Mountain Tree. This tree stood on a small flat on the southeast slope of Sugar Loaf Mountain. Ted Long, who owned Sugar Loaf Mountain run until 1991, often saw the tree. Ted said it was marked with an 'LL' over 1846. It was marked quite high up as if from a horse. Leichhardt marked this tree at the start of his second trip from Drayton to Cecil Plains. The tree burnt down after Ted sold the property. The dot marks the spot where it stood just above the lookout built by the new owner.

LEFT: Comet River Tree. This is one of the trees marked by Leichhardt on his second trip as he travelled down the Comet River. The photo was taken in 1927.

The Marmadilla Tree. The old Marmadilla Station was close to the Comet River and this tree was possibly marked by Leichhardt on his second trip. The photo was taken in 1907.

Tree at the junction of the Comet and Nogoa rivers. This tree was marked by Leichhardt at the end of his disastrous second trip. Leichhardt is reported to have buried some items by this tree and marked the tree with a dig. The photo was taken around 1915.

TREES ATTRIBUTED TO LEICHHARDT'S PROPOSED ROUTE, 1848

The Nangram Tree. This tree marked 'LL' stood on the south side of the Condamine River between the towns of Chinchilla and Condamine. Harold Rennick, who has done a lot of basic research on Leichhardt's movements in the area, believes the explorer marked this tree on the preliminary survey of the route to Mt Abundance. The tree died in 1974 and later fell.

The Barcoo Tree. This tree said to be a Leichhardt tree is just across the Barcoo River from the Russell Station of Swan Hill before you get to where the main road crosses the Barcoo from Tambo to Blackall. Both Leichhardt and Landsborough marked trees on the Barcoo. A. C. Gregory saw at least one tree marked by Leichhardt before Landsborough was in the area. There is some doubt about who marked this particular tree.

Paroo River Tree (pictured right). This tree was seen by the Manager of Yarronvale Station, Paroo River. He attributed the tree to Leichhardt and made a remarkably good sketch of it. In all probability, however, it was marked by Luff, one of Kennedy's men.

The Kell's Creek Tree (no photo of this tree exists). This tree was shown to Ron McKenzie in 1963 by Glen Seymour, the then manager of Cork Station. Ron told me the tree stood on a channel of Kells Creek, a tributary of the Diamantina River. The tree, a big coolabah, had a partly overgrown blaze with the bottom of an 'L' clearly showing. It is unlikely this tree was marked by Landsborough, as I believe it is outside the range of Landsborough's expeditions.

The Glenormiston Tree (above). This tree has long been regarded as one marked by Leichhardt. It gave its name to the nearby Mark Tree Waterhole in the Georgina River and is well outside the range of Landsborough's expeditions. I saw the tree in 1947 but did not take much notice of it, as it was before we found the old camp. Old timers have told me there were marks on the tree similar to those Leichhardt made. The stump of this tree with its burnt out blaze still stands. Bob Moncrieff reported seeing a tree marked by Leichhardt further down the river but as I could not find any confirmation of this, its existence is somewhat doubtful.

TREES MARKED BY WILLIAM LANDSBOROUGH
IN HIS 1861–62 SEARCH FOR BURKE AND WILLS

The Gregory Downs Tree. This tree has definitely been identified as a Landsborough tree. Gregory Downs was taken up in 1872 by the Watson brothers and later owned by Lew Blackmore, who inherited the property from his grand uncle Robert McGregor Watson. This tree was marked by Landsborough at the beginning of his search for Burke and Wills. The photo was taken around 1946 and shows Lew Blackmore standing beside the tree. The blazed portion of the tree has been removed and is now at the Gregory Downs homestead.

RIGHT: The Rocklands
Station Tree. This tree was
marked by Landsborough at
the start of his search for
Burke and Wills. It stood on
what was to become
Rocklands Station close to
Lake Mary, a stretch of water
in the upper Georgina River
named by the explorer. Mr
R. Miller, one time manager
of Rocklands, had the blazed
part of the tree preserved
and it is now on display at
Rocklands Station. The
photo was taken in 1984.

BELOW: The Charleville
Tree. This tree was marked
by Landsborough in May
1862 when he was travelling
south after looking for
Burke and Wills. The photo
was taken in 1985.

EXPLANATORY NOTES ON FINDING THE OLD CAMP AND THE LOSS OF THE STIRRUP IRONS

I wrote my first book *Packhorse Drover* soon after I retired and in it I wrote of finding the remains of the old camp on Glenormiston. I did so from my memories of an event that had happened nearly 50 years before.

Since leaving Glenormiston, I had spoken only twice to Ross Radcliffe, the other survivor of the group who found the old camp site. However, he and I did make contact after *Packhorse Drover* was published and then we discussed trying to locate the camp again. In speaking with Ross, I found that although his memories of the camp site were similar to mine, his recollections of events surrounding the find were somewhat different; for instance I believe we were going mustering when we found the old camp, Ross, however, was adamant we had cattle in hand.

As Ross's memories seemed clearer and more detailed than mine, I changed the story to accommodate them when I wrote of finding the old camp in the first edition of this book. The different versions in the two books may have caused some confusion amongst my readers as no reason for the different version in the first edition of this book was given.

With regard to the loss of the stirrup irons, I believed when writing both books that they went with my droving gear which was sold in Camooweal in the early 1960s. I had given my droving plant to my brother, the late Alan Simpson, to run. He had it for some time and when he was finished, he left both horses and gear in Camooweal where they were later sold separately. Neither he nor I were present at the sale. Sometime after writing the first edition of this book, I spoke with Drover, the late Clive Teece, who ended up with the droving gear. He told me he had no knowledge of the irons; they'd apparently been taken by someone prior to him taking possession.

My readers may question with some justification why I did not take better care of the stirrup irons considering the importance I placed on them as a clue to solving the Leichhardt mystery. My only excuse is at that time all my energy and interest was devoted to establishing a saddle repair business in Winton, and the fate of Ludwig Leichhardt was the last thing on my mind.

It was not until after I retired that I again had the chance to consider the potential importance of what we had found on Glenormiston. It is true that during the intervening years I sometimes thought of the Leichhardt mystery and I even wrote a verse 'Where Leichhardt Lies' that was published in the Sydney *Bulletin*. The responsibility, however, of earning a living and raising a family left no time for the solving of mysteries at that period of my life.

Statutory Declaration

I, JEFFREY FORBES SIMPSON
(FULL NAME OF DECLARANT / PERSON MAKING THE DECLARATION)

of 14 Carnell Road, Severnlea, Qld. 4352
(ADDRESS OF DECLARANT / PERSON MAKING THE DECLARATION)

Postcode 4352

in the State/Territory of Queensland

Insert your occupation(s) Retired

do solemnly and sincerely declare that in 1954 my brother Bruce Simpson, took a mob of 'Avon Downs' steers to deliver to Brighton Downs passing through the pastoral holdings of Glenormiston. One night while yarning about the time he worked on Glenormiston, he recounted the story of finding an old camp with other stockmen and the picking up of a set of stirrup irons. These irons were on his saddle at the time. I had noticed their unusual design but until then attached no great importance to them assuming he had purchased them somewhere in his travels. These irons were still in his possession when I left his employ in 1958.

In 1995 he called on me with a draft of his book "Pack horse & Drover" in which he recounted the story of finding the camp from which the stirrup irons were recovered. We decided at that meeting to see if the camp could be located.

The search has continued since 1996 by Bruce, Ross Ratclife and other members of the original group at considerable personal time and expense without success to this date.

(Your Statutory Declaration ends on the reverse side of this page and that is where you sign it)

A Statutory Declaration signed by my brother Jeff describing the circumstances in 1954 when I told him about finding the old camp and the stirrup irons.

Place your initials in the box beside the State or Territory in which your Statutory Declaration is being made.

☐	**N.S.W.**	– And I make this solemn declaration conscientiously believing the same to be true and by virtue of the provisions of the *Oaths Act 1900*.
☐	**VIC.**	– And I acknowledge that this declaration is true and correct, and I make it in the belief that a person making a false declaration is liable to the penalties of perjury.
J.F.S	**QLD.**	– And I make this solemn declaration conscientiously believing the same to be true and by virtue of the provisions of the *Oaths Act 1867*.
☐	**S.A.**	– And I make this solemn declaration conscientiously believing the same to be true and by virtue of the provisions of the *Oaths Act 1936*.
☐	**W.A.**	– And I make this solemn declaration by virtue of section 106 of the *Evidence Act 1906*.
☐	**TAS.**	– I make this solemn declaration under the *Oaths Act 2001*.
☐	**N.T.**	– And I make this solemn declaration by virtue of the *Oaths Act* and conscientiously believing the statements contained in this declaration to be true in every particular. NOTE: A person wilfully making a false statement in a declaration is liable to a penalty of $2,000 or imprisonment for 12 months, or both.
☐	**CTH/ ACT**	– And I make this solemn declaration by virtue of the *Statutory Declarations Act 1959* statutory declarations, conscientiously believing the statements contained in this declaration to be true in every particular.

Declared at ...... STANTHORPE TUESDAY SECOND .... in the State/Territory of .... QUEENSLAND ......

this ...... 2nd ...... day of ...... MAY ...... 20 06 ....

x .... J.F. Simpson ....
(SIGNATURE OF DECLARANT / PERSON MAKING THE DECLARATION)

before me

.... (SIGNATURE OF WITNESS / PERSON BEFORE WHOM THE DECLARATION IS MADE)

.... MARK ANGUS WICKS ....
(NAME OF WITNESS / PERSON BEFORE WHOM THE DECLARATION IS MADE)

.... MAGISTRATES COURTS OFFICE 51 MARSH STREET ....
(ADDRESS OF WITNESS / PERSON BEFORE WHOM THE DECLARATION IS MADE)

.... STANTHORPE Q. .... Postcode ...4380...

.... JUSTICE OF THE PEACE ....
(TITLE OR QUALIFICATION OF WITNESS / PERSON BEFORE WHOM THE DECLARATION IS MADE)

Lloyd W Linson-Smith
PO BOX 393 Oakey
Qld 4401

To whom it may concern

My name is Lloyd Linson-Smith of 145 Henningsen Rd Oakey 4401,
In 1948 I was a Stockman employed on Glenormiston Station west of Boulia.
During mustering cattle to send to markets the mustering camp was split up
and some stockmen held the cattle while the balance mustered extra cattle to
make the required mob.

When the split camp came back together the news topic was about the site that
the cattle minders discovered while holding the cattle.
Artefacts would describe the items recovered from the site because they were
not items you would expect to find at that time, metal buttons, unknown style
stirrup irons, saddle tree not consistent with those used at that time, signs of a
fire, it was described as a burnt out camp.

Three of the stockmen who discovered the camp were Bruce Simpson, Ross
Ratcliffe, a local black man, Charlie Trotman.
When the camp came back together it was the point of discussion for some
time, the facts pointed to earlier times, the articles were certainly from earlier
times, the camp location as described was consistent with the known camp site
choosing habits of Ludwick Leichardt.

I was a member of two search parties looking for this site in 1996 and 1998.
I declare that the above statement is true and correct.

Signed Lloyd W Linson-Smith on the 24th April 2006

Signature

I was born Lloyd W Smith, I changed my name by deed pole to Lloyd W
Linson-Smith in 1958, a week before my marriage on the 13 September 1958

A statement signed by Lloyd W. Linson-Smith confirming that in 1948,
when he was a stockman on Glenormiston Station, he was a told an old
campsite had been found.

REPORT ON THE 1998 LEICHHARDT SEARCH EXPEDITION

On the morning of the 10th June, the main party left Brisbane, four other members joined the expedition en route to Boulia.

A camp was set up at Mark Tree, west of the Georgina River on the 14th and the search commenced. The main problem we faced in trying to locate the relics was that Ross and I, the survivors of the party who made the discovery, have no recollections of where we were camped at that time. This meant, of course, that most of Glenormiston Station, as well as part of Herbert Downs had to be searched.

The job was not an easy one and I would like to put on record the great help extended to the expedition by the Police Service and the then Police Minister, Mr Cooper. The loan of a vehicle and a very competent driver and team member in Senior Constable Garry Kennedy was of considerable help. The hand-held radios were a boon during the extensive foot searches while the satellite phone gave us contact with the outside world.

Although we did not locate the relics, at the end of five weeks extensive searching we had discarded all but two areas; we are confident the old camp will be found in one of these. If possible, a very thorough search should be conducted there within the next twelve months.

I cannot speak too highly of the unpaid volunteers who used their own time and vehicles in this venture. The expedition members were Ian Tinney, Ross Ratcliffe, Jeff Simpson, Lloyd Linson-Smith, Kerry Kendall, Greg Simpson, Lloyd Ratcliffe, Keith Arnold, Senior Constable Garry Kennedy and myself.

The manager of Glenormiston, Mal Debney, and his wife, were most helpful as was Bob Kirk of Herbert Downs.

Although the expedition returned empty-handed, I believe a great deal was accomplished in isolating the two areas mentioned above.

I trust the search for the relics may be able to be continued.

Yours faithfully,

Bruce Simpson
Expedition Leader
27 July 1998

BIBLIOGRAPHY

Age, The. Melbourne, 3 January 1865.

Armstrong, R. E. M. *The Kalkadoons*, William Brooks & Co., Brisbane. *Australia's First Century*, Child & Henry Publishing, Sydney, 1980.

Barnett, Correlli. *Bonaparte*, Allen & Unwin, London, 1978.

Bull, Jean. *Historic Queensland Stations*, Queensland Country Life Publications, Brisbane, 1968.

Bunce, Daniel. *Travels with Dr Leichhardt*, first published by Steam Press, 1859; facsimile edn by Oxford University Press, Melbourne, 1959.

Cayley, Neville W. *What Bird is That?*, Angus & Robertson, Sydney, 1937.

Chisholm, Alec H. *Strange Journey*, Rigby, Adelaide, 1976, pp. 204, 207, 228.

Cogger, H. *Reptiles and Amphibians of Australia*, A. H. and A. W. Reed Pty Ltd, Sydney, 1979.

Colwell, Max. *The Journey of Burke & Wills*, Child & Assoc., Brookvale, NSW, 1987.

Connell, Gordon. *The Mystery of Ludwig Leichhardt*, Melbourne University Press, Melbourne, 1980.

Corfield, W. H. *Reminiscences of Queensland*, A. H. Frater, Brisbane, 1921.

Cotton, Catherine Drummond. *Ludwig Leichhardt and the Great South Land*, Angus & Robertson, Sydney, 1938.

Dent, Marian K. 'Ruby De Satge, an independent woman', *Mimag*, Mt Isa Mines Ltd, June 1992, pp. 12–13.

Dent, Marian K. 'Ann Topsy Hansen' in *Unsung Heroes and Heroines of Australia*, Greenhouse Publications, Melbourne, 1988.

Dutton, Geoffrey. *In Search of Edward John Eyre*, Macmillan, Melbourne, 1982.

Ericksen, Ray. *Ernest Giles*, William Heinemann, Melbourne, 1978.

Fitzpatrick, Kathleen. *Australian Explorers*, Oxford University Press, London and Melbourne, 1965.

Fysh, Hudson. *Taming the North*, Angus & Robertson, Sydney, 1950.

Gibbney, H. J. *Australian Dictionary of Biography*, Vol. 5, Melbourne University Press, Melbourne, 1974, p. 165.

Hallum, David. 'The Leichhardt Namplate', National Museum of Australia, Canberra, 2006.

Hill, Ernestine. *The Territory*, Angus & Robertson, London, 1951.

Holliday, *A Field Guide to Australian Trees*, rev. edn, Hamlyn Australia, 1989.

Jones, Philip. *Search for the Taipan*, Augus and Robertson, Sydney, 1977.

Keay, John. *Explorers Extraordinary*, John Marray Ltd, London, 1985.

Kemp, The Hon. Rod (Minister for the Arts). Media Release, 23 November 2006.

Kowold, Margaret and Ross-Johnston, W. *You Can't Make it Rain*, Boolarong Publications, Brisbane, 1992.

L'Estrange, Jan. *The Belle of the Barcoo*, self-published, available from author, 'Highfields', Tambo, 4478; 1996.

Lamond, G. H. *Tales of the Overland*, Hesperian Press, Perth, 1986.

Landsborough, William. *Journal of Landsborough' Expedition From Carpentaria, In Search of Burke and Wills*, first published by F. F. Bailliere, 1862; facsimile edition, Melbourne Friends of the State Library of South Australia, Adelaide, 2000.

Leichhardt, Ludwig. *Journal of an Overland Expedition in Australia*, first published by T. and W. Boone, London in 1847; facsimile edition, Doubleday Australia, Sydney, 1980, pp. 309–310.

Letters of F. W Ludwig Leichhardt, collated and translated by M. Aurosseau, Cambridge University Press for the Haklust Society, Cambridge, 1968.

Lewis, Darrell. *The Fate of Leichhardt,* self-published, 2006.

MacLeod, Dr Ian D. 'Surface Analysis of a Brass Plate', Western Australian Museum, Perth, 2006.

Mann, John F. *Eight Months with Dr Leichhardt in the Years 1846–47*, Turner & Henderson, Sydney, 1888.

McLaren, Dr Glen. *Beyond Leichhardt*, Fremantle Arts Centre Press, Fremantle, 1996.

Mitchell, Sir Thomas. *Journal of an Expedition into the Interior of Tropical Australia*, first published by Longman, Green & Longman, 1848; facsimile edn, Greenwood Press, New York, 1969.

Moffit, Ian. 'Discovering Old Australia', *Australian*, 1 January 1970, p. 7.

Moncrieff, R. A. *Australian Women's Weekly*, 3 December 1969, p. 29.

Moorhead, Alan. *Cooper's Creek*, Macmillan, Melbourne, 1977.

North, A. & Hogg, I. V. *The Book of Guns and Gunsmiths*, Quarto Publishing Co., London, 1977.

Perrin, Les. *The Mystery of the Leichhardt Survivor*, self-published, available from author, P.O. Box 1269, Stafford, Qld, 4053; 1991.

Pike, Glenville. *Frontier Territory*, self-published, 1972.

Portus, Prof. G. V. *Fifty Famous Australians*, Colorgravure Publications, Melbourne, 1954.

Price, Dr A. Grenfell. 'The Mystery of Leichhardt, South Australian Government Expedition of 1938' South Australian branch of the Royal Geographical Society of Australasia, May 1939.

Riverina Herald, The. 31 December 1864.

Ross-Johnson, W. *The Long Blue Line*, Boolarong Publications, Brisbane, 1992.

Roth, Dr Walter Edmund. *Ethnological Studies among the North-West-Central Queensland Aborigines*, Government Printer, 1897.

Royal Geographical Society Australasia, South Australian branch. 'The Leichhardt Plate' Vol. 37, 1935–36, Adelaide.

Russell, Henry S. *The Genesis of Queensland*, Vintage, Sydney, 1889.

Sauer, G. C. *John Gould, the Bird Man*, Lansdowne Press, Melbourne, 1982.

Schultz, Dennis. 'Leichhardt Lost and Found', *Bulletin*, January 1996.

Simpson, Bruce. *Packhorse Drover*, ABC Books, Sydney, 1996.

Sturt, Charles. *Journal of Central Australian Expedition,* 1844–1845, ed. by Jill Waterhouse, Caliban Books, London, 1984.

Troughton, Ellis. *Furred Animals of Australia*, Angus & Robertson, Sydney, 1941.

Webster, E. M. *Whirlwinds in the Plain*, Melbourne University Press, Melbourne, 1980, p. 328.